SUBSTANCE ABUSE: FROM PRINCIPLES TO PRACTICE

SUBSTANCE ABUSE: FROM PRINCIPLES TO PRACTICE

David M. McDowell, M.D.

Assistant Professor of Clinical Psychiatry, Columbia University, College of Physicians & Surgeons, The New York State Psychiatric Institute, and Medical Director, Substance Treatment and Research Service (STARS)

Henry I. Spitz, M.D., F.A.P.A.

Clinical Professor of Psychiatry, Columbia University, College of Physicians & Surgeons and Director, Group and Couples Therapy Training Programs, The New York State Psychiatric Institute

Routledge
Taylor & Francis Group
LONDON AND NEW YORK

Substance Abuse: From Principles to Practice

First published 1999 by BRUNNER/MAZEL

2 Park Square, Milton Park, Abingdon, Oxon OX14 4RN
711 Third Avenue, New York, NY 10017, USA

Routledge is an imprint of the Taylor & Francis Group, an informa business

First issued in hardback 2017

Library of Congress Cataloging-in-Publication Data

McDowell, Dawid M.
Substance abuse: from principles to practice/ David M. McDowell & Henry I. Spitz.
p. cm.
Includes bibliographical references and index.
ISBN-13: 978-0-876-30889-9 (pbk)
1. Drug abuse. 2. Narcotic addicts. 3. Narcotics, Control of.
I. Spitz, Henry I., 1941- . II. Title.
HV5801.M343 1999
362.29–dc21 99-13996
CIP

ISBN 978-0-87630-889-9 (pbk)
ISBN 978-1-138-45191-9 (hbk)

For my family and for Kenneth
and
Susan, Becky, and Jake

CONTENTS

PART VIII
COMMONLY ASKED QUESTIONS ABOUT SUBSTANCE ABUSE

ACKNOWLEDGMENTS

The writing of this book, although labor intensive, has been a source of enjoyment. I, David M. McDowell, am particularly indebted to my senior mentors in the field who have taught me so much, in particular Jonah Schein, whose work helped me to have a sense of perspective with this text. I am also equally indebted to Marc Galanter, Marian Fischman (*especially* for her work on stimulants) and Herbert Kleber, who first attracted me to the field, and whose humor and scholarship never cease to inspire. I am also deeply grateful to the following people who are my peers/mentors/collaborators and friends, in particular Fran Levin, Ed Paul, Eric Collins, Eric Rubin, Jami Rothenberg, Ed Nunes, and Lisa Goldfarb who are a constant source of information and joy.

Alex Hammowy's editing and comments were extremely helpful, and we are appreciative of the additional help provided by Sophia Andrade, Emily Robinson, and Ben Small.

We are indebted to our friends and colleagues who have been enthusiastic about this project, in particular Susan Spitz, Henry's spouse, whose love, patience, and support made this possible and Ken Lown, whose gratitude and support was very helpful. In addition, Susan's editorial expertise and clinical wisdom were invaluable in the completion of this text.

PART

I

INTRODUCTORY PRINCIPLES

1

CHAPTER

The Language of Substance Abuse

It is essential to have a common language for understanding the intricacies of substance abuse. There are several definitions of frequently used terms which are necessary to establish a shared baseline of understanding. These terms include:

☐ Abuse

Abuse refers to any use of a given substance which has an unwanted impact upon the user. It is not the amount of the substance that is used that determines abuse, rather it is *the effect that substance has on the individual* and his/her life that dictates whether the substance is being abused. The substance use must interfere with the person's functioning. For instance, certain individuals behave "badly" when they drink. They are said to not be able to hold their liquor well. If such an individual drinks even a small amount, such as a glass of wine, and then acts inappropriately or irresponsibly, that person can be said to be abusing alcohol.

A second factor which defines abuse is *whether or not the substance use is culturally sanctioned.* At certain times and in certain cultures, it is socially acceptable to become intoxicated. The Jewish faith provides for two holidays, Purim, and Simchat Torah—when it is perfectly appropriate for men to drink alcohol and become mildly intoxicated. A man in his mid twenties attending a bachelor party in Russia would be expected to become drunk. Provided he did not try to drive home, and the risks involved with intoxication were kept to a minimum, it is arguable that that person is not *abusing* alcohol. Caution must be exercised here; if that same young man goes to bachelor parties on a regular basis and his drinking begins to interfere with his health or work life, then he would be abusing alcohol. Furthermore, interfering with functioning is a subtle and complex phenomenon. An individual may drink several glasses of wine each evening, stating that he/she is doing it "for my health." He or she may never become intoxicated, but may be emotionally unavailable to his or her children, spouse, or partner. Many would consider this substance abuse.

If it is *acceptable within the context of one's culture* to use a substance, then it is not abuse. For example, members of the North American Indian Church take peyote as part of their monthly religious rites. For such individuals, it is part of their culture. For a young Baptist woman to take the same peyote and discuss her "trip" with her congregation at Sunday church would not be considered normal and would therefore constitute abuse.

□ Addiction

While "addiction" is not a scientific term, it is widely used and broadly understood and will consequently be used throughout this book. The term "addiction" refers to *a global pattern in which the person's substance use (and in this case, abuse) dominates the person's life.* A great deal of time is spent in obtaining the substance, planning for its use, and in using it. For example, a person who spends all of his or her money on cocaine, has lost a job, and had at least some significant relationships suffer because of cocaine dependence, fits the description of an addict. Addiction is a pejorative term and implies a maladaptive pattern of behavior. The term "addict" would be misused when referring to someone who is taking a reinforcing substance responsibly. A person who has been prescribed benzodiazepines for a diagnosed anxiety disorder, and is taking them responsibly, may be physiologically dependent on them, but is not an addict.

Dependence

Dependence has two components:

Physiological Dependence

Physiological dependence refers to an individual's body which has adapted to a substance such that the substance is needed in order for him or her to function normally. The individual craves the substance and must have it or else he or she will not feel normal. With certain substances, such as alcohol, abrupt withdrawal may lead to dangerous consequences.

Physiological dependence does not necessarily imply abuse. The person who needs to take alcohol several times a day and drinks in the morning to avoid withdrawal symptoms is clearly abusing alcohol and is physiologically dependent. The person who is diagnosed with an anxiety disorder may be prescribed benzodiazepine therapy. Abrupt withdrawal of these medicines could be extremely painful and may lead to seizures. This person is dependent upon benzodiazepines, but is not abusing them.

Many people, including many of the readers of this book, are physiologically dependent on caffeine. People who are physiologically addicted to caffeine drink coffee or other caffeinated beverages every day. Withdrawal is sometimes only noticed inadvertently. For example, observant Jewish people may only realize their physiological dependence on caffeine during Yom Kippur, a Jewish holiday when they abstain from ingesting food or beverages of any kind. The same can be said of observant Muslims during the month of Ramadan. Withdrawal symptoms include nervousness, headaches, and irritability. It is believed that many post-surgical headaches are the result of caffeine withdrawal because patients are told to refrain from eating or drinking prior to and immediately after surgery.

Psychological Dependence

People who are non-physiologically dependent do not experience physical withdrawal symptoms when they stop using the substance to which they are addicted. If they still need the substance in order to feel emotionally stable or to function normally, they are said to be *psychologically dependent*. Psychological dependence refers to the perceived need for any given substance.

It is impossible to become physiologically dependent upon any hallucinogens. Certain people feel that LSD helps them to function more successfully in social situations; these people are classified as dependent on hallucinogens, even though they are not physiologically dependent.

Tolerance

Tolerance refers to the need for increasing amounts of a given substance in order to achieve the same effect. Each substance has an index of tolerance, which means that there is an upper limit to what degree any organism can develop tolerance to that substance. Alcohol develops a clear and rapid tolerance, which almost never exceeds more than twice that of the initiate. This means that someone who drinks in large quantities on a frequent basis will be about twice as tolerant as when he/she first began to drink. Tolerance dissipates as well, and with abstinence, it reverts back to its original state. Individuals can develop tolerance to a number of different substances. For example, people often need to use increasing amounts of heroin in order to feel its effects or to feel normal. Another example of the development of tolerance is in the individual abusing benzodiazepines, who requires increasing amounts in order to feel the same effects.

Use

Almost all people have some socially acceptable, mood-altering substance in their culture. In many cases the mood-altering substance adds enjoyment to life. For example, wine can be a social lubricant and has been proven to have some medicinal value. Peyote seems to be an integral part of certain Indian tribal customs. Caffeine is an addictive substance that most people would say is relatively harmless, yet, it is a daily ritual taken in the form of coffee, tea, soda, or chocolate in many parts of the world.

Withdrawal

Withdrawal is the response an individual may experience after an addictive substance of abuse is removed from the body. Withdrawal, as with dependence, may or may not be physiological. Alcohol withdrawal is perhaps the most dramatic and dangerous withdrawal syndrome. Each substance of abuse has its own withdrawal syndrome. Generally, the withdrawal state is the inverse of the intoxication state. Heroin intoxication usually causes relaxation, a feeling of euphoria, complete lack of pain or irritation, and pin point pupils. Heroin withdrawal is characterized by agitation, irritability, depression, aching, and dilated pupils.

2

CHAPTER

Historical Perspectives

Human use of substances to alter mood and consciousness is ubiquitous. Almost all societies, in all eras, have had some substance that enhanced mood, altered consciousness, or promoted spiritual enlightenment.

Substances of abuse act on biological systems that already exist in humans. By altering or enhancing these systems, substances can profoundly change perception, behavior, and experience. This is often pleasurable and it is no wonder that many people have historically turned to exogenous means of enhancement. The Greeks and Romans preferred wine, the Ottomans, opium, the Zulus, cola nut, the Aztecs, high dose caffeine, and the Incas, cocaine from coca leaves. These are but a few of the almost countless cultures that were influenced and, in part, defined by their use of substances.

The following is a brief overview of the history of substance abuse, its surrounding laws, and related treatment issues. An individual history of each substance is found in the introduction to its respective chapter.

The most ubiquitous substance of abuse in American culture is probably tobacco. It was the first cash crop in the New World, and its commerce with the Old World fueled much of the economic growth in the beginning of this nation's history. Alcohol has been the subject of recurrent prohibition crusades since the beginning of American history. These sanctions were influenced by the dominant Protestant ethos of the American ruling class.

Alcohol was associated with immigrant classes during the nineteenth century. Although a nation of immigrants, America has had a tendency to denigrate whoever has comprised the most recent wave of immigration. The scapegoating of the Irish, Italians, and Eastern Europeans for their reliance on whisky, wine, and vodka, eventually led to the passage of the Nineteenth amendment, ratified by all but two states (Connecticut and Rhode Island) in 1919. Although Prohibition did result in decreased health complications due to alcohol abuse, the character of the nation was so intertwined with alcohol, that these new laws were unpopular and frequently broken, even by otherwise law abiding citizens. The amendment was eventually repealed in October of 1933. Franklin Roosevelt, who loved dry martinis, celebrated signing the act by serving the first legal drink in the White House that evening.

Since that time alcohol has been regulated by the Federal government, individual states, and local ordinances. There was a lowering of the drinking age in many states in response to social pressures during the Vietnam war era. The rationale for this was that it seemed hypocritical to allow someone to die for their country and to vote, but not legally drink alcohol. One of the unfortunate consequences was a sharp increase in highway fatalities. Under pressure from the Federal government to restrict highway funds to states that did not raise the drinking age to 21, most states complied.

There is evidence to indicate that the recreational use and abuse of opiates and cocaine increased in the late nineteenth century, resulting in a greater awareness of the pernicious effects of these drugs. In 1914, President Taft declared that, "Cocaine addiction has become the worst public health problem in America." In addition, heroin and morphine addiction was becoming a more and more prevalent problem. This led to the passage of the Harrison Act of 1914, which effectively gave control of the regulation of narcotics and similar substances to the Federal government. It curtailed certain "drug doctors" and made it illegal to prescribe narcotics for the sole purpose of maintaining a dependence on the drug.

In the 1930s, marijuana became associated with another wave of immigrants, this time from Mexico. Fear of marijuana and exaggerated claims of its propensity to create violence, as evidenced in the film "Reefer Madness," led to the adoption of the Marijuana Stamp Act. This made it necessary for an individual to obtain a stamp from the Federal government in order to sell marijuana legally. No stamps were ever issued.

The twentieth century has seen more and more government involvement in the issue of substance abuse. The forties, fifties, and early sixties were characterized by a diminution of drug use in most of the population and a more punitive role on the part of the government. Mandatory sentences were introduced for trafficking in heroin. During the first half of the twentieth century, the Federal government became more and more involved with the regulation of drugs. The response to dangerous drugs escalated from simply requiring accurate labeling of ingredients, to the possibility of the death penalty for drug sales.

President Nixon continued this tough stance, whereby his Comprehensive Drug Abuse and Control Act of 1970 brought together and attempted to organize all previous drug legislation under the interstate commerce powers of the Federal government. That law introduced scheduling for controlled substances, a policy which still exists today. Subsequent legislation created the present structure in the United States which includes the National Institute on Drug Abuse (NIDA), a branch of the National Institute of Health that pursues the drug research component of national policy, and the Drug Enforcement Agency which oversees efforts in law enforcement.

The 1980s saw the introduction of the "war on drugs." This was a combined effort by many governmental forces to reduce both the supply of and demand for drugs. Some of the more prominent features were the so-called "Just say 'No'" campaign championed by Nancy Reagan, and increased efforts at interdiction. In 1988, the Office of National Drug Control Policy (ONDCP) was created. This is headed by the "drug czar," a cabinet-level position.

Another well-known example of noteworthy public health campaigns is the "This is your brain—this is your brain on drugs" ad campaign which showed a frying egg. This commercial was produced by the Partnership for a Drug Free America. The late 1980s saw a marked reduction in the use of cocaine, alcohol, and marijuana, as well as a dramatic decrease in nicotine consumption. Those trends have significantly reversed in recent years, and it appears that the use of the "gateway drugs" such as nicotine and marijuana are on the rise in young people. "Gateway drugs" refer to those substances which are most commonly the first drugs tried by young people. These substances then lead to other "harder" drugs.

An appreciation of the historical pathways of substance abuse enables an understanding of the context in which contemporary treatment efforts have evolved. In order to approach issues of intervention in substance-abusing populations, it is necessary to have a familiarity with some of the basic science involved in addiction.

3

CHAPTER

Neurobiology of Addiction

Anyone who has worked with a substance abuser, especially someone addicted to a substance like cocaine, has witnessed the repetitive, self-destructive, and illogical behavior that can result. One cannot help but wonder about the origins of this behavior, for it is primitive, powerful, and beyond the will. This behavior, like all addictive behaviors, is biologically driven.

Laboratory animals exposed to powerful drugs show striking similarities in behavior to their human counterparts. When given unrestricted access to cocaine, mice, rats, or indeed almost any laboratory animal will do virtually anything to get another dose of the stimulant. A rat who has been exposed to cocaine extensively and has been taught that pressing a lever will be rewarded with one dose of cocaine, will perform that task ***hundreds of thousands of times*** for just one more dose. Furthermore, the animal, if given the option of working for cocaine or any other reward, will work preferentially for cocaine to the exclusion of everything else. A rat or mouse will actually forgo food to the point of death to get cocaine. Such behavior seems remarkably similar to that of human crack addicts, who will work incessantly and act in unimaginably self-destructive ways to obtain just one more dose.

Numerous laboratory models involving animals and addictive substances exist. In one of the first of these experiments, in the early part of the century, chimpanzees exposed to morphine would drag researchers to the cupboard where the morphine, syringes, and needles were stored and voluntarily assume the "proper position" to receive the injection. There is little difference between the behavior of the animals studied and their human counterparts.

When animals are allowed to self-medicate a substance, their intake patterns parallel those of humans. Unlimited ethanol self-administration in animals is characterized by alternating binge and abstinence periods. Barbiturate and dissociative anesthetic self-administration is characterized by maximum self-administration of the available drug without periods of abstinence. Free availability of benzodiazepines results in very modest intake patterns. Unlimited access to opiates results in a self-administration that is quite uniform and constant, characterized by a moderate and measured pattern (though usually with a large initial dose). Opiate intake in this pattern does not have abstinence periods. Unlimited self-administration of stimulants is characterized by alternating periods of administration that sometimes reach frenzied levels. During abstinent periods, a semblance of the normal behavior pattern resumes. Although variations certainly exist, each of these examples closely resembles the pattern of use most typically associated with human addictions.

The reasons for the similarity between these animal behaviors and that of their human counterparts is not coincidental. The axiom that all members of the animal kingdom, including humans, share many characteristics and have "the same architect, just a different floor-plan" applies to the study of addiction. In fact, the brains of all mammals are remarkably similar. Phylogenetically, the human brain is different only in the most recently developed parts which largely control speech, communication, and abstract reasoning. The most primitive parts of the human brain and the ones that control its most primitive and vital functions are remarkably similar to those of our mammalian cousins. It is in these primitive "reptile brain" portions, present in all mammals, that substances of abuse exert their most potent effects.

Animals will self-inject abusable substances directly into their brains if they are given the opportunity. The drug must be introduced into specific parts of the brain that control reward and pleasure. There are only a few parts of the brain where such self-injection will result. If allowed to inject into more primitive portions, they will do so at a remarkable rate. These primitive portions of the brain are located in what is termed the midbrain. Although this portion connects (with projections of neurons) to the "higher" parts of the brain which govern more evolutionarily advanced functions, the midbrain is thought to contain the basic structures of the "brain reward system." The "brain reward system" is a complex and interconnected circuitry with far-reaching radiations to all other parts of the central nervous system. More research is being done on the func-

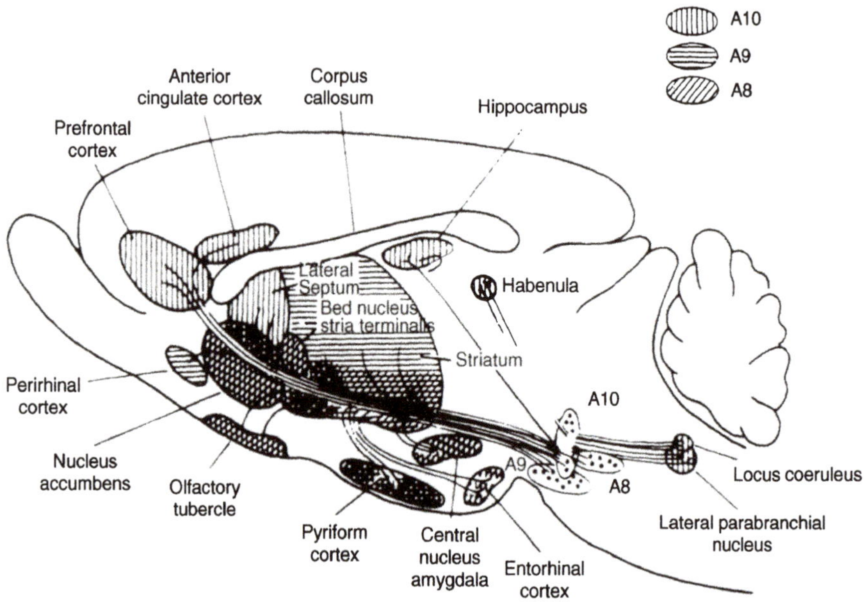

FIGURE 3.1.

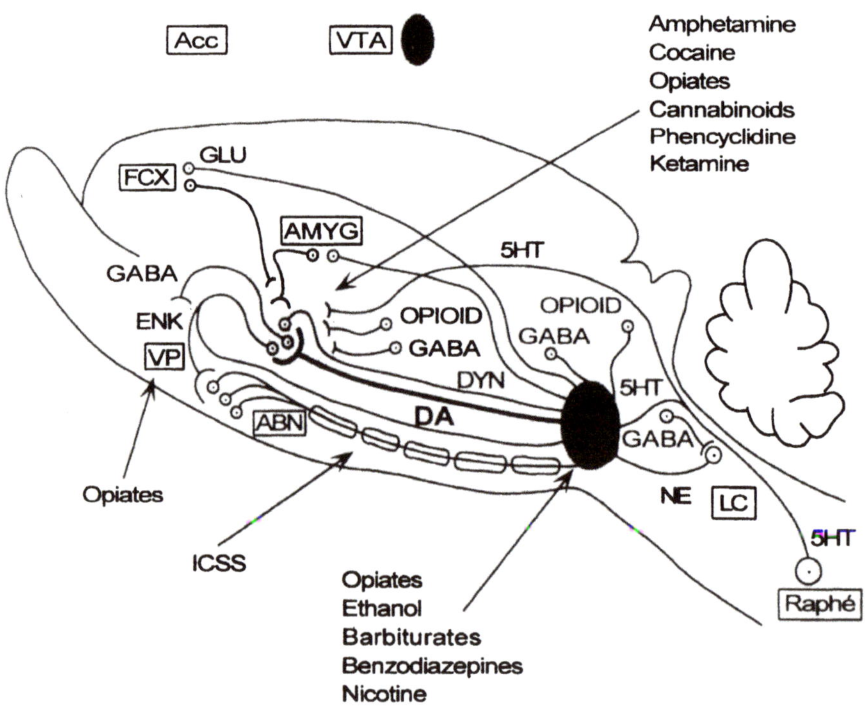

FIGURE 3.2.

tional anatomy of this system and how the dynamics of the molecules that control the system interact, work, and affect behavior.

Substances of abuse work at this portion of the brain, and specific substances act at different sites in the primitive brain to enhance brain-reward. These systems of neurons are located primarily in the deepest and most central of brain structures. The neurons, however, project to other parts of the brain that control such activities as thought and behavior. This is a critical point in understanding why treating addicts can be so hard. The principal areas affected by drugs of abuse are not higher centers, but those most primitive, which are not really under conscious voluntary control. It is thought that these areas, once stimulated, influence behavior and possibly drug craving. In this paradigm, the substances of abuse induce alterations in these primitive pathways, that then have manifestations on more complex phenomena such as behavior. In other words, the part of the brain that is affected is the most basic; the thoughts and feelings that humans later conceptualize are higher functions that are a response to changes in the primitive portions of the brain. This is why addicts so frequently describe feelings of being "out of control."

☐ Principles of Biology

Three billion years ago, about a billion years after the formation of our planet, complex carbon-based molecules were formed in ever-increasing complexity, sparked by the energy of the atmosphere and the abundance of chemicals in the ancient environment. The ability of these molecules to self-replicate marked the advent of what we call life. In the billions of years that followed, increasingly complex and adaptable systems developed. It is from these systems that contemporary mammalian and human species evolved.

Biological organisms developed a system of internal communication, the nervous system. In today's mammals, this consists of a mechanism which responds to the outside world and is termed the "peripheral nervous system." The "central nervous system" (CNS) is a catch all phrase for the pivotal and primary organized system of cells responsible for monitoring, reacting to, and adapting to the outside environment. In simple terms, this is the brain.

The human brain consists of 14 billion individual cells, each with a multitude of connections and interconnections. The cells communicate with one another in electrically charged transmission systems termed neurotransmitters. The following portions of this chapter are divided as follows. First is a brief discussion of the most important neurotransmitters and their synthesis. This is not intended to be comprehensive, but rather to introduce the reader to the most important of these molecules. Next is a discussion of neurotransmission, the process by which these chemicals allow the cells in the CNS and the periphery to "communicate." We will then talk about brain reward circuitry, the neuroanatomy of the systems most involved with this communication. This is the pleasure/reward system, among the most basic and fundamental systems of any organism, and the one that is altered in addiction. Addiction has been described as a process that "hijacks" the brain. We will describe how the systems which usually function to maintain homeostasis are altered by chemicals of abuse. Finally, a clinically useful theory, "the flipped switch" theory of addiction, is described. This is a partially understood model of addictive behavior, but one that the clinician working with an individual substance abuser may find useful.

☐ Neurotransmitters and Their Synthesis

The Mono-amines

The three most studied neurotransmitter systems—dopamine, serotonin, and norepinephrine—are each derived from one amino acid and are termed "the mono-amines." Amino acids are naturally-occurring substances. They are the building blocks of protein and are found in many food sources. Amino acids are ingested and absorbed into the blood on the way to the intestinal tract and cross the blood-brain barrier by way of an uptake pump into the brain. The biosynthesis of the neurotransmitter from its precursors is believed to take place in the neuron itself. It makes sense that the most primitive signals come from such rudimentary building blocks. These are ancient systems that involve the most primitive structures in the animal brain.

Dopamine

Tyrosine, the amino acid precursor of dopamine, is first converted to dihydroxyphenylalanine (dopa) by the enzyme tyrosine hydoxylase. This enzyme is the rate limiting step in the process. Dopa is then converted into dopamine. Dopamine is involved in the regulation of at least three major systems. It is involved in the tonal regulation of muscle coordination. These dopamine neurons are located in the substantia nigra, the so-called "black substance" which is the small, dark area of the brain that degenerates in Parkinson's' disease. Another dopamine pathway has its cell bodies in the hypothalamus, and its processes project toward the pituitary gland. Dopamine tonicly inhibits the hormone prolactin. Prolactin is involved in lactation and the suppression of other hormone responses. It is also likely to be involved in a wide variety of other responses, including some behaviors associated with maternity. The third dopamine system has cell bodies in an area of the brain stem named the ventral tegmentum. It is this pathway (which will be detailed later) that is involved in the most primitive area of brain reward mechanisms and thought to be involved in addictive processes.

Dopamine's effects are widespread, but in general, it serves to make the organism more alert and energized. It has been called the "gotta have it" neurotransmitter. Large amounts of dopamine are associated with heightened responses, and in larger amounts, aggression. When the system has achieved satiety, the effects of dopamine are constrained.

Serotonin

The neurotransmitter serotonin is synthesized from the amino acid tryptophan by the enzyme tryptophan hydroxylase. The product 5-Hydroxy tryptophan is then synthesized into the neurotransmitter 5-Hydroxy tryptamine or serotonin. The serotonin projections in the brain originate from a group of nuclei in the mid-line of the brainstem known as the raphe nuclei. Projections originating from the serotonin cells in this region ascend and branch with particularly dense projections in the limbic system. Serotonin is thought to be responsible for a variety of emotional responses and subsequently has an effect on behavior. Among these effects are a general sense of well-being, feelings of satiety, and the sexual response cycle, satisfaction associated with sex. Serotonin is thought to be a constraining and inhibiting force in the brain reward cycle and, therefore, an important neurotransmitter in the development and maintenance of addictions. In the simplest of models, a relative lack of serotonin leads to the unrestrained effects of dopamine.

Norepinephrine

Norepinephrine is synthesized from dopamine. There are differences, however, in where the cell bodies for the dopamine and norepinephrine neuronal pathways originate. The bulk of the norepinephrine neurons have their origin in a very small nucleus, or cluster of cells, called the locus ceruleus (Latin for "blue place," for its pale bluish-tinged look on dissection). From this small structure, neurons arise that branch out to touch as many as half of all the cells in the brain. Norepinephrine is not thought to be as directly involved with brain reward mechanisms, rather, it is involved in a variety of emotional and muscular actions.

Additional Neurotransmitters

GABA

Gamma amino butyric acid is ubiquitous in mammalian brains. It is the chief inhibitory neurotransmitter whose action is to make related neurons less likely to fire. GABA appears to be related to homeostasis and the regulation of affects and normal arousal. It does not seem to be associated with arousal during emergency situations.

Opioid Receptors

The opiate receptors are important in terms of pain relief and feelings of well-being. They are most likely intimately connected with feelings of pleasure and reward. There are a number of different subtypes of opioid receptors, the most important, best studied, and most understood is the μ (mu) receptor. Recent research has resulted in some confusion regarding the true function of the μ-receptors. A strain of mice bred without the μ-receptor is functionally identical to one with normal receptors. Whatever the evolutionary reason for the receptor, activation does produce feelings of calmness, analgesia, and pleasure.

It is thought that these circuits are intimately involved with normal reward and pleasure. Certain biologically necessary activities such as eating and sex can be enormously pleasurable and rewarding. Indeed, it is hard not to compare descriptions of sexual and gastronomic rapture with the drug addict's initial experience with cocaine or heroin. Much research, both laboratory and neuropsychological, supports this hypothesis. The normal reward and pleasure mechanisms are those that go seriously awry when addiction sets in.

NMDA

The NMDA receptors are perhaps the most common receptors in the mammalian brain but the least well understood. They are most likely involved with brain plasticity as well as learning and cognition. A recent emphasis on the excitatory amino acids has made this receptor the subject of much research which should, in the coming decade, illuminate its role in the functioning of the brain.

☐ Neurotransmission

Neurotransmitters mediate the passage of information via electrical impulses across a gap between neurons known as the synaptic cleft. In ad-

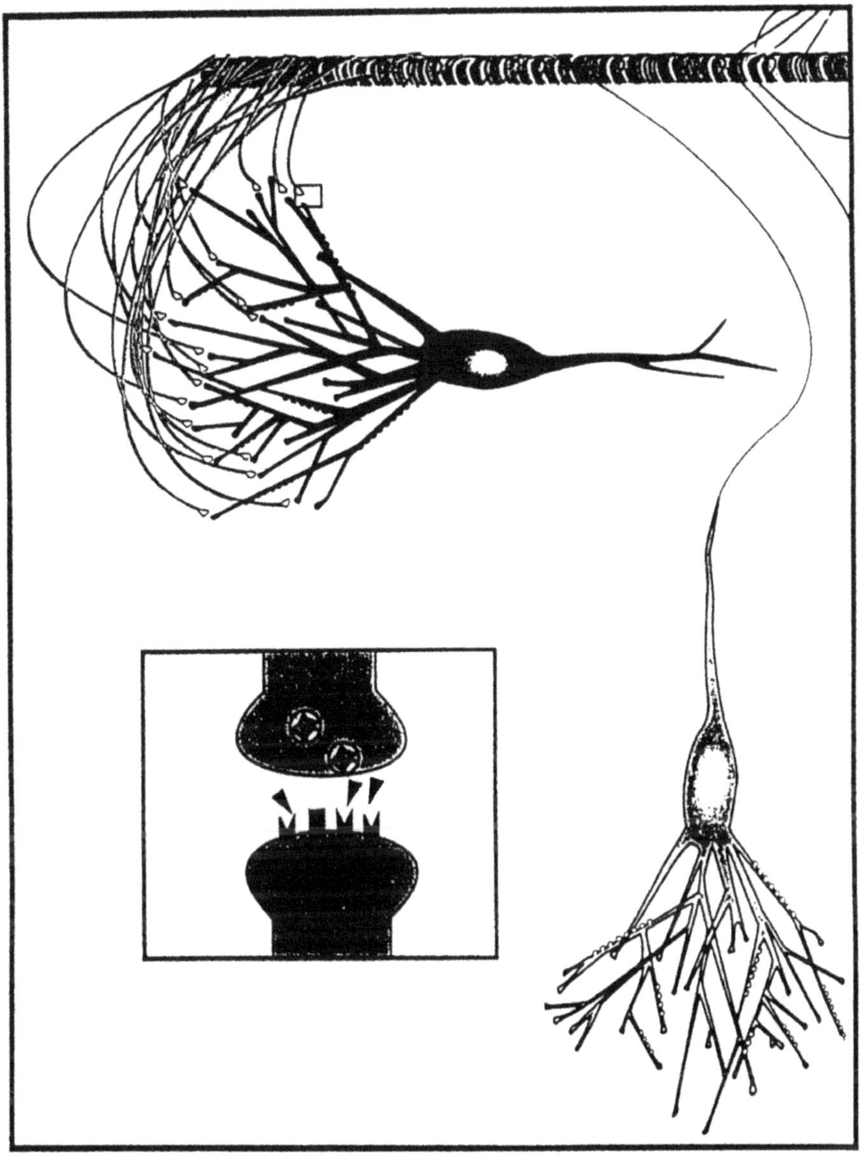

FIGURE 3.3. Shown here is normal communication between two neurons, with the synapse. Normal neurotransmission is being mediated here by neurotransmitter binding to postsynaptic receptors by the usual mechanism of synaptic neurotransmission.

dition, they regulate the frequency of the impulses that are transmitted. What follows is a highly simplified model which can be applied to all known neurotransmitters. Neurons consist of a cell body and numerous projections in the form of axons. For the purpose of clarity, the model shown below consists of only one body with a projecting axon.

Electrical impulses travel down the membrane of the axon and induce permeability changes in the membrane. Before receiving the signal, the membrane would not be permeable to a variety of charged molecules. Neurotransmitter molecules are, in general, stored in membrane-bound vesicles. After receiving the signal, the membrane changes and becomes permeable. This allows for release of the stored neurotransmitter. The neurotransmitter molecule is then released into the synaptic cleft. Neurotransmitters in the cleft naturally alight onto the adjacent receptor. In general, there are specific receptors into which these molecules fit. This fit, which can be conceptualized as a lock and key phenomenon, induces changes in the adjacent neuron (termed the post-synaptic neuron.) If the neurotransmitter is sufficiently powerful to induce chemical changes in this post-synaptic membrane, then these changes will result in the continuation of the signal in this neuron and a subsequent chain of events in neurons along this pathway.

The average neuron has many, many interconnections. Furthermore, many of the most prominent neurotransmitters are excitatory, that is they make it more likely that the signal will commence. However, other neurotransmitters, most notably the GABA system, are inhibitory, making the chemical changes in the membrane less likely to "travel." A given neuron may have a variety of inhibitory and excitatory connections making it more or less likely that the signal will continue.

The neurotransmitters which have effected the receptors float freely back into the synaptic cleft. There, one of two things occurs—the neurotransmitter is degraded by naturally-occurring enzymes, or it is taken back into the original cell in a process known as re-uptake. When the neurotransmitter goes through the process of re-uptake, it is reincorporated into the vesicles and again readied for release. It was first believed that enzymatic breakdown was the primary method in which neurotransmitters were inactivated. This is, however, only true for acetylcholine, a neurotransmitter primarily functional in the neuromuscular system. More commonly, re-uptake into the pre-synaptic nerve terminal is the primary mechanism for inactivation.

☐ Brain Reward Circuitry

The parts of the brain that are involved in these reward system are all located in the midbrain; this includes the nucleus accumbens, the ventral tegmental area, and the medial forebrain bundle. All these midbrain structures are loaded with neurons from various neurotransmitter systems, but are predominately filled with fibers from the dopamine, noradrenergic, and serotonin systems. (The specifics of these and other neurotransmitters are discussed below.) Current research on the neurobiology of addiction indicates that all abusable substances acutely enhance brain reward mechanisms. Another common theme is that all substances that create dependence raise dopamine levels in the nucleus accumbens (some substances may be abused, such as LSD, without raising dopamine, but they do not induce dependence).

The brain reward circuitry is complex and the following discussion is necessarily technical. For the average practicing clinician describing addiction to a patient, it is probably sufficient to explain that addiction is a biological phenomenon which effects the most primitive and vital parts of the mammalian brain. The following discussion is provided for those who want a fuller understanding of what is currently known about this complex system.

Abusable substances, acting on these circuits, effect the brain-reward circuitry in three stages:

1. The "first stage" circuit consists of descending, moderately fast conducting neurons that run caudal within the medial forebrain bundle. These fibers synapse into the ventral mesencephalic nuclei containing the cell bodies of one of the important dopamine pathways. (These dopaminergic neurons are called the meso-telencephalic dopamine pathway.) These project to various limbic structures as well as higher cortical controlling areas (the higher brain which can process, and adds meaning and interpretation to, feelings.)
2. These fibers constitute the "second stage" fibers of the reward system and the most important synapse in the nucleus accumbens "shell."
3. From the nucleus accumbens shell various "third stage" neurons project and interconnect with different neurotransmitter systems from areas both adjacent and quite far removed.

Complex and reciprocal interconnections exist between the "first stage," "second stage," and "third stage" reward mechanism and highlight the complexity of the system. Put more simply, the substances of abuse excite, in a way we do not yet understand, fibers that connect into the nucleus accumbens. These fibers are then excited in the second stage of this paradigm, and connect to fibers in other parts of the emotional and higher brain structures in the third phase of this model.

Chemicals of Abuse

Millions of chemicals are currently known to exist in nature. Given the mathematical complexity of carbon molecule interaction, the possibilities for other chemical compounds are limitless. Only a few dozen compounds, however, are abused by mammals. It is interesting to note that these chemicals are quite different from one another in structure and pharmacological class. The two carbon ethanol molecule, for example, bares little resemblance to the quite complex morphine molecule with its chains of amino acids.

All abusable substances, with a few rare exceptions, have three things in common that distinguish them from other compounds that do not have the same physiological effects. First, the molecules that are abused by humans are those that are self-administered by laboratory animals. The corollary to this is that chemicals that are eschewed by humans are similarly eschewed by lab animals and are not self-administered. Second, nearly all abusable substances studied enhance brain-stimulation reward mechanisms, or they lower the reward threshold in the midbrain dopamine system. Finally, all of these substances enhance the basal rate of firing of neurotransmitter systems in the brain reward circuits.

☐ The "Flipped Switch" Theory

A majority of researchers and clinicians now believe in the so-called "flipped switch" theory of alcoholism and drug addiction. Most people can use most substances without becoming addicted, however, the use of a substance for a long enough time seems to push people over the edge into addiction. The amount needed to become addicted is different for different people. Some people may drink alcohol in large amounts for many years and when they feel that they need to stop—for example, to start a new medication—they have no problem doing so. Others can use a substance for a very short time and become seemingly hopelessly out of control with it. An example of this is smoked coccaine "crack." This is highly addictive and some individuals require only one initial exposure to lose control over its use. As yet, we have no predictive capability for what the vulnerability is for a given person.

The following are two actual clinical examples illustrating the variability of the flipped switch:

> Brian is a 32 year-old Asian man, engaged to be married and working as an assistant manager at a car rental company. Brian had used cocaine intranasally a number of times in his life and liked it, but would not have been considered by himself or any one in his life as having a problem. On a Friday night in October, Brian decided to try crack cocaine, as he had "heard so much about it." He described the "first hit" as the most intense experience of his life, and he felt compelled to have another, and another, and another. He used up all his money from his checking account and in the next four

days, sold all his jewelry and his car to pay for crack. On Tuesday morning, having not slept for four days, he was exhausted, horrified at what he had done, and suicidally depressed. He attempted to cut his jugular vein with a broken glass and was rushed to the hospital emergency room where he was admitted to an in-patient unit.

Barry is a 48 year-old, unemployed married man of Italian descent. He has a long history of drinking, but has never met the criteria for alcohol dependence. On numerous occasions he has stopped drinking, when he had a project due or was taking medication, without any trouble. Barry was cast as an extra in a movie about barflies and hoodlums. This required him to sit in a bar for 12 to 14 hours per day every day for three weeks. The bar where the scenes were filmed was a real one and the kegs were not switched with non-alcoholic beer. Barry drank throughout the filming because it was available and the rest of the crew was doing it as well. When filming stopped, however, Barry found he was shaking in the morning and needed a drink to "steady his nerves." He continued to drink throughout the day and was unable to stop until he presented for a hospital detoxification.

The above examples are of two individuals who were exposed to substances and became addicted. The first needed only one exposure, while the second, although exposed for years to alcohol, had not developed alcoholism until he had a period of heavy and sustained drinking. Why these differences exist is largely unknown. Recently, scientists discovered a gene that seems to protect people from becoming dependent upon nicotine. That is, those individuals who have this gene can smoke for even long periods of time, and stop without much difficulty at all. Currently, with most substances, it is not easy to predict how much exposure an individual will need to become an addict.

This overview of the neuroanatomy and neurochemistry of addiction illustrates the biological substrate upon which brain and behavior interact. Physiological factors also play a role in the development of addiction. Some of these principles form the basis of the next chapter.

4

CHAPTER

Physiology of Addiction

The individual physiological effects of the substances of abuse are discussed in individual chapters concerning those substances. There are, however, a few important principles which apply to all substances. They are important for the clinician to know about in order to better understand how these substances work and how they influence individual addictions.

Route of Administration

In order for a substance to have an effect, it must be taken into the body and then enter the brain. The brain protects itself with a remarkable, but complex mechanism called the blood-brain barrier. While blood carries nourishment to the brain (as well as all of the other organs of the body), the system of the brain is kept separate. Certain substances, however, are able to penetrate, or cross the blood-brain barrier and then affect the central nervous system. These are small molecules or substances that are lipid-soluble, which means they easily dissolve in and pass through membranes.

Before entering the brain, a substance must get into the blood stream. There are several means by which this takes place. Substances may be ingested orally and then pass through the oral mucosa, the stomach lining, or into the intestine. They may be inhaled (insufflated) and absorbed in the nasal mucosa or in some instances, the lungs. Substances may be aerosolized (or pyrolized as in smoking), and taken directly into the lung. In addition, they may also be injected directly into the venous system. (The arterial system leads directly to end organs, and injecting in this way generally leads to localized damage.)

The way a substance is taken into the body has enormous implications for the addictive potential of that substance. In general, *the rate that a substance is taken in and crosses the blood-brain barrier is directly proportional to its level of reinforcement.* This is true of all substances. If a substance is taken in slowly, it is not as reinforcing or as addicting. Cocaine taken in by mouth, as when a Peruvian farmer chews coca leaves, has a gradual rate of absorption and relatively little reinforcement or addictive potential. The user in this example feels mild stimulation, and decreased appetite, much like a strong cup of coffee. "Crack" or injected cocaine, however, both have a rapid, almost instantaneous absorption and are highly addicting. Intranasal cocaine is somewhere in between the former and latter examples just noted.

With alcohol, the level of absorption is responsible for the reinforcing properties experienced as a "buzz." A shot of tequila on an empty stomach will result in a powerful feeling of intoxication as the liquor is absorbed rapidly through the mucosal lining of the stomach. A glass of wine taken over the course of a large meal may only result in a pleasant feeling of relaxation. Both the shot of tequila and the glass of wine contain the same amount of ethanol, but they reach the brain at very different rates and

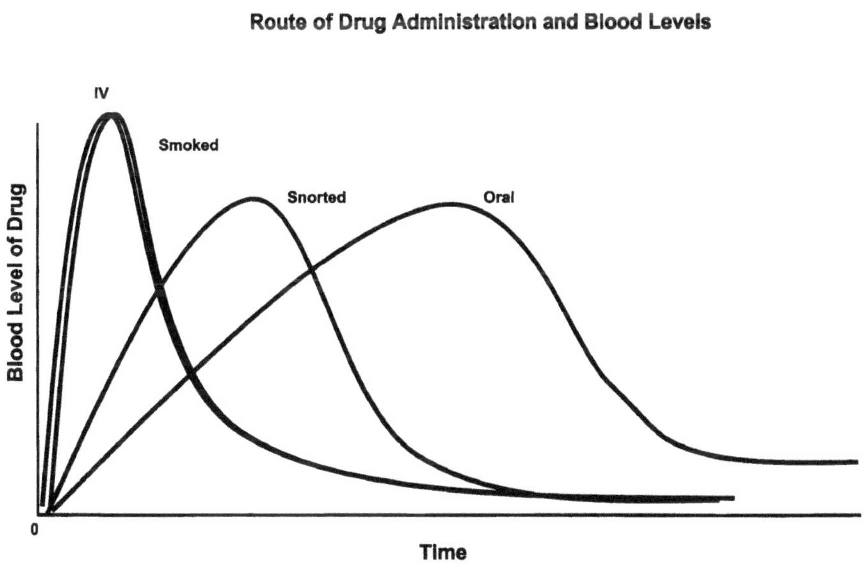

FIGURE 4.1. Route of Administration

therefore, have very different effects. Another way of thinking about this is to imagine the receptors in the brain as buttons. It is how hard and how fast the substance of abuse "hits" the button (or receptor) that determines how reinforcing the substance is, and how great the pleasure/reward experienced.

Figure 4.1 illustrates these principles.

☐ Intoxication and Withdrawal

Another universal principle with addicting substances is that the effects of intoxication with the substance are mirror opposites to the effects of withdrawal. If one does not know what withdrawal from a certain substance is, he/she may think what the intoxication is like. For example, alcohol causes relaxation and lethargy; withdrawal from alcohol is characterized by anxiety and agitation. In the case of opiates, intoxication is characterized by, among other things, feelings of well-being, analgesia, constipation and pin point pupils; withdrawal from opiates is characterized by feelings of misery and discomfort, diarrhea, and large pupils. This is obviously an oversimplification, but the principle, in general, holds and provides a handy guide for the clinician.

The following table describes intoxication and withdrawal from cocaine.

The principles of physiology are intimately intertwined with the experience and effects of abusable substances. The chemicals involved do not exert their effects in a vacuum, but rather combine with the laboratory animal or human being taking them. The physiological makeup of an organism results from a complex interplay between the environment of

TABLE 4.1. Acute and after effects of cocaine use

Acute effects (early during the high)	After effects (late during, or post-binge)
1. Elation	1. Depression
2. Activation	2. Fatigue
3. Confidence	3. Paranoia
4. Friendliness	4. Irritability
5. Calm	5. Panic
6. Disinhibition	6. Self-consciousness
7. Self-admiration	7. Self-loathing
8. Interest	8. Apathy
9. Anorexia	9. Hunger

that organism, and the genes that constitute the code for the organism's makeup. Genetics determine the way these substances of abuse effect an organism and the predilection and susceptibility to addiction. The subject of genetics is the topic of the chapter that follows.

5

CHAPTER

Genetic Factors

The debate over what constitutes the influence of nature versus that of nurture is a perennially controversial theme. As far back as the ancient Greeks, there were arguments about what was learned and what was inherited or given by nature. These discussions have not tempered in modern times. Little more than a century and a half ago, it took Darwin thirty years to gather the courage and stamina to publish his *Origin of Species*, which formulated the theory of evolution. Interestingly enough, that book does not even mention man, but rather concentrates on the evolution of finches.

Modern times have seen increasing amounts of research and discovery in the area of genetics. Today, it is no longer novel to learn of discoveries linking various human illnesses to a particular gene on a particular chromosome.

The same debate about the role of genetics has raged on in the field of substance abuse. It has become increasingly clear that genetics has a significant, yet somewhat ambiguous relationship to substance abuse in the population. For centuries, people believed that drunkenness was a vice, and the product of a weak character, or the result of the devil's work. It is now abundantly clear that the genes an individual inherits interact in a complex way with his or her environment and, in many cases, predispose an individual to a substance-abuse condition. To paraphrase a famous witticism, in terms of substance abuse, as well as many other aspects of life, it is important to choose one's parents wisely.

Most of the genetic research in the field of substance abuse has been focused thus far on alcohol, and the vast majority of research has concentrated on men. Although there is certainly an interest in other substances of abuse, the large majority of data collected centers on the genetic transmission of alcoholism. Therefore, the data from the studies on alcoholism form the basis for the following discussion.

Genetics is the study of genes and their expression. It is the part of a person's makeup that comes entirely from his or her DNA and its expression. It is not fully dependent upon environment, although there is clear, subtle interplay between environment and genetics that is ongoing and dynamic. Environment is a broad term and refers to any external influence. Environmental factors are as varied as hormones in utero with the mother, a person's culture, and family relations.

Methodology

Traditionally, the search for genetic factors that influence substance abuse centered on studies of families, twins, and adoptees who are addicted to drugs or alcohol. The next generation of research has focused on isolating the specific genetic component, gene, or gene expression that predisposes an individual to becoming dependent upon a substance. Although epidemiological studies are filled with contradictions, it is clear that genes play a large role in the predisposition, eventual development, and maintenance of substance abuse problems.

Epidemiological Studies

Family Studies

The majority of family studies tend to support the claim that on some level there is a genetic predisposition to substance abuse. Family studies are usually conducted by comparing individual families and their members with substance abuse histories to similar families without such substance abuse histories. On average, close relatives of individuals with a significant substance abuse disorder are three to five times more likely to develop a substance abuse problem. That is, if a first-degree relative (a relative who is one step away from the index individual (i.e., a parent, sibling or child) has a dependence on a given substance, his or her first degree relative will be three to five times more likely to have a substance dependence problem with that substance. This is independent of environmental factors which also have great influence on this problem.

Twin Studies

Dizygotic twins are commonly referred to as fraternal twins. They are like any other brother/sister pair, with the exception that they share the same uterus and are born at around the same time.

Monozygotic twins are commonly called identical twins. They too share the same uterine environment, but, in addition, they share the same genetic material. They are identical in every way (except for minor spontaneous mutations) genetically. Early in the development of monozygotic twins, for reasons we do not understand, the fully formed zygote completely splits into two separate living beings which grow up to share many, but not all characteristics.

Scientists and researchers believe that they can investigate which traits are learned and which traits are inherited from studying monozygotic twins. If each of the monozygotic twins is not malnourished, height and body build are almost always identical. Intelligence quotient (IQ), a complex measure of the ability to acquire and work with knowledge, but not necessarily the motivation to learn, is also almost always identical. Other factors are much more ambiguous. The logic in these studies is that if there is not one hundred percent similarity or concordance, then the difference can be explained by environmental factors. Homosexuality, being gay, has a 50% concordance among gay male identical twins. That is, if one twin is gay his brother has a 50% chance of also being gay. In fraternal twins, the concordance rate is only 8%. Clearly, sexual orientation has both a genetic and environmental (either intrauterine, or that of the early world of the infant) basis.

Achievement is something that has both a genetic and an environmental component. If an individual is born with an IQ in the retarded range, it is unlikely that he or she will grow to run a large corporation. Similarly, a person may have a genius IQ, but lack motivation and therefore, be as unlikely to run the same corporation.

In Sweden, a country known for its meticulous documentation of genetic records, a large study found that the concordance rates for alcoholism for monozygotic and dizygotic twins was 58% and 28%, respectively. A large study done in the USA showed similar results. The majority of twin studies support the notion that there is a definite genetic role in the establishment and maintenance of alcoholism in any given individual. Most, if not all, experts in the field believe there is a similar genetic basis for *all* substance abuse disorders, not just alcoholism.

Adoption Studies

Adoption studies either look at half siblings, or more classically, look at individuals who were adopted at an early age, and raised apart from their biological families. The index child is studied along with his or her adopted family and his or her biological family. Several large studies have been done using this methodology and most have come to similar conclusions. Biological sons of alcoholics raised by different families have a four times higher risk of alcoholism than other adoptive siblings in the same household.

In summary, adoption studies indicate that there is a strong genetic component which interacts with an individual's environment and predisposes him or her if he or she has genetic links to alcoholism. There are some limitations to these studies. Since most of the studies have examined only men, and most have focused on only alcohol as the abused substance, it is hard to generalize these results to the larger population of substance abusers. Studies of other substances have been harder to duplicate. This is for a variety of complex reasons including the social stigma associated with admitting using these other illicit substances, and the comparatively recent epidemics of abuse of substances such as cocaine. Still, most researchers believe that genetic determinants play a critical role in the development of alcoholism and other substance-abuse conditions.

Biological Studies

Enzymes

Over the years, there have been many intriguing tests for possible biological markers of alcoholism and other forms of drug addition. These are tests which demonstrate and verify the presence or absence of a biological propensity towards substance abuse. These markers have included various isoenzyme forms of aldehyde dehydrogenase, the major enzyme that degrades alcohol in the liver. Other enzymes have included monoamine oxidase and various other blood platelet enzymes. There has been consistent interest in comparing alcoholics and their relatives with control subjects on human leukocyte antigens (HLA). These are complex sets of proteins located on white blood cells and that are quite different in various populations and can be used. The vast majority of researchers believe that someday soon, one of these markers will prove reliable for at least a subtype of alcoholic. There are laboratory tests that demonstrate the heavy use of some substances such as corohydrate-deficient transferrin for alcohol use or dependence, but there is no enzyme test which will identify the future alcoholic.

Other Biological Markers

Equally elusive has been the search for alternative biological markers. Certain physiological markers, such as event-related potentials (ERPs), have been used extensively to study information processing in high- and low-risk populations. ERPs are electrical measures recorded from the scalp and are thought to reflect a variety of brain activities. Some of these patterns change with alcohol ingestion and there is hope that these will someday show more definitive and practical results.

It has also been difficult to find a link between personality profiles and the risk of developing alcoholism. Emphasis has been placed on linking those individuals who thrive on novelty, engage in risk-seeking behaviors, and have low harm avoidance as predicting future alcohol or drug abuse. Some of the results of studies aimed at uncovering personality traits that are correlated with alcoholism have been promising, but have not yet been substantiated. It must be concluded that, at present, the link between personality and substance abuse is probable but the specifics are still theoretical. It is likely that some traits predispose an individual to alcoholism or drug abuse, but these traits interact not only with the environment, but also with genetics. There is no single "alcoholic personality."

The "sway test" has shown more reliability than most tests in response to alcohol consumption. In this type of study, individuals are given various, sometimes prodigious, amounts of alcohol and are asked to walk or simply stand. Complex machines then measure the amount of sway induced by a given amount of alcohol. Generally, the more alcohol ingested, the more apparent the sway. Some individuals can consume a great amount of alcohol and not sway very much at all. These probably are those individuals who are said to have "a wooden or hollow leg" and do not appear to be particularly inebriated at the end of a long night of drinking. In these studies, the hypothesis is that individuals with the least amount of sway are much more likely to eventually develop alcoholism. The understanding is that most individuals, after a few drinks, develop the feeling of being "tipsy." They lose coordination and begin to slur their words. Most people find this aspect of drinking unpleasant and, in response, limit their intake. If an individual did not have those warning signs, he or she might just rush past the point of mild inebriation to full drunkenness. If the "flipped switch" theory of alcoholism does indeed hold true, then these individuals may become alcoholics more readily than the larger population.

The studies of other forms of drug abuse and genetics are equally intriguing but even murkier than the studies of alcoholism. The same theories seem to apply and much work is being done to further elucidate the subject. It is clear that an individual's genes are important in the development of substance-abuse disorders and are probably related to the substance of choice itself, yet its exact nature is still undetermined. That topic will be covered in a later chapter on dual diagnosis and the self-medication hypothesis.

6

CHAPTER

Epidemiology of Substance Abuse

Epidemiology refers to the patterns of occurrence of a disease or its incidence in a given society or population. Epidemiology here represents the rates of either substance use, or abuse. The United States is the leader among all other countries for its development of a sophisticated method of monitoring substance abuse in its population. The clinician, lawmaker, or individual who wishes to be informed about substance abuse has a variety of tools to assess the degree of substance abuse occurring at any given time.

Epidemiology is concerned with incidence, prevalence, and distribution. Incidence refers to the number of times something is done. Prevalence refers to how often that something happens. Distribution refers to the patterns of use in any given group, subgroup, or population.

Prevalence rates are usually discussed in a variety of ways. Point prevalence refers to the frequency at any given time that use occurs. For example, 76% of the population currently drinks at least one alcoholic beverage in any given year. That figure is an example of point prevalence. Lifetime figures refer to the use or abuse of substances at any time in an individual's life. For example, the lifetime figure for alcohol abuse for the American male is 22%. That means that 22% of the male population has, at one time in their lives, met the criteria for alcohol abuse. The term "lifetime figure" does not imply severity or differentiate abuse from dependence.

For substance abuse, incidence is the number of new cases in a specific population. Incidence is particularly important because it allows public health officials to determine if the use of a certain substance is increasing. In recent years, although marijuana smoking on the part of those 25 years and older has declined, the incidence of marijuana use among those younger than 25 has risen substantially. This has prompted government officials to increase efforts to educate younger people and their parents.

☐ Data Collection Techniques

Surveys

Censuses have existed since the dawn of civilization. It was a census of The Holy Roman Empire, called by the emperor Tiberius, that prompted Mary and Joseph to travel to Bethlehem, where Jesus was born. The United States Constitution mandates a census of the United States each decade. In 1933, under the direction of President Roosevelt, epidemiologists developed the probability sample method which is perhaps the most important tool epidemiologists use. Roosevelt wanted to know how many Americans were unemployed. A representative sample was queried, since it was unfeasible to survey all Americans, and the results extrapolated to the entire population. The methods used in these polls are quite sophisticated and can give very accurate and important information.

There are a number of historic and ongoing studies that investigate drug use in America. The first study was conducted in 1972 by the Commission on Marijuana and Drug Abuse in an attempt to assess the degree and severity of marijuana use among the American public.

Each year since 1975, the University of Michigan has sampled approximately 18,000 high school students about their past and present drug use. This study instrument continues to track its subjects as they move into different phases of their lives. It thus provides very useful information about drug trends in America, and the annual publication of its results is eagerly anticipated.

Since 1979, the National Institute on Drug Abuse (NIDA) has convened specialists on epidemiology semiannually to report on the patterns of drug use in 19 key metropolitan areas. This report provides interested parties with a great deal of information on changing rates of drug use, though only in a few urban areas.

In 1984, the National Institute of Mental Health (NIMH) conducted a seminal survey called the Epidemiological Catchment Area Program (ECA). This was a large-scale, comprehensive, and carefully planned study of five mental health catchment areas. Detailed information on substance-use patterns was obtained from those questioned. The information that was obtained was so extensive that papers referring to this data continue to be published regularly.

A pertinent question arises regarding the reliability of these surveys. Do people tell the truth in them? Most researchers are confident that while there are always exceptions, people by-and-large, accurately self report. Consequently, these studies are thought to reliably represent patterns of substance use and abuse in America.

Drug Seizures and Street Investigations

Police and customs officers closely monitor drug activities and seizures. Information about the amounts of drugs seized, purity of substances, and their cost are indirectly valuable in determining the trends of drug use in America. However, caution must be exercised in assessing this data. Arrest rates and amounts seized must be carefully evaluated so as not to be misleading.

Different communities have very different attitudes towards certain drugs of abuse. In California, marijuana use is relatively common, yet arrests for use and possession are infrequent, reflecting a casual attitude toward the drug. In the state of Alabama, on the other hand, where the use is far lower, many more arrests are made. Data from law-enforcement sources reflect the degree of priority given to anti-drug activities, the extent of drug sales, the attitudes of judges, and numerous other external factors.

Collateral Rates of Other Diseases

There is an intertwined and mutually causal relationship between drug abuse, alcoholism, and certain other medical conditions. By tracking these conditions, investigators can gain a clearer picture as to the rates of substance use and abuse. For example, alcohol is by far the greatest cause of cirrhosis of the liver. Rates of cirrhosis can be used as indirect evidence of the rates of drinking in the population. Cirrhosis rates in the United States declined in the years following prohibition, probably because the population drank less. The example of cirrhosis and alcoholism is somewhat problematic because it more likely reflects how much alcohol is consumed, rather than the rates of alcoholism. The rate of cirrhosis of the liver in American Indians is relatively low. This is because, although the pattern of periodic, massive binge drinking is high and is quite destructive in many ways, the gross amount drunk is relatively low. Hence, the causal factor in cirrhosis is not reached. Similarly, in Italy, the rate of alcoholism—the destructive use of alcohol which impairs functioning—is relatively low. However, the population, drinks regularly and often prodigiously, and the rates of cirrhosis are relatively high.

Hepatitis B has been used as an indicator of intravenous drug abuse because of the high incidence of the disease in intravenous drug abusers and the ease of transmission through shared needles. Another indirect method is the rate of death from overdose. The calculations needed to extrapolate this number to an intravenous drug abuse rate in a population, however, are very difficult and although useful, highly problematic.

Still another indirect method of determining substance abuse rates is via prescription audits. An example of this is the National Prescription Audit which provides information on the total number of prescriptions based on the statistically valid sample of 2500 retail drug stores. Information from this survey is useful in determining the prevalence of any given prescription drug and calculating which substances are being diverted to the illegal drug market.

The Drug Abuse Warning Network (DAWN)

A highly useful approach to the epidemiology of substance abuse is provided by DAWN. Established in 1972, DAWN is a national organization of hospital emergency rooms, crisis centers, coroners, and facilities catering to drug users. Any mention of drug use in the medical report of one of these facilities gets reported to DAWN. Also contained in the reporting is the purported reason for using the drug, including suicide attempt, physiological or psychological dependence, or recreation. Reported semiannually, this data provides a very useful glimpse into changing patterns of drug use and misuse. The emergency room physician who is alert to DAWN and realizes that, for example, PCP admissions are on the increase in his/her area, will be more alert to the presence of PCP in diagnosing his/her clinical population.

There are numerous other methods for determining substance abuse. Local surveys can be done either on a large scale (such as by New York State, which has completed several substantial surveys on its population) or, on a much smaller scale (for example, a high school student may conduct an accurate and useful survey of his classmates). There are international organizations, such as the World Health Organization (WHO), that gather data on the development and dissemination of drugs throughout the world. The United Nations Division on Narcotic Drugs collects information on drug-abuse trends throughout the world. The United Nations

Educational Scientific and Cultural Organization (UNESCO) attempts to accumulate data on student drug usage throughout the world.

All of these methods fail to calculate the precise number of drug addicts in the U.S. and throughout the world, or what new wave of drug use the clinician can expect in the coming years. The definition of what constitutes "problematic use" and what is "frank use" is unclear and too relative to permit a truly accurate assessment. Despite this, the clinician can still use epidemiological data to assist in diagnosis and treatment planning for substance-abusing individuals.

PART

I

MAJOR SUBSTANCES OF ABUSE

The following chapters deal with individual substances of abuse. Each of the chapters is intended to be self-contained. For an individual interested in one particular substance, each chapter on that substance can be be read as a separate entity. For this reason, some of the material may be repeated in one form or another in different sections of the book.

The chapters in this section concentrate on the unique aspects of the history, context, physiology, and treatment of a particular substance. Later sections deal with specific treatment modalities. For instance, the chapter on alcohol refers to Alcoholics Anonymous (A.A.), a mainstay in the treatment of alcoholism. A later chapter deals with A.A. specifically, and the reader who is interested in knowing more about that form of treatment is directed to that chapter.

There are many substances of abuse, and this text is intended to be an introduction to the major issues about which the clinician or interested reader is likely to be curious. The authors have chosen to present only those substances that are most commonly abused; therefore, some important substances have been omitted for reasons of space and purpose. In light of this fact, the reader is directed to the section on additional reading, and resources, such as web sites, if he or she is interested in a substance that is not specifically covered.

7

CHAPTER

Alcohol

Introduction

Alcohol has been an integral part of human culture since the beginning of civilization. The earliest known piece of writing mentioning alcohol is a clay tablet found in the Middle East that bears a recipe for a fermented beverage identical to modern-day beer. These types of historical references to alcohol can be found in almost all societies and cultures. In fact, *The Dialogues of Plato* appear to have stemmed from rather drunken evenings at Plato's friend Alcibiades' house. A reading of the works indicates that a great deal of wine was consumed during the development of these discussions. The Mead Hall in *Beowulf* is named for a sweet fermented drink which can be found readily in modern-day England. A good portion of Thomas Jefferson's more rhapsodic writings relays his fondness for claret (red wine from Bordeaux). In his day, in at least some circles, Jefferson was as well known for his wine cellar as he was for his intellect and accomplishments. It appears that alcohol and all its related forms have been an important element of American culture from the beginning to the present.

The world has an ambivalent relationship with alcohol. As fond as people are of describing their favorite beer or wine, or retelling humorous stories that arise from a "night on the town," there are just as many horror stories. Alcohol consumption and abuse are responsible for a large percentage of car accidents, domestic violence, and crime. However, alcohol is used to commemorate important social milestones, is a lubricant for many personal and professional interactions, and has some proven medical benefits. Still, despite these more positive associations, the effects of alcohol abuse are devastating. Even the monetary cost of alcohol abuse, both to society and individuals, cannot be underestimated. Some people do not consider alcohol a drug, and yet this belief could not be further from the truth. Alcohol is a powerful, addictive drug that can have severe physical, personal, and societal consequences.

History

Writings about alcohol and recipes for alcoholic beverages are among the earliest and most pervasive writings found in the ancient world. Different alcoholic beverages are synonymous with certain cultures: the Romans drank wine, the Irish sipped stout, and the colonial Americans guzzled rum.

In the United States, attitudes toward alcohol have a very interesting history. The theory that addictive behavior is a progressive disease is only about two hundred years old. Previously, the assumption had been that people drank alcohol out of desire, rather than out of compulsion. In 1754, Jonathan Edwards, the colonial essayist and intellectual, wrote an analysis of drunkenness. The following is taken from his writings:

> "Thus, when a drunkard has his liquor before him, and he has to choose whether to drink or not...If he wills to drink, then drinking is the proper object of his will: and drinking, on some account or other, now appears most agreeable to him, and suits him best. If he chooses to refrain, then refraining is the immediate object of his will and is most pleasing to him."

Edwards did not take into account the addictive nature of alcohol and the debilitating effect that it had on at least a segment of the population. Alcohol was an ever-present part of life, and those people we would now refer to as alcohol-dependent were previously viewed as moral failures. It is not surprising that the man who coined the rather moralistic phrase "Sinners in the hands of an angry God," viewed a weakness for alcohol as a weakness of the soul, as did most Americans at the time.

However, in 1810, Dr. Benjamin Rush published a seminal work on the subject, suggesting that alcohol was an addictive drug. In fact, he proposed that addiction was a disease. Rush was a leading physician and the first president of what was to become the American Psychiatric Association. According to Rush, drunkards, as they were termed in his day, were "addicted" to alcohol. Rush described the progressive nature of the disease as episodic drinking binges which evolve progressively into more severe occasions that occur in shorter and shorter intervals. Rush was the first to conceptualize the loss of control associated with the addictive process of alcoholism. He anecdotally remarked that, "When strongly urged by one of his friends to leave off drinking, a habitual drunkard said, 'were a keg of rum in one corner of the room, and were a cannon constantly discharging balls between me and it, I could not refrain from passing before that cannon, in order to get the rum.' " Rush understood the nature of addiction and the need for total abstinence in some individuals. His advice for those with a problem with alcohol was, "Taste not, handle not, and touch not."

These writings, along with a general shift in cultural attitudes, led to an expanding temperance movement that gained and lost popularity during the next century. In the early part of the twentieth century, the passage of the eighteenth amendment created Prohibition, which curbed drinking. Popular attitudes led to the reversal of Prohibition in 1933. Since that time, the attitude toward alcohol and its effects have fluctuated. The fifties and sixties were fairly permissive in terms of alcohol consumption. The famous "three martini lunch" actually had a place in American social and business life.

During the 1960s, E. M. Jellinik wrote the definitive work on the concept of alcoholism as a disease. His main thesis was that alcoholism was a disease from which only some people suffered, and that certain individuals were more susceptible to alcohol addiction than others. While the finer points of this theory are still debated, it has become an accepted conceptualization of the difficulties many people have with alcohol and the progressive nature of their dependence upon the substance.

In the 1980s, health-conscious Americans frowned upon over-indulgence, and the sales of hard liquor plummeted. In recent years, this trend has reversed, and with the newly rediscovered popularity of the martini cocktail, alcohol sales, at least for the "trend-setting" population, seem to be climbing.

☐ Epidemiology

Alcohol can interact negatively with medications, contribute to or exacerbate medical and psychological conditions, and wreak havoc on a person's life as well as the lives of those around him or her. Clinicians should be aware of the possibility that a large portion of their patients have temporary, but potentially important, alcohol-related problems.

At some time during their lives, 90% of the population in the United States drinks alcohol. In the adult population, 60–70% are current drinkers at any given time. For the purposes of this discussion, a drinker is defined as anyone who has consumed alcohol during the past month.

Over 40% of the population has had, or will have, a temporary problem with alcohol during his or her lifetime. Twenty percent of men, and 10% of women will meet the rather strict criteria of alcohol abuse, and 10% of men, and 5% of women will be physiologically dependent upon alcohol.

Alcohol consumption throughout a person's life often follows a typical pattern. There are, of course, many exceptions to the following generalization, but it is offered as a common scenario. Alcohol is first consumed during the early teens, when "adolescent experimentation" is considered to be normal. This acceptance is common in many cultures; even the notoriously strict Amish allow for and expect a period of "rebellion" before "settling down" in adulthood (in the case of the Amish, this is after baptism, which occurs as an adult). The heaviest period of drinking alcohol occurs during the late teens and early twenties. It is during these times, that individuals who will go on to develop drinking problems part company from their peers. Most people appear to grow out of the binge drinking that may take place during their youth. This observation is important, especially when evaluating younger drinkers. The vast majority can and do spontaneously decrease their consumption as they grow and mature.

The typical heavy drinker in his or her teens or twenties continues to drink heavily throughout the twenties and thirties, and begins to develop increasing health and social problems. These problems include blackouts, fatigue, depression, and difficulties with family, jobs, and social relationships. It is important to note that despite heavy drinking and its associated

FIGURE 7.1. A Prototypical Course of Alcoholism

Age 13–first drink from parents' liquor cabinet
Age 16–begins drinking regularly on weekends with friends
Age 20–continues to drink regularly, now on weeknights as well

Age 24–begins to experience blackouts, becomes annoyed at friends who comment on excessive drinking
Age 28–first DWI, unsuccessful attempts to cut down, or stop drinking
Age 32–second DWI, more frequent blackouts

Age 35–problems at work because of effects of drinking and frequent hangovers, similar problems with relationships. Continued efforts to cut down or stop drinking.
Age 38–health problems become apparent (weight gain, gastritis, etc.)
Age 42–continued problems with family, work, career
Age 45–first hospitalization for detoxification
Age 52–third hospitalization for detoxification
Age 57–death from effects of cirrhosis

problems, the individual problem drinker is likely to have numerous areas in his or her life that are going quite well. Many business leaders, statespeople, and other prominent individuals are alcoholics.

As the alcoholic ages, his or her problems tend to intensify. Individuals may become alcohol-dependent, and in this case, trying to stop leads to all of the manifestations of withdrawal (e.g., jitteriness, agitation, elevations in vital signs, and perhaps frank delirium tremens). The disruptions in an alcoholic's personal and professional life also intensify. The alcoholic can expect increasing health problems throughout his or her forties and fifties. Although there are many exceptions to this, the typical alcoholic dies in his or her late fifties or early sixties.

The following is offered as a clinical example of an individual with a progressive course of alcoholism.

> Linda first tried alcohol at the age of 13, when she snuck a drink during one of her parents' frequent parties. She bragged to her friends that she liked the taste, which was untrue, but she genuinely enjoyed the way alcohol made her feel. At parties during high school, and then at college, she would frequently drink many beers, but not a great deal more than her friends. After college, she continued to drink, with morning hangovers becoming more and more of a problem for her (although she did not admit this to herself—rationalizing about the terrible way she felt). She began to notice that her friends no longer became drunk as frequently as they used to and she began to resent their comments about her drinking. As a result, she tended to socialize with those people who drank and didn't criticize her. In her mid-thirties, she began drinking at lunch time, at first because she convinced herself that it was fashionable, and then to quiet the shaky feeling she had throughout the morning. She did not achieve the kind of success she had expected in her career, and her personal life was more and more unfulfilling as potential mates were turned off by her drinking, and her friends drifted away. She was arrested for driving while intoxicated. Her doctor told her of abnormalities on her physical exam and laboratory tests, but she ignored him and her drinking continued. In her forties, she had progressively more problems with her health, more hospitalizations, and eventually died of complications from her alcoholism at the age of 54.

☐ Mechanism of Action

Ethanol (beverage alcohol) is a simple two-carbon molecule that is well absorbed through the mucosal lining of the digestive tract in the mouth, esophagus, and the stomach. The majority of alcohol is absorbed in the initial part of the small intestine (the duodenum). The rate of absorption is quite variable, and is influenced by a number of factors, including the contents of the stomach which accounts for the increased feeling of intoxication in those who drink on an empty stomach. Other factors, such as carbonation, influence the rate of absorption and the associated "buzz" or feeling of intoxication. Ethanol is highly fat-soluble and can be found in all the lipid-rich parts of the body. It can be detected in the blood, and is measured by a simple laboratory test. Ethanol passes easily through the blood brain barrier, and enters the central nervous system. It is here that it exerts its physiological and psychological effects.

A drink is usually defined as between 10 and 12 grams of ethanol. This is approximately the amount found in 12 ounces of regular beer, 4 ounces of wine, and 1.5 ounces of 80-proof spirits. "Proof" is double the percentage of alcohol, and 80 proof represents 40% ethanol-containing spirits. It should be remembered that beer's alcohol content, although regulated by law, is quite variable. Wine also is quite variable, ranging, for example, from the lighter German wines which typically contain 7% alcohol, to the fortified Rhone wines, and wines from California made from Cabernet Savignon and Chardonnay grapes which contain as much as double the lighter German wines. While some of the other ingredients in alcoholic beverages are in part responsible for the hangover effect of drinking large quantities, it is the *amount* of alcohol consumed that is responsible for the intoxication and the subsequent withdrawal effects. The popular conception that mixing different types of alcohol increases the risk of a hangover is better explained by understanding that if an individual is mixing several different types of liquor, he or she is likely drinking a large quantity of alcohol.

John, a 28-year old construction worker, went out with his friends. They consumed three gin and tonics at a local tavern before going for dinner and drinking four beers each. This was followed by three scotches on the rocks. After a fitful sleep, the next morning John awoke with a terrible headache and dry (cotton) mouth. He explained his terrible hangover to "mixing all those different kinds of liquor," making little of the fact that he had consumed the equivalent of 10 drinks during the previous evening.

Alcohol is filtered through the liver where it is metabolized. The first breakdown product is acetaldehyde, which in turn is rapidly broken down by acetaldehyde dehydrogenase, and these products are then excreted in the urine. There is considerable genetic variability in terms of alcohol metabolism, but generally for men, the average drink raises the blood level of alcohol by 0.02%. Therefore, it takes five rapid drinks to achieve a blood alcohol level of 0.1%, the most common definition of legal intoxication. Some states have an intoxication definition of 0.08%, and some states differentiate between driving while under the influence of alcohol and driving while intoxicated. On average, the liver is able to metabolize one drink equivalent per hour.

Women tend to absorb alcohol more readily than men, and one drink equivalent raises their alcohol level almost twice as rapidly as that of a man. The reasons for this are complex, but are primarily due to differences in fat distribution and absorption rates. This is important clinically, since it takes considerably less alcohol to achieve intoxication for a woman. Estrogen has an impact on the absorption rate of alcohol in women. Thus, birth control pills, estrogen replacement therapy, and premenstrual status all play a role in the rate of absorbtion, blood levels of alcohol and levels of intoxication. Similarly, long-term health problems occur with less total accumulation of alcohol consumed for women than for men. Some researchers believe that the cut-off criteria for all of the definitions and classifications for problems with alcohol ought to be considerably less for women than for men. For example, a man who drinks two to three alcoholic beverages and has no impairment might not induce worry in the astute clinician. If this consumption were reported by a woman, then it ought to raise more concern and the clinician treating such a woman should be aware of the possibility that problems associated with alcohol could occur.

The actual neurophysiological mechanism of alcohol remains elusive. It seems to operate on a variety of neurotransmitter mechanisms such as gamma amino butyric acid (GABA) and N-methyl d-aspartate (NMDA). In general, alcohol is a central nervous system depressant. This effect is more readily seen in higher doses. At lower doses, under two drink equivalents for the average person, its effects seem to be more anxiolytic (something that makes a person less tense). The behavioral corollary can be observed by the sober guest at a New Year's Eve party. After one or two glasses of champagne, the guests are likely to be festive, gregarious, and enjoying alcohol's effect of reducing social anxiety. At 3:00 a.m., the drunk individuals are all lethargic and likely to be sprawled out, while the activities of moving and thinking are quite slow, if at all.

☐ Effects

Acute Effects of Alcohol

The problems with alcohol fall into three categories: acute effects, chronic effects, and withdrawal. There are many effects of acute intoxication and long-term use. Initially small amounts of alcohol produce a feeling of relaxation and well-being; motor performance and thinking ability are slowed, but only subtly. At higher doses, motor and cognitive impairments increase and judgment is also impaired. This impairment is proportional to the amount of alcohol imbibed. The motor effects at higher doses can include slurred speech, diminishment of coordination, unsteady gait, and nystagmus (the uncontrolled movement of the pupils). Memory also suffers and at high enough doses blackouts can occur. This memory impairment includes all forms and functions of memory including short term, long term, recall, and acquisition.

Blackouts are a memory impairment for the period of time when the individual was drinking heavily. These occur in anyone who drinks enough alcohol, but are more common in the alcoholic individual. The presence of blackouts indicates a state when new memories are not consolidated or acquired. The individual in a blackout may or may not appear drunk, but little else seems awry. He or she is walking and talking, but not recording. The related phenomenon may be termed a "brownout" in which the details of the evening before are recalled only "fuzzily."

Blackouts and brownouts are common phenomena and are cause for concern if they occur frequently. They are common in individuals who would not be described as having an alcohol problem and who, for example, in their early twenties drank heavily on a social occasion and did not remember the details in the morning. This phenomenon is typified by the very funny Dorothy Parker story "You Were Perfectly Fine." The premise of the story is the conversation of a young woman and her very hung-over new fiancée. She recalls his outrageous drunken exploits the night before, which he does not remember and is ambivalent about learning.

Chronic Effects of Alcohol

Alcohol has significant long-term effects on those who drink heavily. Alcohol use affects the nervous system; it causes significant, permanent cognitive impairment and memory problems. The most dramatic form of this memory loss is the Wernicke-Korsakoff syndrome. Wernicke's encephalopathy occurs acutely, is caused by alcohol and a thiamine deficiency and manifests itself in eye coordination disturbances, ataxia (an unsteady gait), and confusion. This lasts for several days and, if left untreated, can lead to Korsakoff's syndrome.

Korsakoff's syndrome is a long-term, permanent, and dramatic deficit in memory. In its most extreme form, the person affected is unable to acquire new memories and is locked forever in the time during which they developed the syndrome. Such individuals appear to be in control of themselves, but they are not. The maxim which states that they "walk and talk, but do not record," applies to patients with Korsakoff's syndrome. They are unable to register new information.

> A 52 year-old divorced insurance salesman is admitted to the hospital with a history of 30 years of heavy drinking. He had two previous admissions for detoxification. He appears malnourished and confused. On examination, he is ataxic and has bilateral sixth nerve palsy. Within weeks, he appears much more robust and pleasant. His long-term memory and recall of long past events is good. However, he is unable to retain any new information. His doctors must reintroduce themselves each time they meet him. He is able to recognize his family, but does not recall any of their recent visits. He is calm, alert, and friendly. One could be with him for a short time without noticing that something is very wrong. This short-term memory deficit appears to be permanent. For the rest of his life when he greets his doctor he will need to be reintroduced and as he gets older he will be more and more surprised at his appearance when he looks into the mirror.

Alcohol causes difficulties with the peripheral nervous system. Estimates indicate that 10% of alcoholics have peripheral neuropathies. These include either a lack of sensation or pain in the limbs. Once these appear, both of these symptoms may very well be permanent. The only treatment for these symptoms is to treat the individual's alcoholism, a step which hopefully may lead to improvement.

Alcohol also causes problems with the digestive system. Gastric ulcers can be caused, or at least exacerbated by alcohol. Liver damage is the most serious effect of alcohol on the gastrointestinal tract. The liver damage caused by alcohol is variable for different individuals, but is related to the gross amount of alcohol consumed by a given individual. If caught early enough, the damage is usually reversible; the liver has a remarkable capacity for regeneration. The end result of alcohol damage to the liver is called cirrhosis. Cirrhosis of the liver is caused by alcohol, possibly with the additional interaction of an inadequate diet. It results in significant scarring of the liver and loss of its function. End-stage cirrhosis is curable only by a liver transplant, and is a fatal condition.

Alcohol abuse also induces a general depression of immune function and the alcoholic is much more likely to acquire infections. Other problems that are caused by alcohol are blood disorders including anemia, and cardiomyopathy (a disorder of the heart muscle which involves a loss of function). Fetal alcohol syndrome is caused by alcohol consumption by the mother during pregnancy. The abnormalities most typically associated with fetal alcohol syndrome include central nervous system dysfunction, birth deficiencies, a characteristic facial abnormality, and other malformations throughout the infant's system.

Withdrawal

The term alcohol withdrawal refers to the phenomenon which occurs when an individual who has become dependent upon alcohol attempts to quit, or in some cases cut down. Tremendous anxiety, agitation, and increases in blood pressure can all occur. This is currently conceptualized as autonomic nervous system overdrive. The symptoms also exist on a spectrum of mild to severe effects. On the most mild end of the spectrum is the non-dependent individual who feels shaky the morning after being drunk. Such a "hangover" can be understood as a mini-withdrawal. It is for this reason that "a bit of the hair of the dog" *is* effective in treating the effects of a hangover. Though not advised for obvious reasons, moderate amounts of alcohol will relieve most of the symptoms of a hangover. A hangover is the least complicated form of withdrawal, but the symptoms can be much more severe. At the other end of the spectrum is frank withdrawal and delirium tremens ("the DTs") which is a medical emergency and needs to be treated in an intensive care unit.

The end stage of withdrawal is essentially autonomic nervous system collapse. Withdrawal is generally treated with vitamins, particularly thiamine, to prevent Wernicke-Korsakoff syndrome, and benzodiazepines such as valium or librium. The amount of prescribed medication can vary, but is usually proportional to the level of alcohol dependence. A typical regimen will begin with 10 mg of valium, or another benzodiazepine every six hours and a gradual taper over the next five days. Individuals who are highly dependent may require massive amounts of benzodiazepines to prevent withdrawal. Benzodiazapines are slowly tapered off over the course of several days until the patient is free of either alcohol or sedatives. Since this can be accomplished in a matter of days, most detoxification units of local hospitals are short-term units.

Because of the high degree of cross-addiction between alcohol and benzodiazepines, the astute clinician should be watchful that the patient, once free of alcohol withdrawal symptoms, does not go into a second phase of withdrawal from long-acting benzodiazepines.

Treatment

Treatment exists in a wide range of options for people with alcohol problems. The first, most basic, and medically important question is whether or not the patient is physiologically dependent upon alcohol. While the current DSM-IV criteria are useful, the most pressing question to ask is "Does the patient have withdrawal symptoms?" If the patient does, then he or she needs medical attention and, in most instances, needs to be in a hospital setting for the detoxification procedure. Outpatient detoxification can take place, but requires a great deal of monitoring and is therefore more difficult and dangerous. In general, it is far safer to admit a person in withdrawal into a detoxification unit, a general medical, or a psychiatric unit, than to attempt to treat that person as an outpatient.

Pharmacotherapy for alcoholism can be divided into two categories: medicines that treat the alcohol condition itself, and those that treat related conditions. The individual who has been in withdrawn from alcohol has, at present, two options for pharmacotherapy: disulfiram and naltrexone. Disulfiram, also known as Antabuse®, is taken each morning by the patient in either a 250 mg or 500 mg preparation. There are relatively few side effects unless the individual drinks or comes into contact with alcohol. Disulfiram works by inhibiting the liver enzyme acetaldehyde dehydrogenase. This enzyme is the second in the alcohol degradation pathway and is responsible for converting acetaldehyde into its harmless byproducts. Alcohol consumed by an individual on disulfiram is therefore broken down into acetaldehyde, but goes no further. This results in a buildup of serum acetaldehyde, characterized by physical symptoms of hot flashes, nausea, and increased blood pressure. In some cases, the results of drinking while on disulfiram can be quite severe and dangerous. Any individual on disulfiram should be clearly warned of this, and carry a medical identification card or bracelet. Similar effects may occur with a number of other medications.

An important clinical consideration is that the effectiveness of disulfiram is variable. A reckless patient might be able to sip some alcohol on one occasion with mild, or even no effects. Emboldened by this experiment he or she might drink more with disastrous results. Disulfiram is a very effective tool for *some*, but certainly not all patients. Taken in the morning, when motivation for sobriety is highest and temptation to drink the least, it can remove the constant nagging desire to drink for many patients. It is also quite useful in some situations where mandatory treatment and abstinence is warranted. It is often helpful to have the medication monitored by either the clinician or a family member. Disulfiram unfortunately earned a negative reputation when it was studied in several large-scale clinical trials. A major flaw with these studies was that the intake was not monitored. Had the trials been more closely monitored, most clinicians believe disulfiram would have proven quite effective.

Naltrexone, a mu opioid receptor antagonist, has recently been demonstrated to have applicability in the treatment of alcoholism. It is more commonly used in the treatment of heroin addiction, where it completely blocks the euphoric effects of narcotics. Naltrexone is taken as a 50 mg tablet each morning, or three times per week, in a

100 mg/100 mg/150 mg schedule. Recent studies indicate that people on naltrexone have less severe relapses with alcohol than those who are on placebo. It does not decrease the amount of relapse events an individual may have, but definitely decreases the severity of such slips. In recovery parlance, "it prevents a lapse from becoming a relapse."

Individuals with alcohol disorders are more likely than the general public to have concomitant psychiatric conditions such as anxiety disorders or depression. The relationship between alcohol and depression or anxiety is complex. It is often clinically difficult to sort out the complexities of these "dual diagnosis" conditions, and represents a chicken/egg dilemma for the clinician. Alcohol abuse itself can be responsible for many of the symptoms associated with depression and anxiety, such as lethargy, low mood, and difficulty sleeping. After making sure that physiological withdrawal will not occur, an individual complaining of such symptoms should be advised to stop drinking to see if the symptoms remit. With the wide range of relatively safe pharmacological options available for depression and anxiety, a trial of such medications in the anxious or depressed person is often warranted, even if he or she continues to drink. In an individual with an alcohol disorder, conservative pharmacological interventions to treat the anxiety or depression may make the overall treatment of alcoholism more effective.

Sleep disorders are extremely common in individuals with alcohol problems. Alcohol is deceptive, as it does initially increase sleepiness, and helps the individual fall asleep. This sedation has a rebound effect, and such an individual frequently wakes up in the very early part of the next morning feeling anxious. In addition, alcohol interferes with the normal sleep/wake cycle in adults, and interferes with restful sleep.

> Melinda K. is a 49 year-old housewife who presented to her internist complaining of a sleep disturbance. The internist was convinced that his patient had a problem with alcohol. Melinda freely admitted that she was worried about her alcohol consumption, but was terrified about not being able to sleep, and believed that the alcohol at least helped her fall asleep. She had no signs of withdrawal, and the internist suggested that he would, at least on a temporary basis, ensure that she would get a good night's sleep with the use of a prescription soporific, if she would attempt abstinence. The experiment worked very well, and Melinda did stop drinking. After two weeks of sobriety (with her sleeping) it was clear that she was suffering from a mild case of depression which was treated, allowing for the discontinuation of the sleep aid.

While sleep aids should be used with extreme caution in this population, the above example is a scenario where the judicious use of a medication accomplished a greater good for the patient's health.

The psychosocial component of alcoholism can be treated in a variety of ways. In general, as in most addictions, the more severe the problem, the more comprehensive the treatment program recommended. An individual who has only a mild problem with alcohol may need only a serious warning from his or her doctor, or brief counseling from a professional. The severely dependent individual will likely need a more comprehensive program, perhaps an inpatient rehabilitation, or in more extreme cases, a stay at a therapeutic community, followed by observed intake of disulfiram. In between is the full range of individual and group counseling. While Alcoholics Anonymous is not effective for everyone, individuals suffering from alcoholism ought to be encouraged to attend at least a few meetings, as they are at least educational. The spectrum of treatment options available to substance abusing individuals is discussed in detail in later portions of this text which deal with specific therapeutic techniques for treating addiction.

8

CHAPTER

Hallucinogens

Introduction

The term *hallucinogen* refers to any naturally occurring or synthetically derived substance which, when ingested, induces an alteration in the sensory and perceptive systems. This disturbance exists on a broad spectrum and can range from a mild alteration, such as a perceived increase in the intensity of colors, to symptoms that are quite severe, with the user experiencing frank and intense delusions. The term *hallucinogen* can be used interchangeably with the term *psychedelic*. The term *hallucinogen* is often more commonly used in scientific circles, while the term *psychedelic* is reserved for the drug user.

Hallucinogens are used by a variety of individuals for a variety of purposes. This class of drugs, perhaps more than any other, relies on *the set and the setting* to explain the subjective effects. Certain substances are used in religious ceremonies to enhance the participants' sense of the otherworld and to form a communion with that spiritual place. The Church of the American Indian is currently permitted by the American government to use peyote in its religious rites. Some individuals use hallucinogens to engage in spiritual journeys. In other instances, people take drugs such as lysergic acid diethylamide (LSD) to hallucinate and become high. In many instances the same hallucinogen may be used for either purpose. Peyote, as mentioned before, is used for religious purposes, and is also taken by some others to "get high," with no thought to religion or ritual. In the

United States, hallucinogens hit their peak in popularity during "the sixties," which actually refers to the period between 1965 and 1974. Their use decreased substantially until the very early nineties. Hallucinogens have made a "comeback," increasing in use especially among younger teens.

Methylenedioxymethamphetamine (MDMA), also known as "Ecstasy," has had a similar pattern in terms of popularity. It is not a "designer drug," but is much more related to the hallucinogens. It was first synthesized in 1914 by Merck in Darmstad, Germany, but was not popularized until the early sixties. Ecstasy was not classified as an abusable substance, and therefore its use was legal until the middle of the 1970s. It has been illegal since 1985. Before that time it was unregulated, and hence its manufacuture, distribution, and ingestion were legal. Like other hallucinogens, the use of Ecstasy has increased since the early 1990s. Its history and physiology are covered in the next chapter.

☐ Classification

Hallucinogens share common properties in terms of effects and mechanism of action. In general, they are classified in terms of their chemical structure.

These classifications include:

1. The Indoles, examples are LSD, dimethyltriptamine (DMT) and psylocybin (mushrooms).
2. The substituted phenethylamines, examples are mescaline and 2,5 Dimethoxy, 4-methylamphetamine (DOM).

☐ History

Naturally occurring hallucinogens can be found in a variety of plants throughout the world. These range from morning glory seeds to "magic" mushrooms, which contain psylocybin. The ingestion of these substances, either inadvertently or with intent, has occurred throughout history. Some scholars have suggested that the book of Ezekiel of the Old Testament, with its fiery images and glowing wheels from the skies, is remarkably similar to accounts of someone having taken a hallucinogen, and that perhaps the author of Ezekiel was "tripping."

Other scholars have argued that the young women of the Salem witch trials were exhibiting hallucinogenic symptoms from ingesting morning glory seeds, which contain a hallucinogen, and can be found in the fields near Salem, Massachusetts. These two examples are of course speculative, but they are intriguing. History abounds with examples of behavior which may have been influenced by hallucinogen ingestion. In any case, the use of hallucinogens, whether for religious rites or recreational purposes, has occurred in many cultures throughout history. Accounts can be found in sources as diverse as the poems of Catullus, or the descriptions concerning the prophesies of the Oracle at Delphi.

The first human creation of a synthetic hallucinogen, LSD, occurred in April 1944 by Albert Hoffman, a young scientist working for Sandoz. He was investigating compounds that might be psychoactive and in the process he synthesized LSD. After coming into contact with a small amount of the substance on his skin, Hoffman began to feel strange and emotionally dissociated. Pondering this strange circumstance, he began to wonder whether this may have been caused by the LSD. If his hypothesis were correct, then LSD would have to be active in extraordinarily small amounts. Hoffman did not know how small the amounts would actually be.

The next day he ingested some in a self-experiment to see what manifestations would occur. At first nothing happened and he decided to go home. He then began what would eventually be known as "the bicycle trip." He peddled homeward, and began experiencing intense and frightening hallucinations along the way. He felt he was being engulfed by the gates of Hell. These terrifying experiences lasted for the next two days. Later understanding would indicate that he had ingested over 100 times the effective dose of LSD and had experienced the first documented "bad trip."

Because of its unique properties, LSD was the subject of numerous scientific investigations. By the mid 1960s, over 1,000 articles relating to LSD appeared in medical journals. Today there are at least 5,000 scholarly studies of LSD. Many scientists advocated that the drug had a number of legitimate uses, ranging from a role in psychotherapy to a cure for alcoholism. The Central Intelligence Agency studied LSD as the elusive "truth serum." Despite this volume of research, no useful clinical application for LSD was ever confirmed. The question as to whether or not there are beneficial effects of LSD remains controversial to this day.

In the late 1960s, the illicit use of LSD was gaining popularity. Sandoz, the manufacturer, stopped distributing the drug at that time in response to reported adverse reactions and the resulting public outcry. LSD was not made illegal until 1966. Perhaps the most famous proponents of LSD were Timothy Leary and Ram Doss. Their exploits, and those of their friends—"The Leary Pranksters" are chronicled in Tom Wolfe's hilarious *The Electric Kool Aid Acid Test.* Its use escalated through the sixties and seventies, but declined after that and hit a nadir in 1992, probably as a result of the aggressive anti-drug campaign advocated by the U.S. government. However, since then, the combination of a more relaxed social climate and the rise of psychedelic subcultures has led to a renewed increase in LSD use. Other hallucinogens have had similarly waxing and waning popularity, which have depended on a variety of factors such as publicity and availability.

Mechanism of Action

The exact mechanism of action of hallucinogens remains unclear. Although the administration of hallucinogenic drugs can affect several neurotransmitter systems, they seem to affect the serotonin system the most. This neurotransmitter is very important in the regulation of perception and affect, and thus appears to be the most likely candidate for the main effects of the drug. There also seems to be indirect effects on the dopamine system as well, as separate neurotransmitter systems communicate with one another.

Historically, it had been thought that the effects of hallucinogens provided a good model for psychosis. This theory no longer holds true, as the perceptual disturbances experienced by hallucinogen users are thought to be quite different in origin.

Effects

The effects from the classic hallucinogens are experienced in a range from mild to severe. This depends on the individual drug, as well as the dosage. The individual who ingests a very small amount of LSD, or a milder hallucinogen such as peyote, may experience a heightened perceptual sensation. In addition, colors and sounds may become more dramatic or intense. The individual who takes larger doses or concentrations of hallucinogens may have delusions or hallucinations. These experiences may be pleasurable, and can be accompanied by minor changes in behavior. Alternatively, the "trip" may be a profoundly negative one where the individual experiences paranoid and violent delusions, as well as other psychotic features.

LSD is the archetypal hallucinogen; other drugs in this category have similar pharmacology and effects, but are commonly less intense or have a longer or shorter acting period. Other hallucinogens include peyote, psylocybin, and DMT. Hallucinogens cause somatic sensations and the user frequently experiences dizziness, weakness, and tremors. Altered visual states, changes in perception, and synesthesia are common. Synesthesia is a condition where the individual experiences one sensory perception through the realm of another sense. For example, a person may smell a color or taste a sound. "Trails" are a perceptual disturbance in which an individual sees visual images following a moving object, much like the effect seen with a strobe light. There are numerous psychic effects including changes in mood, dream-like feelings, and an altered perception of time which occur as a regular byproduct of hallucinogen use.

The experience of being on a hallucinogen itself is usually not dangerous, but more like a frightening movie, full of dramatic sensation. Still, it is the behavior that accompanies these experiences that can lead to serious consequences. A family member or friend that is attempting to deal with an inconsolable person in the throes of a bad hallucinogen experience can find himself or herself in the path of danger. The hallucinating individual may also act upon a delusional belief and here is, perhaps, where these drugs have real dangers. Someone who believes he or she is able to fly, may just jump off a building. Someone who believes he or she is invincible may walk into traffic. While statistics for these incidents are hard to find, the overwhelming anecdotal evidence indicates that these tragedies do occur, and perhaps more frequently than one might assume. The technical term for the dangerous behavior that individuals engage in while under the influence of drugs is "behavioral toxicity."

There are also chronic reactions to hallucinogens. These are rare, but when they occur, are life-compromising. These include prolonged psychosis and depression, sufficiently severe to require long-term treatment and hospitalization. Another potential consequence to hallucinogen use are "flashbacks" or the re-experience of the hallucination, even months after the last use. In an individual with a psychotic disorder, hallucinogens can cause a re-emergence of the underlying psychosis. Consequently, these drugs must be avoided by anyone with a history of psychosis or an anxiety disorder.

The most serious long-term disorder caused by this class of drugs or other is Post Hallucinogenic Perceptual Disorder. This syndrome is a prolonged, often dramatic, sometimes low-grade, but unremitting re-experience of the hallucinogenic experience. Post Hallucinogenic Perceptual Disorder can last for months, even years, and when it happens, it can be devastating. Unfortunately, there are no effective treatments for this, except to medicate any severe psychiatric symptoms and keep the patient safe from harm to himself and others.

> Jacque was fifteen when he tried his first "hit" of acid. He enjoyed the high very much. He especially liked the feeling of floating, and the way colors seemed more intense. He used LSD without incident every month or so with his friends, often at raves, the all night dance marathon parties he and his friends loved. On his seventeenth birthday, he took a hit of acid and had a particularly disturbing trip, thinking that his friends were turning into wild

animals. He was able to realize that this was part of the trip, but was only barely reassured. He couldn't wait for the trip to end. The next morning, he continued to experience hallucinations, seeing trails, and experiencing numbness and a feeling as though he was "out of my body." He became alarmed and told his parents, who took him to the local emergency room. The doctors there kept him for observation, but the symptoms persisted. He was admitted to the psychiatric ward, and was treated symptomatically for anxiety symptoms, but the hallucinations and out-of-body feeling continued. He was released from the hospital after three weeks, and attempted to return to school but was unable to because of the prolonged hallucinations. At a two-year follow-up visit, Jacque felt better, was able to complete his GED, but still continues to have occasional hallucinations. He has not used LSD, or any other hallucinogen since.

Withdrawal

There is no withdrawal syndrome for any hallucinogen. Immediately stopping the drug causes no ill effects. A corollary to this is that tolerance develops very rapidly, usually over the course of several days. It is, therefore, from a physiological standpoint, impossible to become "addicted" to any hallucinogen. Nonetheless, certain individuals exhibit an attachment to the drugs, which might be termed a psychological addiction. People who use the drug compulsively and in a destructive pattern are thus considered to be "addicted" to hallucinogens.

Treatment

Although neuroleptics, in theory, ought to be beneficial for treatment of the acute psychosis, they sometimes lead to increased agitation. Clinical experience indicates that they should not be used for treatment of a severe symptomatic state caused by a hallucinogen. The chief stress is usually the anxiety associated with drug-induced psychosis. This may be treated accordingly, with an anxiolytic agent such as diazepam. In general, removing all noxious stimuli will relieve the patient. Talking with him or her in a calm, reassuring manner may also be effective. Most clubs where people take hallucinogens have a section called a "chill out lounge." Such an area is usually dimly lit and has only soothing music. This is often all that is needed to help someone ease down from a disturbing trip.

Since there is no known, definitive cure for Post Hallucinogenic Perceptual Disorder, such individuals must be treated symptomatically to help them as much as possible while their symptoms persist.

9

CHAPTER

"Club Drugs": MDMA (Ecstasy), Ketamine, GHB, and Rohypnol

Introduction

Methylenedioxymethamphetamine (MDMA), Ketamine, Gamma Hydroxybutyrate (GHB), and Rohypnol are unique compounds, differing in terms of their pharmacological properties and their phenomenological effects. The common thread linking these disparate drugs is the people who use them. These substances are used throughout the world most frequently by a sophisticated, adolescent or twenty-something constituency, as well as within the gay subculture. The drugs are widely used and abused at urban social gatherings both in commercial and informal settings. They are most commonly used in nightclubs and all-night dance marathon parties known as "raves" and at gay "circuit parties." Composed primarily of affluent gay men, "circuit parties" are large social gatherings held in many different countries, usually on weekends and holidays. These drugs, which will be discussed extensively, and several others, which will be described more briefly, are widely known as "club drugs."

Club drugs have been associated with the rise of the rave movement. At raves, groups of young people, typically in their teens, dance to rapid, electronically synthesized "techno music" (i.e., music with no lyrics).

These events traditionally take place in unregulated and unlicensed locations such as stadiums, abandoned warehouses, and other surreptitious arenas. Since the early nineties, the venues have become increasingly mainstream. The "club drugs" are seen by teenagers and young adults as the perfect match for this scene. These drugs, along with marijuana and LSD, are extremely popular at these events.

MDMA

(±) 3,4-Methylenedioxymethamphetamine (MDMA), better known as Ecstasy, has been known as "Adam," "XTC," "E," and "X." A synthetic amphetamine analog with stimulant properties, MDMA has some unique properties and effects. MDMA has been illegal since it was made a Schedule I drug in July 1985. In recent years, it has become increasingly popular.

The compound's appeal rests principally on its psychological effect, a dramatic and consistent ability to induce in the user a profound feeling of attachment and connection. "Ecstasy" is perhaps a misnomer. The L.A. dealer who coined the term wanted to call the drug *Empathy*, ". . .but who would know what that means?"

History

MDMA was first patented in 1914 by Merck in Darmstadt, Germany. MDMA was not, as is sometimes thought, initially intended as an appetite suppressant, but was originally developed as a parent compound. The United States Army experimented with the compound during the 1950s. MDMA was first used by humans in the late 1960s. It was discovered by free-thinking pop aficionados (New Age seekers), people who liked its properties of inducing feelings of well-being and interpersonal connection. It was used by clinical therapists, at first on the West coast and then the East. Given MDMA's capacity to induce feelings of warmth and openness, a number of practitioners and researchers interested in insight-oriented psychotherapy believed it would be an ideal agent to enhance the therapeutic process. Before the compound was made illegal in 1985, it was used extensively for this purpose.

MDMA was also popular, as it is today, with young people. For this group, the drug's capacity to induce feelings of interpersonal relatedness and a motor agitation that can be pleasurably relieved by dancing, makes it an ideal "party drug." In spite of widespread usage during the early 1980s, the drug did not attract much attention from the media.

This widespread anonymity was changed by events in Texas. Until 1985, MDMA was not scheduled and its use was unregulated and legal. A distribution network in Texas began an aggressive marketing campaign and, for a time, it was available over the counter at bars, convenience stores, and even through a toll-free number. This widespread use attracted the attention of the media, and of Texas Senator Lloyd Bentsen. He petitioned the FDA, and the compound was subsequently placed on Schedule I on an emergency basis as of July 1, 1985. Despite some protests from reputable sources, the compound's possible neurotoxicity, combined with concern about illicit drug use in general, resulted in MDMA's permanent placement on Schedule I. According to law, that makes it a compound with high abuse potential and no therapeutic value.

☐ Effects

MDMA is usually ingested orally, in pill form. The usual single dose is between 100–150 mg.

The initial effects begin about 20–40 minutes after ingestion and are experienced as a sudden, amphetamine-like "rush." Nausea, usually mild, but sometimes severe enough to cause vomiting, often accompanies this initial feeling.

The plateau stage of the drug lasts between three and four hours. The principal desired effect is a profound feeling of relatedness to the rest of the world. In addition, people on the drug feel restless. Other side effects commonly experienced are jaw clenching, teeth gnashing, sweating, decreased appetite, and hot flashes. Although the desire for sex can increase, the ability to achieve orgasm for men and arousal for women is greatly diminished. It has thus been termed a sensual, not a sexual, drug.

After-effects can be quite pronounced, sometimes lasting 24 hours or more. The most dramatic "hangover" effect is a sometimes profound lack of interest in life, and even severe depression. Users of MDMA can experience lethargy, anorexia, and decreased motivation which can sometimes last for days.

☐ Mechanism of Action

MDMA's primary mechanism of action involves the serotonin system. It also affects a number of other receptors. MDMA is taken up by serotonin-containing neurons, causes the release of serotonin stores, and then blocks re-uptake. Like some other drugs of abuse, notably cocaine,

MDMA is a "messy drug," affecting serotonin- and dopamine-containing neurons as well as a host of other neurotransmitter systems. The drug's various effects of anorexia, psychomotor agitation, difficulty in completing the human sexual response cycle, and a profound feeling of empathy can all be explained as actions precipitated by the flooding of the serotonin system.

Because of the physiological mechanism of the compound, the patterns of usage are unusual for a drug of abuse. It is uncommon to find a pattern of escalating usage with this drug. Because the drug depletes serotonin stores, subsequent doses are increasingly less effective and are accompanied by an elevation of side effects rather than an increase in the desired effect. People who use the drug quickly discover this and adjust their usage patterns. In addition, many users who are at first enamored with the drug, subsequently lose interest, usually citing the substantial side effects. There is an adage about Ecstasy which captures this phenomenon: "Freshmen love it, Sophomores like it, Juniors are ambivalent, and Seniors are afraid of it." Those who continue to use the drug over longer periods of time usually tend to do so only periodically.

In the summer of 1992, there were as many as fifteen deaths associated with the use of Ecstasy in England. These deaths appear to be similar to certain features of both the serotonin (5-HT) syndrome and the neuroleptic malignant syndrome. Raves are often held in hot, crowded conditions. That summer, some of the clubs which had organized raves turned off their water supplies in an effort to maximize profits by selling bottled water. Hot conditions, the physical exertion, and the dehydration caused by decreased fluid intake and increased sweating may have contributed to the deaths when combined with the drug's effects. Since the British government mandated an open water supply at all clubs, the deaths have apparently stopped.

The drug's neurotoxicity is the most important area of concern about its use. This has been the subject of much research, some of it controversial. MDMA probably does permanently damage serotonin neurons in higher primates, including humans. The functional implication of that effect, however, remains open to question. The issue of serotonin damage in humans must be taken seriously. In general, the higher up the evolutionary chain the mammal, the more serotonin damage is done by MDMA. For humans, this means that MDMA is probably quite toxic to serotonin axons and the damage is permanent. This likely has a negative impact on mood; especially in those people who have, or have a propensity to develop affective illness. While it is not advisable to use the drug at all, individuals with affective illness appear to be especially at risk.

MDMA's high price, usually 25 dollars a tablet, deters more widespread use and makes the use of the much cheaper LSD and amphetamines more compelling. MDMA, while the drug of choice at raves, is probably not the most common. Young people initiated into the world of raves with MDMA often use other drugs as well, most commonly LSD, mushrooms, and marijuana.

Treatment

Since MDMA does not usually have an escalating pattern of abuse, it is somewhat different than a number of other drugs, such as alcohol or heroin. It is more common to find MDMA abused along with some other drug, with that drug, not MDMA, becoming the focus of treatment. The treatment for MDMA abuse is, therefore, quite similar to that of other substances.

There are, however, a number of complicating issues with MDMA. The first is that it is often abused by adolescents, so the treatment needs to take into account their particular needs and issues. The second is that for

TABLE 9.1. MDMA intoxication: Stage I

20–40 minutes after ingestion
Experienced as a sudden amphetamine-like rush and increase in sensory perception. This feeling is also accompanied by mild nausea, sometimes severe enough to cause vomiting.
It is immediately followed by the plateau phase of intoxication.

TABLE 9.2. Subjective effects of MDMA (Plateau Phase)

Altered time perception
Increased ability to interact with others
Decreased defensiveness
Changes in visual perception
Increased awareness of emotions
Decreased aggression
Speech changes
Decreased obsessiveness
Decreased restlessness
Decreased impulsivity

TABLE 9.3. Adverse effects of the use of MDMA

Decreased desire to perform mental or physical tasks
Decreased appetite
Jaw clenching
Gnashing of teeth
Decreased libido
Inability to complete the sexual response cycle
Increased restlessness
Increased anxiety
Decreased ability to perform mental or physical tasks
Depressed mood
Nystagmus
Motor tics
Headaches

TABLE 9.4. Short-term sequelae of MDMA use (less than one week)

Decreased sleep
Decreased appetite
Increased sensitivity to emotions
Decreased ability to perform mental or physical tasks
Decreased desire to perform mental or physical tasks
Increased ability to interact with or be open with others
Fatigue
Decreased aggression
Decreased fear
Depressed mood
Decreased obsessiveness
Increased restlessness
Altered perception of time
Decreased anxiety
Decreased libido

those with a co-morbid affective illness, MDMA has profound effects on mood and anxiety. Someone who is struggling with cocaine dependence, is depressed, and takes MDMA is likely to become even more depressed. This depression can last for a significant period of time. As always, clinical judgment is critical at these points. In most cases, the depressive symptoms will return to baseline in a few days. If they persist, perhaps pharmacological treatment and/or psychotherapeutic treatment is recommended.

Ketamine

Ketamine, also known as "Special K," is a powdered substance which is popular with a small segment of the population, usually people in their twenties living in urban areas. Originally derived from PCP, it is currently used medically as an anesthetic for animals and in human pediatric populations. Its mechanism of action is poorly understood, but it causes the user to feel disassociated from his or her body. In small doses, the sniffed powder causes a mild feeling of being "out of it." Higher doses result in more profound feelings of dissociation, popularly known as a "K-hole."

Ketamine is definitely reinforcing, and although ketamine addiction is rare, it does occur. Treatment occurs in two phases: (a) Acute intoxication can usually be treated with observation. Acidifying the urine with vitamin C, or an acidic juice such as cranberry, may make excretion more rapid; (b) In the case of overdose, the patient should be supported and treated in the emergency room. Since it is possible to become dependent upon Ketamine, the treatment of Ketamine addiction follows the principles of other substance abuse treatment options covered in later sections of this text.

GHB

Gamma Hydroxy Butyrate (GHB) is an abusable substance that is becoming more popular on the East and West coasts with the same populations that use MDMA and Ketamine. GHB is probably a naturally occurring neurotransmitter, as receptors to it are found in mammalian brains. Its precise functions are cause for speculation at this time. It was originally sold in health food stores and marketed to body builders who wanted to increase their weight. This practice was stopped in 1990. It is, however, quite available from inner-city drug dealers, especially those found in nightclubs.

GHB is known as "liquid ecstasy," or as an inversion of its acronym, Grievous Bodily Harm. Although other forms exist, it is usually purchased in liquid form, with 5 mg being the most common initial dose. The effects begin after about 20 minutes and last for several hours. Subjects report feeling "woozy" and pleasantly "disconnected." Reaction time and sensory perception are delayed. If the individual is drinking alcohol along with the drug, the two may produce a synergistic effect. At higher doses, this can lead to respiratory suppression, coma, and death. In recent years such deaths have become more frequent. Although GHB addiction is rare, GHB does cause dependence in some users. It causes an increase in dopamine levels in the nucleus accumbens, and is therefore reinforcing.

Treatment consists of two phases: (a) Acute intoxication can usually be treated with observation. In the case of overdose, the patient should be supported and treated in the emergency room, being especially mindful of the effect of respiratory suppression; (b) Individuals who are dependent on GHB may go through a withdrawal phase characterized by restlessness, jitteriness, and difficulty sleeping. These symptoms should be treated symptomatically. Since it appears to be so similar to alcohol and benzodiazepine withdrawal, GHB withdrawal should probably be treated in much the same fashion (although no formal studies have investigated this). The treatment of a more significant addiction to GHB follows the principles of other substance abuse treatments.

□ Rohypnol

Flunitrazepam is a synthetically derived short-acting benzodiazepine, marketed in a number of countries (most notably Mexico, where it is manufactured) as Rohypnol. It is known in underground circles as "roofies." There are a number of explanations of how the name was derived. While the term roofies sounds vaguely similar to the brand name, the most likely explanation is that it was popular with the Mexican workers who, after Hurricane Andrew, were imported to work on the roofs of destroyed homes in Southern Florida. These "roof workers" used the drug to relax in the evening.

Rohypnol is a benziodiazepine. It is passes through the blood brain barrier and exerts its main effects to benzodiazepine receptors. Intake of the drug results in an induction of drowsiness, feelings of relaxation, and, depending upon how awake the user is, sleepiness. It also creates short-term memory problems. Technically, this is known as anterograde amnesia, which means the user has a cloudy and incomplete memory of events occurring after the use of Rohypnol. If high doses are taken, the individual can become very drowsy and not remember anything occurring after the use.

The drug gained notoriety as some individuals were surreptitiously putting it into others' drinks at bars. The synergistic action of alcohol and benzodiazepines produced somnolence, disinhibition, and impaired memory of events. It therefore became known as the "date rape drug."

Like all benzodiazepines, significant use of Rohypnol can induce tolerance to the drug. Individuals using very large doses are at risk for severe withdrawal if the drug is abruptly stopped. Because of the short half life (2–4 hours), dependence is rare but should be considered in treating a Rohypnol abuser. In overdose, especially combined with alcohol, breathing may be compromised. The treatment of a Rohypnol user mirrors that of an individual with problems with alcohol or any other benzodiazepine.

Conclusion

The drugs discussed above are by no means the only ones found at clubs, raves, or circuit parties. They are, however, the most emblematic. Attendees also use more "traditional" drugs such as LSD, and other hallucinogens. Marijuana is perennially popular, and alcohol use is also high. Furthermore, each week seems to bring a report of some "new" drug of abuse. Often this is just an older, well-known drug, packaged differently or with a new name.

These drugs are used at clubs, often in combination, and often by very young people. This is cause for concern for several reasons. The younger a person begins using drugs, and the more often, the more likely he or she is to develop serious problems with these or other substances. In the future, we are likely to see more and more use of such drugs, and the problems that come with their use.

10

CHAPTER

Marijuana

Introduction

Marijuana refers to the dried-out leaves, flowers, stems, and seeds of the hemp plant, *Marijuana Sativa*. The plant is a common weed that grows freely in most areas of the world. Marijuana, also known as cannabis, is also probably the most commonly used abusable substance in the world, with estimates in the hundreds of millions of daily users. It is most frequently smoked in small, hand-rolled cigarettes called "joints." Alternatively, users employ regular pipes, or water pipes called "bongs." The resin from the flowering tips, or hashish, is more potent and may also be smoked.

Marijuana can also be ingested. Usually this occurs when it is baked into lipid-rich foods such as brownies. Marijuana has been used since antiquity and can be found in numerous ancient texts. Peak popularity occurred in the late 1970s and then steadily declined until 1992. Since that time, marijuana's use has been on the rise, and whether or not its current level of use has reached a plateu phase is still a subject of debate. Marijuana has many purported uses and in recent years the debate over its controversial role as a medicine has been revised.

History

The oldest known reference to marijuana is in a 15th century B.C. Chinese text on herbal remedies. There are Paleolithic cave drawings that appear to be images of people smoking marijuana. Marijuana was first brought to Western Europe and used for intoxicating purposes by the troops of Napoleon's armies returning from Egypt. In Europe, it was quite popular in 19th century high society. In the United States in the beginning of this century, it was popular principally in the West, and was mostly associated with ethnic groups and jazz musicians. Marijuana's social stigma, epitomized in the now popular cult classic film "Reefer Madness," led Congress to enact the Marijuana Stamp Act in 1935. This legislation called for the requirement of a federally approved stamp for commerce with marijuana.

Marijuana, considered benign by many, became a more popular and mainstream drug in the late 1960s, coinciding with the growing drug subculture. Its peak use was in 1978 when approximately 60% of high school seniors admitted to having tried it, and 25% admitted to having used it in the past month.

Probably because of the exposure to individuals who used the drug frequently and suffered lethargy and impairment from it, as well as pressure from the newly emerging war on drugs, marijuana use declined substantially throughout the 1980s. The mid 1980s saw a substantial increase in popularity of the drug with the image of the marijuana plant appearing on numerous articles of clothing worn by "pot aficionados" attesting to the resurgence in interest among users.

Mechanism of Action/Pharmacology

Marijuana smoke is usually inhaled deeply, with the user keeping the smoke in his or her lungs for as long as possible. This allows for absorption of 25–50% of the 9-delta-tetrahydrocannabinol (THC) in the marijuana cigarette. THC is the most potent, but by no means the only, active ingredient in marijuana. THC is the psychoactive substance most studied, and the one most researchers are discussing when talking about the pharmacology of marijuana. THC is quickly absorbed, and this lipophilic molecule quickly passes through the blood-brain barrier.

The THC level in the blood quickly gets redistributed throughout the body, especially in those areas of the body that have high fat content, such as the brain, and the testes for men. THC then leeches out and small levels of the drug can be detected in the bloodstream. This effect lasts for two to four days in the naive user, and as long as three to four weeks in the heavy daily user. As with other drugs of abuse, it is the rise in concentration that is intoxicating, and this residual amount which leeches out into the bloodstream probably does not have much of an effect on the user.

While the effects of the drug can be felt almost immediately (usually heralded by "the giggles" for the new initiate), the peak effect occurs after about 20 minutes. The user feels a mild euphoria, an alteration of sensory acuity, and a distortion of time perception. These effects gradually diminish over the next three to four hours. For the person who ingests marijuana, the effects begin in 20 to 30 minutes and peak at about two hours. The effects of the orally ingested drug usually last for up to eight hours.

The molecular basis of THC's actions are only now being understood. It has a number of physiological properties. It acts like a barbiturate and has anticonvulsant activity as well as opioid properties, causing weak analgesia and anti-diarrheal action. In addition, it suppresses REM (dream period) sleep. Smokers of marijuana usually report an increase in non-restorative sleep. It increases brain limbic stimulation and is thought to activate the pleasure–reward system in the brain. It is for this reason that it is an addictive agent.

In recent years, a specific receptor in the mammalian (and hence human) brain has been discovered and cloned. There are at least two subtypes of the receptor. Along with this, the natural ligand of marijuana, anandamide, has been identified. A ligand is the naturally occurring molecule in the brain that a drug of abuse mimics. Interestingly, the term anandamide is derived from the Hindu word for bliss. At present, pharmaceutical companies have synthesized both an agonist and antagonist to the receptor. Much research is being conducted to identify the properties of these compounds, but at present, it is unclear what function they serve in the mammalian and human brains. Cannabinoid receptors have been described in various regions of the brain with the greatest abundance in the basal ganglia and hippocampus, areas involved with memory function.

The hemp plant synthesizes at least 400 chemicals, of which more than 60 are cannabinoids. Pyrolizing the plant may create even more molecules. Very little is known about the vast majority of these molecules. The most psychologically and physiologically active compound is delta-9-tetrahydrocannabinol. In the pyrolized form, it is delta-11-tetrahydrocannabinol. This molecule is believed to account for most of marijuana's effects. There are, however, numerous other compounds whose effects remain completely unknown. For instance, it is known that marijuana use *raises* the seizure threshold, or makes it more difficult to have a seizure. THC alone *decreases* the seizure threshold. This property of marijuana, therefore, is not the result of THC, but rather of some other cannabinoids. The two most abundant of the cannabinoids are cannabinol and canabidiol. Much research is currently underway regarding the possible uses of marijuana in clinical and other settings.

☐ Effects

Cannabis intoxication commonly heightens the user's sensitivity to external stimuli, thus making colors seem brighter and smells more pungent. It also distorts, sometimes severely, the user's sense of time. The term "temporal disintegration" has been coined to describe the slowing of subjective time after use of the drug. In addition, at least in low doses, marijuana causes mild euphoria and feelings of relaxation. It is also known to increase appetite.

There is some controversy over whether individuals who are intoxicated with cannabis pase a hazard, as they do not seem to be attracted to thrill-seeking behavior, and are usually subdued. Some people have argued that individuals who smoke marijuana are less likely to drive fast. However, reaction time to complex and unforeseen situations is slowed, and muscle strength and hand steadiness is decreased. Because it delays reaction time, alters time perception, and for many other reasons, marijuana must be considered a danger to those who would operate a motor vehicle or use complex machinery or equipment.

At higher dose levels and with chronic patterns of use, cannabis can induce panic attacks. This is especially common in first-time users or older experimenters who have not used marijuana in a long time. Hypervigilance, sometimes resembling frank paranoia, is seen with higher doses. Cannabis-induced psychosis is rare but does occur, especially in countries where heavy smoking is more common and the THC concentration of the plant is higher. The term "hemp insanity" refers to this type of psychosis. The question of whether the drug causes long-term psychotic disorders is more difficult to answer. Clearly, first break psychotic episodes are commonly associated with marijuana ingestion. Whether marijuana was actually a contributing factor in the a priori cause is a matter of dispute and speculation. More probably, individuals who are prone to psychosis are attracted to the drug. In a population which is prone to psychosis, such as in individuals with schizophrenia, marijuana is a risk factor for relapse and psychosis.

> Phyllis, a 45 year-old secretary, was offered marijuana by her neighbors, long-time marijuana users, at a dinner party after inquiring about its effects. She said that she had tried it once in college and only got "the giggles" but had heard so much about it she was eager to try it again. After a few

large puffs, Phyllis began to giggle uncontrollably. Five minutes later, she became anxious and agitated with feelings of suspiciousness and worry. This was manifest in her concern that the police would arrive and the exposure of her marijuana use would ruin her standing in the community. Her husband, who also had tried the marijuana, but was experiencing only mild feelings of pleasant euphoria, tried to reassure her. When it became clear she was still panicky, he took her home and put her to bed. She experienced the suspiciousness for several more hours and her dreams that night were disturbing. After a non-restorative sleep, she vowed never to experiment with illicit drugs again, but would prefer to stick with her occasional glass of wine.

Amotivational Syndrome

Much has been written about the amotivational syndrome, and it remains a controversial entity. It is marked by apathy, poor concentration, social withdrawal, and loss of interest in achievement. It is unclear at this time if marijuana causes a permanent, irreversible impairment in cerebral function, as research on the topic is contradictory. Still, individuals who are chronic users tend to smoke marijuana often and in high doses. Cannabis has a long half-life, and these users can be thought of as chronically "stoned." Marijuana clearly causes impairment in the acquisition of short-term memory, at least at the time an individual is intoxicated. If an individual, especially a young person, is "stoned" nearly all the time, their accumulation of knowledge will be seriously impaired. If the intoxication continues for long enough during critical growing times, it may have permanent consequences. This is the most dangerous and insidious aspect of marijuana use. A high school student who is constantly "stoned" will not learn to the degree to which he or she is capable of functioning. For many people, this will lead to a lifetime deficit that can never be completely repaired.

☐ Treatment

Marijuana withdrawal has been demonstrated in laboratory animals, and has recently been described in humans. Chronic, heavy users of cannabis may experience some withdrawal in the form of irritability, general discomfort, and sleeplessness. Still, the syndrome is not as painful as with heroin, dangerous as with alcohol, or long-lasting as with cocaine. It may contribute to relapse in some individuals.

The clinician is confronted by a wide range of marijuana users. On one end is the individual who uses the drug only rarely but whose use is detected on a routine drug screen and brought to the clinician's attention.

Brief assessment to make sure the problem is not more serious than it appears is all that is necessary. Subsequent follow-up to ensure that the initial impression was correct is part of a thorough assessment. In this instance, the user is usually embarrassed and repentant, and has no objection to future monitoring. The user who does not have a problem with marijuana does not have a problem giving it up.

On the other end is the person—most critically, the adolescent—who uses the drug both daily and heavily. For this case, the individual may need much more intensive rehabilitation and may need to be admitted to a residential drug treatment facility. In any case, the clinician must be alert to any underlying co-morbid condition.

Many researchers believe that marijuana is administered as a form of self-medication. The co-morbid conditions which have been suggested to be associated with marijuana use range from the personality disorders to psychotic spectrum illnesses. In certain personality disorders, the drug's sedating and anxiolitic properties may be used to reduce painful affects. In some mood disorders, marijuana may be a form of self-medication for agitation and even manic or hypomanic states. This hypothesis is still quite intriguing and controversial. At the present time, there is only anecdotal and circumstantial evidence for its existence.

In recent years there has been a great interest in marijuana as a medicine. Advocates see usage for such conditions as glaucoma and nausea. In general there are better and safer agents for such medical conditions. Marijuana may however have some use, and the issue has not been satisfactorily tested in a sound scientific manner.

11

CHAPTER

Nicotine

Introduction

European explorers to the new world found many new and fascinating things. They found land in abundance, new plants such as potato and corn, new flavorings such as chocolate and vanilla, and new cultures quite distinct from their transatlantic counterparts. They also found tobacco. The natives grew the plant, dried it, and either chewed it, or more commonly, smoked the dried leaves. The European settlers quickly adopted this custom. Tobacco became the first "cash crop" of the new world, and financed a good deal of the economic growth of the early colonies.

Tobacco is the plant which contains nicotine. It is nicotine that is the reinforcing and addicting substance in the plant. The delivery system in smoking the cigarette, the cigar, or chewing the leaves is responsible for the severe health consequences. As noted by former Surgeon General Antonia Novello, "smoking represents the most extensively documented cause of disease ever investigated in the history of biomedical research." Cigarette smoking is a profound contributor to mortality. Each year more that 400,000 deaths, or 20% of the total deaths, in the U.S. are caused by smoking.

Many health care professionals ignore smoking in their patients for a variety of reasons. Smoking is so common that it may seem the norm. Intoxication with nicotine is not readily apparent and, in fact, may be associated with diminishing of anxiety and satisfaction. Health care workers often smoke and may be self-conscious about mentioning smoking to patients. This is a profound disservice to patients. The health benefits of quitting are substantial and well documented. Furthermore, there are a number of behavioral and pharmacological tools which are efficacious in the treatment of smoking cessation. Advocacy of quitting and knowledge about effective means to do so are necessary elements in the well-informed clinician.

History

The tobacco plant is short with broad leaves and grows in moderate climates. It is indigenous to the East coast of North America. It was probably cultivated from the time people first settled the region. Tobacco was introduced to Europeans during the age of exploration. Sir Walter Raleigh is credited with bringing it to the court of Queen Elizabeth. From there its use and popularity spread throughout Europe and the world. Sometimes tobacco is taken as snuff and held against the buccal mucosa of the cheek, but it is more commonly smoked. It can be smoked in a pipe, in a large cigar, or in smaller "cigarettes" which were invented in the early part of this century.

Many Americans became hooked on cigarettes while in the military. Cigarettes were included in rations and became a staple of everyday life, and a pleasure that could be counted on. "Smoke 'em if you got 'em" was the refrain heard by servicemen on the eve of important battles. Cigarettes took on a majestic and masculine air. Advertisers played on this and romanticized the notion of smoking. Smoking achieved its peak popularity in the 1950s. In the 1970s, with the advent of the women's movement, advertisers emphasized that equality for women meant equality in smoking rates (probably accounting for the rising rates of smoking-related cancer seen in women today).

That smoking causes health consequences is evident to anyone who has ever had or heard a "smokers' cough," the hacking associated with even moderate smoking. In 1965, the Surgeon General's report confirmed what everyone knew: smoking is dangerous to one's health. In 1971, the FDA banned cigarette advertising on television, but not in print. Currently, the tobacco industry, dominated by the five largest manufacturers, is in negotiation with the Federal government over its future and the future of cigarette advertising.

Smoking rates have decreased in recent years except in a few discrete segments of the population, perhaps the most troubling of which is younger people. Furthermore, the rates are higher in the lower socioeconomic classes with less access to health care. Worldwide cigarette smoking continues to increase, which may be a reason for the cigarette manufacturers' willingness to cede to public health officials' demands about smoking in the U.S. In other countries, particularly in the developing world, smoking is increasingly common and American cigarettes have the most caché. For example, in Vietnam, American manufactured cigarettes are exceedingly popular and account for the bulk of sales to the astoundingly high 77% of individuals who smoke.

Nicotine is highly addictive. Given the political dimension in this very complex issue, it does not appear likely, or even possible, that smoking will end. The National Health Objectives of attaining a smoke-free society by the year 2000 seems desirable but unrealistic at this point in history.

Mechanism of Action

Tobacco smoke is composed of the constituents of cigarettes themselves—the paper and the tobacco leaf. This includes organic matter, nicotinic akyloids, and various additives and flavorings. It also includes the products of the pyrolysis of tobacco, including carbon dioxide, carbon monoxide, and tar. Nicotine is the addicting substance in cigarettes, but it is quite controversial whether nicotine itself is dangerous. It has effects that would seem to be detrimental to one's health. Most notably, it increases blood pressure and heart rate. Theoretically, this ought to place a burden on the cardiovascular systems of smokers. The evidence is mixed, however, and some studies even show a mild tendency towards cardiovascular protection in users of nicotine alone. In any case, nicotine's potential toxicity appears to be substantially less than that associated with tobacco use. It is smoking and its byproducts that are responsible for the very serious health consequences associated with smoking.

Nicotine is readily absorbed from every site on or in the body including the lungs, nasal and buccal mucosa, the gastrointestinal tract, and the skin. Smoking delivers nicotine very rapidly and efficiently. It is almost immediately absorbed and permeates the central nervous system. Delivery into the brain is estimated to take less than 20 seconds. Nicotine has a half life of about 10 to 20 minutes, although this seems to be dose dependent. It is eliminated from the body in 2 to 3 hours. Most nicotine is metabolized into cotinine. Cotinine has a long biological half life of about 24 hours, and does not appear to be physiologically active. Cotinine's presence provides a reliable marker for detecting whether a person uses tobacco. Insurance-related blood work almost always tests for the presence of cotinine.

Nicotine receptors are found throughout the central nervous system and muscular system of mammals. Recent advances in neurobiological research have increased our understanding of the diversity of nicotinic receptors and sites of activity in the brain. Recent evidence indicates that there are many types of these receptors and they likely provide a variety of functions in maintaining emotional, cognitive, and neurophysiological homeostasis. More work needs to be done before the precise function of the nicotine receptors can be fully understood.

Peripherally, nicotine increases blood pressure, heart rate, cardiac output, coronary blood flow, and cutaneous vasoconstriction. Endocrine and metabolic effects are known to occur. These include the release of growth hormone, vasopressin, Prolactin, B endorphins, cortisone, and adrenocorticotrophic hormone. Research is being conducted on the relationship of nicotine to many of these physiological and endocrinological functions.

Like all substances of abuse, nicotine raises the level of dopamine in the nucleus accumbens. It stimulates the dopaminergic system in a complex way. There are numerous animal models for smoking, and if nicotine is made available, animals tend to take it the way humans do, in fairly regular intervals throughout the waking day. It is highly reinforcing. This reinforcement is most likely responsible for the highly addictive nature of nicotine. The individual who smokes more than 12 cigarettes, has an 80% chance of developing a dependence on smoking.

☐ Effects

Smoking itself is a highly dangerous activity and contributes to monumental forms of morbidity and mortality. It is a direct contributor to the development of cancer, lung and heart disease, and many other illnesses. Some of the major effects of smoking and nicotine include the areas of cognition, hunger and body weight, and mood.

Cognition

Smokers often report that smoking enhances their feeling of calmness and ability to concentrate. This has been difficult to reproduce in nonsmokers, but is definitely seen in individuals in withdrawal from smoking. Nicotine may or may not be performance enhancing for non-smokers, but for those who are in withdrawal from nicotine, it is performance enhancing. Therefore, a smoker may in fact need to be smoking in order to think normally.

Hunger and Body Weight

Smokers frequently complain that smoking cessation results in a ravenous appetite and increase in weight. The reasons for this are complex. Nicotine administration probably does result in modest weight loss and the resultant weight gain from cessation may be unavoidable. This may be cosmetically significant for people, however the weight gain is not nearly as problematic as the health consequences of continued nicotine use.

Mood

Smokers report that nicotine helps improve their mood. The best research to date indicates that this probably results from two interrelated factors: rather than promote an improved mood, nicotine probably relieves, albeit mildly, some negative feelings such as anxiety and stress. In addition, for the dependent individual, withdrawal is quite unpleasant, and smoking does relieve the pain associated with withdrawal. It therefore appears to enhance mood, when in fact, it is just relieving symptoms associated with nicotine cessation.

Withdrawal

Nicotine-specific withdrawal is measurable in the laboratory setting. Nicotine deprivation in heavy smokers produces increases in the subjective desire to smoke, impaired performance on computerized cognitive tasks, and decreases in heart rate. Diagnostic criteria for nicotine withdrawal according to the DSM-IV include at least four of the following signs occurring within 24 hours of abrupt cessation of nicotine use or reduction in the amount of nicotine use: (a) dysphoric or depressed mood; (b) insomnia; (c) irritability; (d) frustration or anger; (e) anxiety; (f) difficulty concentrating; (g) restlessness; (h) decreased heart rate; and (i) increased appetite or weight gain. A table listing the most common side effects associated with nicotine withdrawal is next.

Treatment

The treatment of nicotine dependence can be divided into the pharmacological and the non-pharmacological therapies. Both means are effective to a degree, and the evidence indicates that the most efficacious means is a combination of the two. As with the treatment of any other addictive

TABLE 11.1. Selected signs and symptoms of nicotine withdrawal

Signs
Constipation
Decrease in adrenaline, noradrenaline, and cortisol as measured in urine
EEG changes
Decrease in heart rate
Increased coughing
Mouth ulcers
Sleep disturbances
Weight gain
Symptoms
Craving
Drowsiness
Difficulty concentrating
Decreased alertness
Stomach upset
Lightheadedness
Headache
Chest tightening
Aches and pains
Restlessness
Hunger
Mood changes
Irritability/Frustration/Anger
Anxiety
Depression
Hostility
Impatience

disorder, persistence on the part of the clinician is often needed. Similarly, since there is no universal smoking cessation model, the clinician needs to be creative in designing specialized treatment plans which address the specific needs of each smoker.

There are many psychosocial treatments for nicotine dependence. Most formal smoking cessation programs consist of multiple treatment sessions, delivered in a group setting by trained facilitators. Other methods commonly employed include gradual diminution of cigarettes (i.e., either limiting the number of cigarettes, or the potency of the ones purchased) eventually ceasing, contingency management, relapse prevention, and cue exposure. Nicotine dependence is a multifaceted disorder involving biological, social, behavioral, and psychological factors. Effective behavioral treatments must focus on as many aspects of a smoker's life as possible. The principles of relapse prevention treatment can be extremely useful in dealing with people who want to quit smoking. Education about cues and relapse triggers, and how to handle them, is often quite effective.

Pharmacotherapy

In recent years, a number of pharmacological treatments of nicotine dependence have been developed. These include nicotine replacement therapies, other pharmacotherapies, and those that treat co-morbid conditions.

Nicotine replacement is just what the name implies. Given that nicotine is not very harmful, and its delivery system is the problem in smoking, nicotine replacement systems deliver pure nicotine to an individual and then gradually decrease the levels. This can take several months. The eventual goal is complete smoking cessation. In recent years, several of these systems have become available over the counter. This method has advantages and disadvantages. It will likely increase the number of those attempting to quit, but because of the lack of concomitant behavioral counseling and therapy, will likely result in an increased failure rate. In addition, the over-the-counter status has allowed some prescription plans to drop payment for nicotine replacement therapy. Since it is relatively expensive, this will undoubtedly decrease its use.

Nicotine replacement comes in a variety of forms: a gum, a patch, and a nasal spray. It also comes as an inhaler, both as an aerosol and as so-called "safer cigarettes" that heat enough to aerosolize the nicotine but do not create the other harmful byproducts of smoking. Transmucosally-delivered nicotine in the form of polacrilex is available in a commercially available gum. The user chews the gum and then places it in the cheek. Nicotine is absorbed and a significant blood level is achieved. Advantages to this form are that individuals can take the gum ad libidum. A lengthy and gradual discontinuation phase is recommended in order to achieve abstinence. Anecdotal clinical experience indicates that most successful treatments result in an individual gradually decreasing his or her dose over an extended period of time, often six months or more.

A nicotine skin patch is available in several strengths and is recommended to be used for either 16 or 24 hours. The 24 hour form sometimes results in difficulty sleeping. Nicotine is absorbed through the skin, and over the course of 6 to 8 weeks the patient decreases the dosage form of the patch. The nasal spray and nicotine inhalers are less well-studied but may also be helpful in encouraging smoking cessation.

Recently, Buproprion has been approved for smoking cessation and represents the first approved indication for a non-nicotine replacement therapy. The medication is marketed under the name Zyban®. It is the same chemical compound as the antidepressant Wellbutrin®. The recommended dosage is 200–300 mg per day in a twice daily fashion. Nicotine dependence rates are increased in dual diagnosis conditions and any condition, such as depression or an anxiety disorder, ought to be treated with pharmacotherapy when indicated.

Research suggests that the most effective treatment results from a combination of behavioral support, education, and pharmacotherapy. Persistence is necessary and often rewarded since this is a difficult addiction to treat. Mark Twain is quoted as saying, "It's easy to quit smoking, I've done it hundreds of times," emphasizing the ease with which people stop, but the difficulty in doing so for long periods of time. The responsible clinician, however, recognizes how much quitting can benefit a patient, does not collude with the patient's denial defenses, and perseveres through many ups and downs in the individual's efforts to stop smoking.

12

CHAPTER

Opioids

Introduction

The term "opiate" refers to any compound which is derived from the opium plant or poppy. An opiate is by definition a naturally occurring substance. The more inclusive term, opioid, refers to all naturally occurring opiates as well as those molecularly similar compounds which are synthetically derived. Unlike some substances of abuse, such as alcohol and cocaine, which act more generally upon the central nervous system, opioids act through specific receptors. There are naturally occurring opioid receptors in all mammalian brains. Although there are several different subtypes of receptors (such as kappa and delta), the most prominent and the one most responsible for the physiological and psychological consequences of opioid ingestion, including analgesia, is the (mu) μ-receptor. All known opioids exert their most important actions principally through the μ-receptor.

This class of drugs has many therapeutic uses and opioids remain the gold standard for pain relief. Unfortunately, in addition to the therapeutic value of opioids, they are also dangerously addictive and often lead to abuse. Morphine and heroin use have been social problems for many years. At the turn of the century, the U.S. saw a substantial problem with morphine. In the 1960s and 1970s, the purity range of heroin purchased on the street varied tremendously but averaged about 20%. Nowadays, it is not uncommon to find heroin that is 70–80% pure. The implications of this and the dangers it poses to society are striking. Heroin that is less pure can be smoked or snorted and produces the same effect as purer forms of heroin that are injected. Although many people are averse to the injection of any substance into their bodies, with these alternative methods of administration the fear of injecting heroin no longer acts as a deterrent to its use. A whole new dimension of opiate abuse has emerged.

☐ History

Opioids have been used for at least 3,500 years. For most of that time, they were found in the form of crude opium or in alcohol solutions derived from the poppy plant. Morphine and codeine were first isolated from the poppy plant in the beginning of the 1800s. In the first decade of the nineteenth century, morphine was isolated from opium. Codeine was isolated in 1832. Heroin was a trade name used by the Bayer Company for diacetylmorphine and was introduced commercially in 1898. The hope was that acetylation of the morphine molecule would reduce its side effects while maintaining its effectiveness in the suppression of the cough reflex.

These initial opiates were used not only for medicinal purposes, but also for recreational purposes. Opioid dependence, or at least withdrawal from this class of drugs, was first recognized as a medical problem in the middle of the nineteenth century. There was an increasing awareness of social consequences to permitting the sale of opioids as an over-the-counter medication. At the beginning of this century, there were significant numbers of people who were dependent upon opium. The Harrison Narcotic Act of 1914 made the usage of opioids for the treatment of addiction and prevention of withdrawal illegal. Thus, opiates could not be used for "maintenance." All of the clinics established to maintain heroin dependent individuals with opium substitutes closed by the early 1920s.

Heroin use has remained a social ill throughout the twentieth century and was a particularly difficult problem for veterans in both World War II and Vietnam. Debates about how to deal with heroin addiction flared and continue to do so today. The treatment of heroin dependence was influenced by the development of therapeutic communities. The first, Synanon, began in California in 1958, under the direction of Charles Dederich. At about the same time, Vincent Dole and Marie Nyswander demonstrated the effectiveness of oral methadone in decreasing heroin use and related crime. Heroin continues to be a significant social problem. Despite the fact that effective treatments and medications that deal with heroin dependence and abuse exist, there is often difficulty implementing these treatments. Most experts view the beurocracy created to distribute methadone as needlessly complex and not at an "user friendly."

Mechanism of Action

The actions of M-agonist opioids are exerted primarily at receptors on neural tissues in the central nervous system, the autonomic nervous system, and to some extent, white blood cells. Three distinct neurobiological opioid systems, or families, have now been described. Each of these systems has both a distinct genetic basis and precursor molecules. It is unclear what the complete functional and developmental role played by these molecules and receptor systems is. However, the exogenous opioids share a structure and function with them, and are probably involved in basic and primal reward and pleasure systems. All opioid receptors are activated by these molecules, causing changes in ion channel permeability. The changes induced by this action presumably mediate a myriad of effects in these substances, as well as resulting in tolerance and dependence upon them.

Interestingly, in recent years, scientists have bred a strain of mice that are identical to all other lab mice with one exception: they do not have μ-receptors. As far as these scientists can tell, the mice seem to be identical both behaviorally and morphologically. This presents a puzzle to researchers and seems to imply that while integral to species adaptation mechanisms, μ-receptors are not essential for existence. Further implications of this will undoubtedly be a continued source of investigation in future years.

Effects

The effects of all opioids are dose dependent, and the intensity and severity experienced are proportional to the amount and relative potency of the compound. Examples of opiates are heroin, morphine, dilaudid, meperidine, oxycodone, and codeine. These are all commercially available analgesics. When abused, the initial and desired effects are euphoria and analgesia. Heroin users describe a profoundly pleasing experience of calmness and pleasure. This is usually accompanied by lethargy and a lack of motivation. The user may appear to "nod off" or be stuporous, with impairments in attention and memory. Motor effects are pronounced, and slurred speech is common. Pupils become quite constricted, a phenomenon called "pinpoint pupils."

Overdoses with these drugs are common, in part because it is difficult to calculate accurate dosages given the extreme variability in purity of the street version of the drug. In higher doses of opiates, respiratory depression is common and can lead to death.

Tolerance to these drugs develops rapidly with frequent usage. This means that in order for the user to continue to get the same amount of pleasure from the drug, he or she must use increasing amounts. Hence, a standard dose of methadone might lead to the death of a more naive user. The physiological opposite of tolerance is dependence. That is, if an individual stops taking the drugs abruptly, he or she may experience withdrawal symptoms. Dependence on heroin may develop in as little as a week of daily use.

☐ Withdrawal

Withdrawal from opioids is unpleasant, painful, and prolonged, but in a healthy individual is never dangerous or fatal. The adage "No one ever died of heroin withdrawal—they just wish they did" is quite accurate. Opiate withdrawal may vary from mild feelings of discomfort to severe, dramatic, and painful full-blown symptoms. The most common symptoms include irritability, dysphoria, nausea or vomiting, muscle aches, runny nose, dilated pupils, goose bumps (from which the term "cold turkey" originates), diarrhea, yawning, fever, and insomnia. The duration of the withdrawal is directly proportional to the length of action of the opioid. The longer the half life, the longer the withdrawal phase. Methadone has a particularly long half life of over 24 hours. A methadone maintained patient attempting to withdraw has a particularly severe and protracted withdrawal. This is one reason for the very high relapse rate in the population that attempts to stop taking methadone.

☐ Treatment

The treatment of heroin dependence is divided into two main areas: dealing with the withdrawal effects, and the physical and psychological dependence on the drug. The treatment of withdrawal is principally pharmacological, although the treatment setting should follow common sense guidelines which suggest a comfortable and safe setting. There are a number of medications that relieve the symptoms of withdrawal. These can make the experience of withdrawal much easier to tolerate and the chances of a successful recovery much greater. Clonidine is an antagonist which is currently only officially approved for the treatment of hypertension. It is, however, highly useful in the treatment of withdrawal from opiates. By suppressing the sympathetic outflow of the locus ceruleus and the concomitant feelings of overdrive, it greatly relieves the suffering of those in withdrawal. Benzodiazepines are also helpful for the anxiety and insomnia which accompany withdrawal. Analgesics such as acetaminophen and ibuprofen may be used, but in cases where nausea

TABLE 12.1. Sample withdrawal schedule for opiate dependence

Day 1

The first eight hours patient observed in a clinical setting but after that the patient may be sent home as long as he or she has a support system such as a friend or family member.
0.1 mg of Clonidine PO every four hours (monitoring blood pressure)
Klonazepam–1 to 2 mg every eight hours
Ibuprofen–800 mg every eight hours
Loperimide–one 2 mg tablet then one 2 mg tablet after each subsequent bowel movement. The daily dosage should not exceed 16 mg
Odansetron–8 mg twice per day

Day 2

Hour 1: 0.1 to 0.2 mg of Clonidine
Klonazepam–2 mg
Ibuprofen–800 mg
Loperimide–one 2 mg tablet then one 2 mg tablet after each subsequent bowel movement. The daily dosage should not exceed 16 mg
Odansetron–8 mg twice per day
Hour 2: Naltrexone–12.5 mg (one quarter of a tablet). Observe for one hour if patient is clinically healthy, give an additional 12.5 mg and observe for one more hour. If no problems exist, the patient may be sent home with instructions to take the Clonidine 0.1–0.2 mg every four hours as needed, as well as the Klonazepam every eight hours as needed.

Day 3

Hour 1: 0.1 to 0.2 mg of Clonidine
Klonazepam–2 mg
Ibuprofen–800 mg
Loperimide–one 2 mg tablet then one 2 mg tablet after each subsequent bowel movement. The daily dosage should not exceed 16 mg
Odansetron–8 mg twice per day
Hour 2: The patient may be given 50 mg of Naltrexone, be observed for one hour and released. The patient should then continue to take the naltrexone on a daily basis (preferably observed).

and vomiting do not permit their intake, then the intramuscular form of toredol is often used instead.

Table 12.1 contains following an example of a detoxifying protocol; the clinician should use this only as a guide, and remember that only a medically stable individual ought to be detoxified as an outpatient. More complicated cases should be referred to a specialty facility. Furthermore, outpatient detoxifications are rarely successful if the person is more than moderately dependent on opiates. As a rule of thumb, the individual who is using more than four "bags" of heroin a day will require an inpatient detoxification.

If, in the future, there is any doubt about the patient's level of use of opiates, a "Narcan challenge" is recommended. Narcan is the short-acting, intravenously administered opiate blocker. This involves drawing up 2 cc of .4 mg/ml of Narcan into a syringe. Inject 0.5 cc intravenously, wait 30 seconds while observing for signs and symptoms of opiate withdrawal. If none are noted, administer the remaining 1.5 cc intravenously. If signs and symptoms of opiate withdrawal are still not observed, Naltrexone may be administered.

The clinician should keep in mind that this is only a prototypical schedule and that the specific symptoms of each opiate addict should be treated on an individual basis.

Recently, several for-profit firms have developed an "ultra-rapid" detoxification procedure. Patients are admitted and given what is essentially general anesthesia. They are detoxified from the opiates and put on a blocking agent such as Naltrexone. Sufficient studies have not been conducted on this method of detoxification. Anecdotal reports suggest that this model is effective in the short term but does expose the patient to the risk of anesthesia.

Treatment of opioid dependence can be divided into the pharmacological and the nonpharmacological. This is a difficult condition to treat and the clinician will often need to employ both modalities. Most individuals who have developed an addiction to heroin or other opioids will need to be treated with a combination of pharmacological and psychosocial therapy.

Pharmacotherapy

Pharmacotherapies can be categorized as agonists, legal forms of opioids that stimulate the μ-receptor, and antagonists, which block the effect of morphine or heroin. Agonists include the opioid itself, such as morphine. In the earlier part of the century in the United States, and in some parts of the world, morphine was legally available for the treatment of dependence and abuse.

Methadone is the most common form of agonist available in this country. First created by the Germans during World War II, it was the first synthetic opioid. (Its commercial name, Dolophin, is derived from the Latin root for "pain", not from the first name of Adolph Hitler, as is sometimes rumored.) Its relatively long half life of 18–24 hours successfully blocks the reinforcement of other opioids; however, it must be used in high enough doses to be effective. This has been an ongoing problem as many clinics do not give adequate doses. In general, *at least* 60 mg per day is necessary. A longer-acting form, levo acetyl acetyl morphine (LAAM) should be commercially available shortly. Buprenorphine, an agonist/antagonist is presently undergoing clinical trials as well. In the future, it is likely that Buprenorphine will be a useful and more widely used agent to deal with detoxification.

Methadone is available only at licensed clinics. The individuals enrolled usually come to the clinic on a daily basis to receive their dose. While some of these clinics are well run, a large number are poorly administered. In addition, there is an insufficient number of methadone programs to deal with the large population of addicts requesting treatment. Research indicates that once a person is treated with methadone, the likelihood of successfully stopping methadone is remote. Therefore in most cases, once an opiate addict becomes a methadone patient, they will remain so for life. There are obviously some individuals who are successful in withdrawing from methadone, but they are the exception.

The μ-receptor may be successfully blocked with either a short term or long term agent. Naloxone, which is administered intravenously, immediately blocks the receptor and will immediately precipitate withdrawal. This is used in emergency rooms in actual or suspected overdoses. A longer-acting oral form is available. Naltrexone taken daily, usually in 50 mg doses, or three times per week (e.g., Monday/Wednesday/Friday at 100 mg/100 mg/150 mg) will completely block the effects of administering opioids. In many cases, this is an effective means of treating the heroin abuser. Caution must be taken so that the individual does not take toxic amounts of opioids to override the blockade. If an individual on Naltrexone is involved in an automobile accident and suffers trauma, normal analgesia is not an option and the person may need sedation. In such a case, a trained anesthesiologist must be involved.

The non-pharmacological treatments run the gamut, and can be as informal as occasional attendance at a Twelve Step meeting, to much more aggressive interventions, such as active participation in an intensive drug treatment-focused therapeutic community. These specific forms of psy-

TABLE 12.2. Signs and symptoms of opiate withdrawal

Signs	Symptoms
Stomach Cramps	Diarrhea
Anxiety	Increased heart rate and blood pressure
Loss of appetite	Tearing
Sleeplessness	Restlessness
Craving	Fever
Muscle aches	Muscle spasms
Perspiration	Runny nose
Yawning	Vomiting
Dysphoria	Goose pimples

chosocial treatment are not necessarily specific to heroin or opiate addiction and are covered later in this text.

13

CHAPTER

Stimulants: Cocaine and Methamphetamine

Introduction

The term stimulant refers to a chemical which serves to increase the level of alertness of the individual who takes them. Although quite different chemically, all stimulants activate the CNS to one degree or another. In general, these chemicals increase the level of dopamine transmission and therefore increase the organism or person taking the stimulants general level of activity, both mentally and physically.

A stimulant is a stimulant is a stimulant. In general these compounds all cause the same effect. What differs is the intensity of the effect that the compound has on the CNS. Matters such as route of administration are also important, but each of these compounds affects the CNS to a varying degree. It is the intensity with which the stimulant activates the CNS that determines its effectiveness, as well as its potential for abuse. Some mild stimulants such as caffeine are considered relatively safe. So to are therapeutic agents such as methylphenidate (Ritalin) or dextroamphetamine (Dextrostat). These have abuse potential, but they are much less than the more potent agents such as cocaine and Methamphetamine. The therapeutically used agents are useful for a variety of conditions including attention deficit hyperactivity disorder. When used therapeutically, they are usually quite useful and safe.

We have chosen to focus on cocaine and methamphetamine, as these are the most well known, and most widely and dangerously abused of the stimulants.

Cocaine

Before the 1980s, cocaine was not widely thought to be addictive. A leading psychiatric textbook (Kaplan & Sadock) in 1980 described cocaine as not particularly addicting, and a substance that could be taken 2 to 3 times per week, without danger, resulting in only mild feelings of euphoria. Clinicians who deal with patients who abuse cocaine know that this is not true. It has become increasingly evident in recent years that although cocaine dependence does not have the systemic physiological impact of alcohol and heroin, it does indeed create a physiological dependence. In the case of cocaine, this dependence most likely occurs in the neural networks of the person's brain. Hundreds of thousands of individuals each year realize that the substance they once felt they could control is now controlling them.

Cocaine is a 6-carbon molecule that is derived from the coca plant. The plant is a mid-sized shrub which grows wildly in parts of Central and South America where the climate is particularly conducive to its growth. Natives chew the coca plant leaves or brew them into a tea. The products of the coca plant are highly prized for their capacity to increase energy and decrease appetite. The plants are crushed into a milky-white liquid which is then dried into the familiar powder that is commonly referred to as cocaine.

Most users in the United States place the powder on a flat surface and divide it into "lines" which are then insufflated, or snorted, through a straw or rolled up dollar bill. (The affluent use 100 dollar bills, and at the height of the cocaine epidemic in the middle of the 1980s, over 75% of 100 dollar bills passing through the Federal Reserve in Miami were supposedly found to have traces of cocaine.) Low to average doses resulting in cocaine intoxication range from 25 to 150 mg. The average "line" of cocaine contains approximately 25 to 30 mg. Cocaine can also be injected or, if the user engages in a process called "freebasing," where the cocaine molecule is chemically altered to allow it to be pyrolized, it can be inhaled. If the precipitate of this pyrolization process is allowed to dry, it is known as *crack*, or *rock*. This potent form of cocaine is also smoked.

Cocaine has been popular for many years. Since the severe and damaging epidemic during the eighties, cocaine use appears to have diminished, although there are indications that it will be increasing in the coming years.

History

Cocaine has been cultivated for at least four thousand years in the areas that were once controlled by the Incas. Knowledge of and a market for cocaine first spread to Europe in the mid to late 1800s coinciding with the popular trend of world exploration. At that time, figures such as Sir Richard Burton and Alexander Von Humbolt were household names because of their exploits. Europeans were eager for anything new, and a white powder which made its users euphoric was intriguing to say the least.

In 1884, Sigmund Freud, then a young and prominent neurologist, published his essay "Uber Coca" in which he advocated the therapeutic use of cocaine for a wide variety of ailments, such as a cure for morphine addiction, migraine headaches, and hysteria. He used this remedy for his great friend and mentor Willhelm Fleiss who suffered from morphine addiction. The unfortunate Fleiss merely ended up addicted to both morphine and cocaine. Freud, also a regular user of cocaine for a time, never seemed to have become addicted to it. He did, however, die from consequences of another addiction: nicotine. (Freud took an overdose of morphine administered knowingly by his physician, after enduring over thirty operations for cancer of the mouth.)

Cocaine's popularity in Europe was mirrored in the United States. An Atlanta druggist, John Pemberton, devised a patent medicine that contained two stimulants, cocaine and caffeine. He called his product "Coca-Cola," and it contained about 60 mg of cocaine per 8 ounce serving. As cocaine use spread in the last century, so did the common observations that it had numerous adverse consequences. This led to the voluntary removal of cocaine from the cola's formulation (The Coca-Cola Bottling Company still imports coca leaves, denuded of cocaine, for flavoring purposes only).

The American Medical Association, seeking to raise the standards of medical practice and protect the public's health, advocated for the Harrison Narcotic Act of 1914. The bill (which mistakenly listed cocaine as a narcotic) banned the use of cocaine in proprietary medications. Cocaine lost favor as a stimulant for a variety of reasons, among them its lack of availability. The 1930s and the 1960s are considered stimulant epidemic periods, but the drug of choice was amphetamine, which was cheaper and more available because of the ease of manufacturing it.

The late 1970s and early 1980s saw the rise of cocaine use among middle class Americans. The perception at that time, echoing Freud's forgotten errors of a century before, was that cocaine was a safe and pleasant stimulant. It was expensive and became a status symbol. By the mid 1980s, it was clear in the public domain that cocaine was indeed a highly dangerous and addictive drug. Numerous national education and treatment initiatives were begun.

In the middle 1980s, a smokeable form of cocaine, which became known as "crack," appeared in the drug markets. Crack is low priced (2 to 4 dollars per vial) and, as such, far more available to younger and poorer users. It is not cheaper, it can just be bought in smaller amounts and, as a result, it is cheaper to get high. Almost anyone can afford a 2 dollar vial of crack. The effect of crack on the inner city was profound. Cocaine itself is quite toxic and the heavy use of it leads to a number of serious physical consequences. In addition, the behavior of those on crack can be very dangerous, violent, and paranoid. The drug has also been a contributing factor in increased crime rates. Almost anything could be stolen and sold to buy another vial of crack. If a criminal wants to buy $100 worth of powdered cocaine, thought and planning need to occur in the contemplation and execution of the crime. The same is not true for crack. The addict needs only 2 dollars worth of goods to acquire it. In recent years, crack use seems to have stabilized because of the high visibility of problems encountered by and with "crack-heads." At the present time, cocaine continues to be an enormous public health problem.

Mechanism of Action

The rate of the rise of cocaine within the blood-brain barrier is related to the route of administration. Like all drugs of abuse, the quicker the rise, the more intense the subjective feeling experienced by the user. Crack, and intravenous (IV) administration of cocaine produce an almost instantaneously measurable rise, while nasal and oral administration is much slower and much less reinforcing. The slowest route, oral ingestion, produces the most gradual rise and the least intense "high." This form of cocaine use is the least powerful and is not nearly as addicting as intranasal or crack forms of cocaine.

Cocaine is considered a "dirty drug," since it affects numerous neurotransmitter systems. It does not purely affect one receptor or system, but rather has a multitude of effects and actions in the brain. It has an impact on the release and re-uptake blockade of dopamine, norepinephrine, and serotonin. As a result of its complex neurochemical effects, an inclusive understanding of its neuropharmacology is not yet within the grasp of science. Much is known, however, about the neurophysiology of cocaine even if the information is incomplete.

Cocaine is perhaps the most reinforcing of all the drugs of abuse. As noted in earlier chapters, laboratory animals, if given unblocked access to cocaine, will self-administer cocaine in preference to any other reward including sex or food. In the laboratory, this can actually end with the animal's death from exhaustion. Among humans, users tend to become exhausted by trying to obtain more of the drug, and consequently "crash" before they are able to abuse cocaine to the point of lethality.

It has long been thought that the principal reinforcing effect of cocaine is related to the inhibition of dopamine re-uptake. While much research points to this conclusion, it cannot be the sole explanation or else dopamine blocking agents would block cocaine's effects—which they do not. Cocaine probably affects its mechanism through a variety of receptors at the most primitive reaches of the mammalian brain. Although dramatic strides continue to illustrate the mechanism of action of cocaine and other stimulants, the true neurochemistry of cocaine has yet to be elucidated.

Effects

The principle effects of cocaine are similar regardless of the route of administration. The substantial difference is in the intensity and duration of the effect (and the propensity to induce an addictive process). Chewing the coca leaves, along with a small amount of base, usually bicarbonate, to make the molecule more absorbable, results in a pleasant feeling of well-being, increases sensory awareness, and reduces appetite. The effects of this begin after 10 to 20 minutes, last for several hours, and then gradually diminish. It is for these properties that it is prized among the farmers of Bolivia, who must work for long hours at a very high altitude, and sometimes need to go with little food or sleep. (This led to the colloquial appellation "Bolivian Marching Powder.")

Smoked cocaine, or crack, produces an almost instantaneous sense of intense euphoria, followed several minutes later by a severe reduction in energy or the "crash." The user feels the results of the more intermediate form of cocaine administration or intranasal absorption (snorting), just minutes after insufflation, and experiences a peak in about 20 minutes. The individual feels mildly euphoric, with an increased sense of energy, enhanced sense of confidence, decreased appetite, and a state of general well-being. To the naive user, the enhancement of self esteem is highly rewarding and reinforcing. This is the beginning of addictive use. It should be noted that only about 15% of those who try cocaine ever go on to have a problem with it, but for substantial numbers of people, this initial use may lead to much more chronic, regular use and more severe consequences.

Continued use of cocaine can have very severe side effects. Initial euphoria is replaced by depression, an increased sense of energy is replaced

TABLE 13.1. The most common effects of cocaine at low to moderate doses (25 to 150 mg).

1. Euphoria and a sense of well-being and connectedness
2. Increased sense of energy
3. Enhanced acuity and ability to problem solve
4. Anorexia or decreased appetite
5. Increased sensory arousal
6. Increased desire for sex
7. Increased self confidence which may be disproportionate to reality
8. Suspiciousness and increased arousal which can progress to frank paranoia
9. Delusions (often paranoid), clinically indistinguishable from chronic paranoid schizophrenia

by fatigue, increased sensory awareness can become frank delusion, the decreased need for sleep is replaced by extreme lethargy, and it is not uncommon for someone coming off of a severe binge to sleep for 3 or 4 days, rising only occasionally to go to the bathroom or eat (usually ravenously).

☐ Withdrawal

While neither as physiologically dramatic as alcohol withdrawal, nor as painful as heroin or opioid withdrawal, a physiological withdrawal from cocaine definitively exists. In recent years, it has become increasingly clear that cocaine indeed has a distinctive and profound withdrawal syndrome. It is probably best to think of this withdrawal syndrome, and easiest to explain to patients, as something that occurs deep in the brain structures of patients weaning themselves from cocaine.

The cocaine withdrawal syndrome is perhaps best understood as occurring over three phases. It must be emphasized that these three phases blend into one another and are described here in more distinctive terms than the clinician may encounter. In addition, just as all intoxication is in large part subjective and influenced by the *set and setting* of the drug use, so is the withdrawal phase. Generally, the intensity of the withdrawal phase is directly proportional to the amount and time of the cocaine consumption. The individual who has insufflated one or two lines of cocaine may experience only some mild tiredness, while the individual who has been on a "run" of several days may sleep for four days during the first phase of the crash.

Crash Phases

Phase 1: The crash

Preceded by the intoxication phase, the crash generally lasts from 9 hours to 4 days. The early part of the crash phase is characterized by agitation, depression, anorexia, and a highly intense craving for cocaine, as the individual tries to extend the "run." The middle part of this phase is characterized by the diminution and extinction of cocaine craving as well as fatigue and depression. Later on, as mentioned earlier, the individual user becomes exhausted, may sleep for hours or even days, and has an uncontrollable appetite.

Patients in this phase do not crave cocaine. If the patient has been admitted to an emergency room, the caregivers, if unfamiliar with the withdrawal syndrome, are often perplexed. Upon admission, the patient may have been extremely paranoid, hostile, and agitated, followed by the long stretch of sleep. The staff may be very surprised that upon the patient's awakening, he or she is often calm and may actually be pleasant. When asked if he or she is still craving the drug, the user may respond with absolute sincerity: "No." Because the patient is calm and does not crave cocaine, a most critical therapeutic mistake is often made if the staff determines that the need for treatment is no longer pressing. **This is a serious error.** This individual will be in need of support and help to deal with this serious dependence. Like the eye of the hurricane, which can give false comfort and sunshine, this period of euthymia, normal blood, and low craving should be thought of as a brief respite between the violence of the binge and the difficulty of the next phases of withdrawal.

Phase 2: Withdrawal

This portion of the withdrawal phase generally lasts anywhere from the end of the crash phase to 10 weeks. The early phase is characterized by a gradual normalization of sleep and mood. In the first few weeks, there is often a low level of cocaine craving and a low level of anxiety. This is a major reason why 30 day rehabilitation programs can be unsuccessful with this population of primarily cocaine-abusing patients. Individuals may spend the entire program at a time when they are not craving cocaine very intensely, and thus develop a false sense of security about how easy it will be when they attempt to return to their previous environment. After 30 days or so, when they are released, the cravings become much more pronounced.

The middle and late portion of the withdrawal phase is characterized by anhedonia (lack of pleasure), low energy, anxiety, and high cocaine craving. This is exacerbated by cues that may induce craving, an example of classical conditioning. The sight of cocaine paraphernalia or hearing a few bars from a song associated with past days of revelry, may induce intense craving with physiological responses such as rhinorhea (runny nose), taste sensations, fidgetiness, and intense drug craving. Individuals in treatment need to be warned repeatedly about how difficult and common this occasional experience will be and how to plan for this likely phenomenon.

Phase 3: Extinction

This is the final, and by far longest, of the withdrawal phases. It lasts for at least six months and for many cocaine users, the rest of their lifetime. Stories of experiencing cravings, when faced with particularly strong cues, even years after the final use, are not uncommon. As the individual firms up his or her abstinence and recovery, mood returns to baseline and gradually becomes normalized. It must be emphasized that current research supports the notion that any drug use for the cocaine-dependent individual, even on a casual and occasional basis, is extremely dangerous and will likely propel the whole cycle of addiction and recovery back into gear. **The knowledgeable clinician will not condone "social use" of cocaine by the previously dependent user.**

☐ Treatment

The overall treatment of cocaine dependence does not differ greatly from the general treatment models discussed in other chapters of this text. The treatment plan needs to be correlated with the severity of the addiction. An occasional user who is escalating the amount and use of the drug may only need goading from a concerned friend, or education from a health professional, that this activity is life-threatening. Research has demonstrated that this can be enormously powerful. The heavy user needs much more intensive treatment, such as within the supportive structure of a therapeutic community lasting as long as 2 years. Such an individual may never be able to live apart from a sober and supportive environment.

Pharmacotherapy

A large number of agents, mainly antidepressants and dopamine agonists, have been tested as treatments for cocaine abuse, but none have demonstrated clear efficacy. Tricyclic antidepressants, mainly desipramine, have been most studied, but have shown limited promise. Trials of most other pharmacological agents for cocaine abuse have been more unsuccessful. Tricyclics were originally proposed because they reverse the effects of cocaine in the intra-cranial self-stimulation model, thought to represent cocaine-induced disregulation and blunting of the brain-reward system. There is probably a small to medium-sized effect on cocaine "craving" and a marginal effect on cocaine use, which may be restricted to the early weeks of treatment, or perhaps limited to intranasal users or depressed users.

Tricyclic antidepressants cannot, therefore, be recommended as a routine treatment for cocaine abuse, although they might be considered in patients who have failed other approaches or who have depressive symptoms. Depression is common in cocaine abusers and is associated with poor outcome. As with alcohol, cocaine induces a lot of depressive symptoms, making differential diagnosis difficult.

Although not definitively demonstrated, several clinical trials have suggested that *depressed* cocaine abusers may benefit selectively from tricyclic antidepressants. Except in patients with cardiac conduction disease, these agents are safe and a trial with an antidepressant is often warranted. It may also have the added benefit of increasing a person's motivation for psychosocial treatment.

The evaluation of anxiety disorders is difficult in cocaine abusers because cocaine is a stimulant and, as such, is anxiogenic (causes anxiety). Cocaine use is associated with the induction of panic attacks. In many instances, the anxiety will lessen—and even cease—when the substance abuse remits. The clinical principles for differential diagnosis of substance-induced versus independent psychopathology (discussed in the chapter on comorbidity) can be applied in this situation.

If an independent anxiety disorder is suspected, then treatment either with a tricyclic antidepressant (TCA) or a selective serotonin reuptake inhibitor (SSRI) is warranted. Buspirone also appears to be safe. As with all substance abusers, caution should be employed in considering the choice of whether or not to prescribe benzodiazepines with this population. This section deals with pharmotherapies, but it should always be kept in mind that other types of simultaneous treatment such as relaxation techniques, hypnosis, cognitive/behavioral therapies, and acupuncture may be simultaneously useful in assuaging anxiety.

Cocaine, either intranasal or in the smokeable form ("freebase" or "crack"), has had a profoundly negative effect on the urban poor and homeless population. A large number of these people carry the diagnosis of schizophrenia. At least part of the symptomatology of the acute psychotic phase of schizophrenia is a manifestation of excessive dopamine neurotransmission. Cocaine increases dopamine neurotransmission and, therefore, can mimic psychosis or exacerbate an underlying psychotic condition such as schizophrenia. Although formal clinical trials in schizophrenic substance abusers are lacking, clinical experience suggests that neuroleptics are useful in this population. Equally important is prompt attention to the substance dependence. These patients need a great deal of social and therapeutic support and may require hospitalization to manage periods of increased cocaine use and psychosis.

Further Treatments

General treatment for cocaine dependence runs the same gamut as that for other substance abuse disorders. Individual counseling or dynamic therapy has been discounted as a primary treatment plan. Therapy groups are the mainstay of cocaine abuse treatment and equip the participant with specific coping strategies, awareness of cues and patterns, and the feeling that he or she is not alone. The most impaired and recalcitrant user may need to be admitted to a rehabilitation facility or to a therapeutic community. The important thing in the treatment of a cocaine abuser, as in the treatment of almost anyone with an addiction, is for the clinician to be patient and persistent. Failures, although discouraging, may lead eventually to success even with patients deemed least likely to recover. The details of psychotherapeutic and other non-pharmacological treatments will be the focus of other chapters later in this text.

☐ Methamphetamine

"Speed kills" is a famous catch phrase which describes the dangerousness and lethality of methamphetamine. Other names for the drug include "ice", "meth", and "crystal". Methamphetamine has been a substantial drug of abuse for at least three decades and it periodically increases in popularity. In recent years its use has been rising, particularly in the West, Southwest, and rural areas. It is fairly easy to manufacture, and can be "cooked up" in a matter of hours with easily obtainable ingredients. As such, it is often manufactured in home "laboratories" and then distributed. It is quite similar in action and effect to cocaine but has several important differences. Compared to cocaine, methamphetamine is cheaper and longer acting.

Crystal methamphetamine (methamphetamine HCl) is a large, usually clear crystal of high purity (greater than 90%) that is smoked in a glass pipe. The smoke is odorless and residue of the drug stays in the pipe and can be resmoked. The cost fluctuates, but in general a gram sells for approximately 200 to 300 dollars, and a "paper" (one-tenth of a gram or less) sells for 25 dollars. The drug may also be snorted or ingested orally and these forms are more common in certain subcultures. For example, rural youths usually snort the drug, as do people attending dance clubs on the West coast.

Amphetamines are controlled under Schedule II of the Controlled Substances Act. Substances classified as such have both a high potential for abuse and are also accepted for medical use within the United States. Amphetamine, methamphetamine, cocaine, methylphenidate, and phentermine are all stimulants included in this category.

History

Amphetamine was first synthesized in 1887, but its central nervous system stimulant effects were not noted at that time. It was rediscovered as a bronchial dilator and was widely used for this medical indication by the early 1930s. It was introduced in pill form in 1937. As with cocaine products when they were first introduced in the 1880s, the medical profession enthusiastically explored this new compound for potential uses. Exaggerated publicity and claims about the drug contributed to public interest in amphetamine, and it was promoted as being effective for a variety of ailments without being addictive.

In the 1930s, derivatives of amphetamine were developed and both oral and intravenous preparations became available for therapeutic use. Amphetamines were hailed as wonder drugs. The most popular and effective form of this was methamphetamine. Despite early reports of an occasional adverse reaction, enormous quantities were consumed in the 1940s and 1950s, and their liability for abuse was not recognized. Indeed many health care professionals used them as "pep pills." Medical students and physicians routinely used the drugs to deal with fatigue and exhaustion from long hours on call.

Although amphetamine abuse is typically thought of as an American phenomenon, abuse has been reported in many countries and there have been major epidemics in at least three of these countries. Japan was the first country to experience a methamphetamine epidemic. Production of this drug was substantial during World War II. Military personnel needed sustained energy and individuals in wartime industries were required to work long hours in order to meet the requirements of the war effort. Methamphetamine use became widespread, and for practical purposes was almost required. This widespread use during World War II resulted in a substantial portion of the post-war Japanese population being dependent on methamphetamine. The Japanese government recognized the public health problems associated with this epidemic and instituted drug control laws. This substantially lowered the use of methamphetamine but its abuse remains a significant health problem in Japan to this day.

Reports of Germany using methamphetamine for its troops during World War II encouraged other countries to evaluate its utility as well. This led to methamphetamine and amphetamines being widely used by the military in the U.S., Great Britain, and Japan. They were used as stimulants to increase alertness during battle and on night watches. It has been estimated that approximately 2 million Benzedrine tablets were dispensed to the U.S. Armed Forces during World War II. Much of the research on performance effects of amphetamines was carried out on enlisted personnel during this period.

In the 1950s, college students, athletes, truck drivers, and housewives were all using amphetamines for non-medical purposes. Amphetamines were being marketed in an unregulated fashion to treat obesity, narcolepsy, and depression. People took them to increase energy, decrease the need for sleep, and elevate mood. Pills were the first form to be widely abused. Use of the drug expanded as production of amphetamine and methamphetamine increased significantly. In 1966, the FDA estimated that more than 25 tons of amphetamine were illegally distributed. An extensive black market in amphetamines developed, and it has been estimated that 50% to 90% of the quantity commercially produced was diverted into illicit channels.

Intravenous methamphetamine abuse became prominent in the U.S. during the late 1960s. It was at this time that the name "speed" emerged. Abuse was particularly severe in the Haight-Ashbury district of San Francisco, where in the late '50s and early '60s several Bay Area physicians were prescribing Methedrine as a substitute for heroin. Injectable ampules of methamphetamine were voluntarily taken off the market by the manufacturer at the request of the California Attorney General in 1963. When sale of intravenous methamphetamine to retail pharmacies was curtailed, illicitly synthesized methamphetamine began to appear. The summer of 1967 is fondly remembered as "the summer of love" in San Francisco. The summer of 1968, however, saw an increased abuse of methamphetamine resulting in a substantial increase in violence and trauma. The public health campaign responding to this was: "Speed Kills." Speed did indeed kill the summer of love.

An intensive public health campaign probably caused a reduction in the use of methamphetamine and levels remained stable until the early 1990s. In recent years, it is apparent that although nationwide use has probably not increased, in certain areas use is still quite common. This is particularly the case in parts of the southern U.S., the midwest, and Southern California.

Amphetamines do not have to be imported and can be synthesized locally. The illicit methamphetamine industry shows every indication of expanding. The chemicals required would cost about $700 per pound, with a street value of $225,000, based on a price of $50 per 100 mg. These are huge profit margins and manufacturers could reduce the price substantially to increase the number of consumers.

☐ Mechanism of Action

As with all substances of abuse, the stimulants methamphetamine and amphetamines increase dopamine release in the nucleus accumbens. This increase in dopaminergic transmission is probably the chief mechanism for its associated effects of increased attention and energy. An increase in dopamine is also responsible for the development of psychosis in individuals who use a great deal of methamphetamine. The psychosis develops more readily and more quickly than in the case of cocaine.

☐ Effects

Laboratory data with both non-human and human research subjects indicate that the behavioral and subjective effects of amphetamine and methamphetamine are similar to those of cocaine. The subjective effects are increased energy, euphoria, a feeling of well-being, and heightened sensation. As with cocaine, in higher doses the increased energy can lead to a manic state and to psychosis. The chief physiological difference between cocaine and methamphetamine is that the duration of effects of methamphetamine are much longer, from 6 to 24 hours as compared to 1/2 hour to 1 hour for cocaine. People taking methamphetamine also report an increased feeling of "jitteriness" as compared to cocaine. In drug parlance, it is a "less smooth high."

Under most conditions, amphetamines are not general performance enhancers, although they do bring a mood that has ebbed due to boredom or fatigue back to pre-fatigue levels. Though not widely publicized, NASA astronauts carry supplies of amphetamine in their medical kits, in case of an emergency where they would need to remain awake for long periods of time.

In trained athletes whose behavior is sharp and barely variable, small improvements can be induced with the use of stimulants. Some researchers have argued persuasively that the small changes in performance induced by amphetamines can result in the 1 to 2 percent improvement that can make the difference in a close athletic competition. Although the facilitation of performance after amphetamine intake does not appear to be substantial, it is sufficient to "spell the difference between a gold medal and a sixth place." All performance enhancing drugs are banned in international competition and competing athletes are routinely urine tested.

Of particular concern for the clinician in treating methamphetamine abusers is its propensity to cause psychosis. Administration of amphetamine to normal volunteers with no histories of psychosis by researchers in 1968 resulted in clear-cut paranoid psychosis in five of the six subjects who received d-amphetamine for 1 to 5 days (120–220 mg/day). Unless the user continues to use the drug, the psychosis usually clears within a week, although there is the possibility of long-term symptoms. This amphetamine psychosis has been thought to represent a reasonably accurate model of schizophrenia, including symptoms of persecution, hyperactivity and excitation, visual and auditory hallucinations, and changes in body image. In addition, sensitization occurs to the development of stimulant psychosis; once an individual has experienced this toxic effect, it is readily evoked, even after long drug-free periods. Once patients have had an episode of paranoia while on methamphetamine, they are likely to have another one.

Methamphetamine, by weight, sells for about the same amount of money as cocaine. This is deceptive because the effects last much longer than cocaine. It is, therefore, relatively cheap. In certain urban areas, such as New York City, in an odd twist, the price accounts for its relative lack of availability. The organized crime forces that sell and distribute cocaine do not want to see their profits decrease by increased sales of the more affordable methamphetamine. It is joked in some psychiatric circles in New York that one sure suicide plan is to announce that you are going to become a methamphetamine salesman. The response from the criminal dealers would be swift and certain.

TABLE 13.2. The most common effects of methamphetamine at low to moderate doses

1. Euphoria and a sense of well-being
2. Increased sense of energy
3. Enhanced acuity and ability to problem solve
4. Decreased appetite
5. Increased libido
6. Increased self-confidence, which may be disproportionate to reality
7. Suspiciousness and increased arousal
8. Paranoia (greater incidence than with cocaine)
9. Delusions clinically indistinguishable from chronic paranoid schizophrenia

Amphetamines are generally abused in binges, in which people take the drug repeatedly for some period of hours or days, followed by a period in which they take no drug. This is comparable to the way rhesus monkeys take the drug when given free access to it.

Therapeutic Effects

Amphetamines are frequently indicated for the treatment of narcolepsy, obesity, childhood hyperactivity, and childhood as well as adult attention deficit hyperactivity disorder (ADHD). Although patients with narcolepsy require large doses of amphetamine for prolonged periods of time, unwanted sudden bouts sleep can generally be prevented. Tolerance does not seem to develop; therefore, the therapeutic effects of the drug are not inhibited. The use of amphetamines in the treatment of hyperkinetic behavioral disorders in children, however, remains more controversial. It has been found that amphetamines have a dramatic effect in reducing restlessness and distractibility as well as lengthening attention span, but there are definite side-effects, such as irritability, restlessness, and paranoia. Proponents point to their potential benefits and advocate care in limiting treatment dose and duration. Although the major therapeutic utility of amphetamine is in the short-term treatment of obesity, considerable evidence exists for a rapid development of tolerance to the anorectic effects of the drugs. These drugs should be used with extreme caution for this purpose, if at all. If used, a patient should only be given 4–6 weeks worth of the drug for the treatment of obesity.

□ Withdrawal

As with cocaine, methamphetamine has a definite but subtle withdrawal phase. It also is not as physiologically apparent as withdrawal from alcohol or heroin, but it does have some recognizable features. The most notable features are depression, decreased energy, increased appetite, and low self-esteem. These effects can linger and be quite protracted. The experimental evidence for how long these symptoms last is not clear, but experience indicates they certainly last several weeks, probably months or even longer. There is also evidence that methamphetamine, when abused, may after the CN's reward system permanently.

TABLE 13.3. The most common characteristics of methamphetamine withdrawal

1. Depression and a feeling of sadness and isolation
2. Decreased sense of energy
3. Mental dullness
4. Increased appetite
5. Decreased libido
6. Decreased self confidence
7. Continued suspiciousness with decreased arousal
8. Paranoia (greater incidence than with cocaine)
9. Delusions clinically indistinguishable from chronic paranoid schizophrenia (this symptom may persist)

Treatment

Treatment for methamphetamine dependence parallels that established for cocaine addiction. Individual counseling or dynamic therapy has been discounted as a primary treatment. Therapy groups are the mainstay of stimulant abuse treatment. They equip the participant with specific coping strategies and the feeling that he or she is not alone in attempting to overcome this addiction. The most impaired and recalcitrant user may need to be referred to a rehabilitation center or to a therapeutic community. The important element in the treatment of a stimulant abuser, as in the treatment of almost anyone with an addiction, is to expect exacerbations and remissions over the course of time. The treating clinician has to guard against feeling defeated or dispirited and needs to persevere in the face of many "false starts" on the road to recovery.

PART

II

EVALUATION AND EARLY TREATMENT

The previous sections have dealt with individual substances that are abused. The purpose was to intoduce the reader to the most commonly encountered substances. Each of these chapters, provided an overview of the history, mechanism of action, effects, and a description of the particular associated withdrawal syndrome. In addition, treatment issues were discussed only in terms of what was unique to the given substance.

Individuals who abuse substances and become dependent upon them are often unable to curb use or stop on their own. Such loss of control is the sine qua non of addiction. This next section is an overview of evaluation and treatment common to all substance abuse issues. As with other sections of this text, and the text itself, it is not intended to represent an exhaustive description of all the issues of detection, evaluation, diagnosis, and treatment. Rather, it should serve as an introduction and orientation to the many treatment options that are available for these conditions.

CHAPTER 14

The Initial Interview and Screening

Substance abuse is so prevalent that it needs to be considered in any health or psycho-social assessment. This is especially true if a patient complains of any psychiatric symptoms. Anxiety, sleeplessness, depression, psychosis, and many common complaints may be clues that there is a substance abuse issue for the patient. In addition, certain medical conditions should alert the clinician that substance abuse may be the problem. For example, chronic gastritis is common in alcoholism, a perforated nasal septum may be caused by severe cocaine use, and needle marks almost always mean intravenous drug abuse.

The patient should be asked detailed and specific questions about substance abuse, although patients notoriously minimize the amount of drugs and alcohol they use. If substance abuse is the presenting complaint, then the interviewer may be more direct. The manner in which questions are asked is vital. The interviewer who asks an open-ended question such as "How much do you drink?" will not get much useful information. That patient is likely to say something like, "I drink socially, you know, one or two." One technique to deal with the tendency to minimize is to assume that the patient drinks a great deal and ask it in that context. For example, asking, "How many six packs of beer do you drink in a night?" gives the interviewee the idea that the clinician knows he or she drinks a lot. An alcoholic might reply, "I only drink two six packs per night," revealing that the person does indeed drink a great deal. The person who seems genuinely shocked and admits to drinking one or two beers per week probably does not have a problem. A useful clinical tool is the assumption that anyone who says, "I can take it or I can leave it," probably has a substance abuse problem.

The opposite case is the substance user who exaggerates the amount used in order to obtain more medicine for detoxification. This is more common in an opiate or benzodiazepine user being admitted for evaluation and detoxification. This can be dangerous and lead to an iatrogenic overdose. Independent verification of the actual dose the patient is taking is necessary in these cases in order to most closely approximate the actual degree of drug intake.

☐ Screening

There are a variety of well-known and useful screening instruments which are helpful in identifying whether a person has a problem with substances. If the evaluation is suggestive of a more significant problem, then a more detailed investigation can be planned.

There are numerous screening tests for problems with substances. These range from simple, few-item questions, to lengthy, complicated, and more sophisticated measures. One of the simplest methods for detecting a problem with alcohol, which can be adapted for other substances, is the "CAGE" model. This is an acronym for a set of four questions: (1) Have you ever tried to **C**ut down on your drinking? (2) Have you become **A**nnoyed at others' criticism of your drinking? (3) Have you ever felt **G**uilty about your drinking? and (4) Have you ever had an **E**ye-opener to steady your nerves in the morning? Three out of four affirmative answers is highly suggestive of a problem with alcohol. Four out of four is almost certain to indicate a problem.

A widely used screen in obstetric patients follows the mnemonic "T-A-C-E." This consists of four questions: (1) **T**olerance: "How many drinks does it take to make you feel high?" An answer of two or more, scores 2 points. A yes to the following three questions earns one point; (2) Have you become **A**nnoyed at others' criticism of your drinking? (3) Have you ever tried to **C**ut down on your drinking? and (4) Have you ever had an **E**ye-opener to steady your nerves in the morning (or taken medication to relieve the effects of your drinking)? A score of two or more is indicative of "risk drinking" during pregnancy, and warrants further investigation. Both the "CAGE" and the "T-A-C-E" questions can be modified to apply to other drugs as well.

The MAST is the Michigan Alcoholism Screening Test and its sister test is the Drug Abuse Screening Test. These are 25-item instruments that can be personally administered or handed out to a group. The answers are scored and can be useful in defining whether a substance abuse problem exists.

Information

The previous discussion concerned screening instruments that can be employed with a wide variety of patients or populations to identify those that may need further evaluation. If a substance use disorder is suspected, then there are several questions that need to be part of any thorough evaluation. These questions include:

–When did your use begin and when did it become a problem?
–What were the influences that caused you to start?
–What do these substances do for you? What are the positive effects? What are the negative ones?
–What has your pattern of use been in the past month?
–When were your periods of heaviest use?
–What were your periods of abstinence like? How long? How did you do it?
–What led to your relapsing?
–Have you ever attended a rehab program, or A.A./N.A. (Narcotics)/C.A. (Cocaine)?

There are obviously many other questions that are relevant to a good history, but these provide a starting point.

Substance Use Disorders

One of the central goals of the initial evaluation and screening process is to arrive at a decision regarding the presence or absence of a true substance abuse or dependence state. Substance abuse refers to a maladaptive pattern in which continued or periodic use of a given substance leads to negative consequences. These negative consequences can be blatant, like repeated car accidents, or far more subtle, as in the case of those whose drug use makes them less emotionally available to their children. Maladaptive behaviors, of course, are subject to interpretation. It is generally acceptable for a 27 year-old man to do a shot of tequila at his bachelor party. The same behavior is inappropriate for his 5 year-old niece. The DSM-IV criteria for substance abuse are listed in Table 14.1.:

TABLE 14.1. DSM-IV criteria for substance abuse

A. A maladaptive pattern of substance use, leading to clinically significant impairment or distress, as manifested by three (or more) of the following, occurring at any time in the same 12-month period:

(1) recurrent substance use resulting in a failure to fulfill major role obligations at work, school, or home (e.g., repeated absences or poor work performance related to substance use; substance-related absences, suspensions, or expulsions from school; neglect of children or household).

(2) recurrent substance use in situations in which it is physically hazardous (e.g., driving an automobile or operating a machine when impaired by substance use).

(3) recurrent substance-related legal problems (e.g., arrests for substance-related disorderly conduct).

(4) continued substance use despite having persistent or recurrent social or interpersonal problems caused or exacerbated by the effects of the substance (e.g., arguments with spouse about consequences of intoxication, physical fights).

B. The symptoms have never met the criteria for Substance Dependence for this class of substance.

Substance dependence occurs when a patient has lost control over the use of a substance. A good clinical rule is that the substance has become integral, not enhancing. Both psychological and physiological factors are crucial to making the diagnosis of dependence. Physical dependence and tolerance to a substance are important in making the determination of substance dependence. Tolerance refers to the need for increased amounts of a drug in order to obtain the same desired effect. Patients are considered to be physically dependent if they must continue to use substances in order to avoid withdrawal. In addition, these symptoms must cause distress or functional impairment in order to qualify as evidence of dependence. The DSM-IV criteria for dependence can be seen in Table 14.2.

Once an assessment of the extent of substance use has been made, the clinician is in a position to make a treatment plan.

TABLE 14.2. DSM-IV criteria for substance dependence

A maladaptive pattern of substance use, leading to clinically significant impairment or distress, as manifested by three (or more) of the following, occurring at any time in the same 12-month period:

(1) tolerance, as defined by either of the following:

(A) a need for markedly increased amounts of the substance to achieve intoxication or desired effect.

(B) markedly diminished effect with continued use of the same amount of the substance.

(2) withdrawal, as manifested by either of the following:

(A) the characteristic withdrawal syndrome for the substance.

(B) the same (or closely related) substance is taken to relieve or avoid withdrawal symptoms

(3) the substance is often taken in larger amounts or over a longer period than was intended.

(4) there is a persistent desire or unsuccessful efforts to cut down or control substance use.

(5) a great deal of time is spent in activities necessary to obtain the substance (e.g., visiting multiple doctors or driving long distances), use the substance (e.g., chain smoking), or recover from its effects.

(6) important social, occupational, or recreational activities are given up or reduced because of substance use.

(7) the substance use is continued despite knowledge of having a persistent or recurrent physical, or psychological problem that is likely to have been caused or exacerbated by the substance
(e.g., current cocaine use despite recognition of cocaine-induced depression, or continued drinking despite recognition that an ulcer was made worse by alcohol consumption).

Specify if:
With Physiological Dependence: evidence of tolerance or withdrawal (i.e., either item 1 or 2 is present).

Without Physiological Dependence: no evidence of tolerance or withdrawal (i.e., neither item 1 or 2 is present).

15

CHAPTER

The Emergency Management of Acute Drug Intoxication

When asked to treat a person who is intoxicated, the clinician must clarify the severity of the situation. Some important questions to ask include: What is the patient's clinical condition and behavior? Is the patient alert, agitated, or comatose? What are the vital signs? With mild intoxication, the person may need to be observed in a safe environment which can sometimes be done at the patient's home, as commonly occurs in the case of an adolescent who got drunk for the first time and aroused concern in his or her parents. Other cases, such as severe opiate intoxication, are medical emergencies that may require treatment in the Intensive Care Unit (ICU).

Secondly, it is essential to determine what substance or substances the patient abused. It is important to remember that many patients take several drugs simultaneously, so the clinician may be dealing with more than one form of intoxication. In addition, many street drugs are not what they are promoted to be and may contain additives and mixtures of other drugs.

Intoxicated patients can be divided into two categories: agitated and obtunded. Agitation can result from intoxication with stimulants such as cocaine and methamphetamine, and hallucinogens such as LSD and PCP. Alcohol in either the early intoxication phase or the later withdrawal phases also produces agitation. If the patient is obtunded, then it is wise to think of opiate intoxication, benzodiazepines, sedative hypnotics, or alcohol in later intoxication phases.

The following sections of this chapter describe some general regimens for dealing with the acutely intoxicated patient. These regimens are intended as a basic guide and should not be used in a "cookbook" fashion. They are presented here so that the reader may have an idea of how intoxication is handled in an emergency setting. If such a situation presents itself, the reader is urged to obtain professional and expert consultation. If the person's behavior or presentation is disturbing, it is imperative that the patient be taken for medical evaluation.

☐ Intoxication and Management of Selected Substances

Alcohol

Signs and Symptoms

These include slurred speech, ataxia (uncoordinated walking), aggression, elevated heart rate, and in extreme cases of intoxication, coma.

Management

–Evaluate the patient in a quiet area, being careful to monitor vital signs at regular intervals (at least every 15 minutes).

–Treat agitation with a benzodiazepine such as Lorezapam 1 or 2 mg, either orally or intravenously.

–Any patient who presents for evaluation of alcohol dependence should be treated with thiamine 100 mg IM, then 100 mg by mouth for six days in order to provide prophylaxis for Wernicke's encephalopathy.

–Unconscious patients are probably severely intoxicated and need physiological support, thiamine, intensive care monitoring, and careful evaluation for withdrawal. This is best treated, if possible, in the intensive care unit.

Hallucinogens

Signs and Symptoms

–Variable periods of lucidity and hallucinations.
–Perceptual distortions which can be hallucinations.
–Extreme emotional lability.
–Tremor and lack of coordination.
–Hyperthermia (high temperature, generally above 101.5 degrees Fahrenheit; this is a serious problem and needs to be treated with hydration and other medication in a hospital emergency room).

Management

–Reassurance in a calm environment is sometimes all that is needed and is often an extremely important factor in treatment.
–Observation is crucial; behavioral toxicity in someone hallucinating can be perilous. These are the people who act impulsively while under the influence of delusional beliefs. This is rare, and it is avoidable.
–Agitation should be treated with a benzodiazepine such as Lorezapam 1 or 2 mg IM or PO. This may be given every hour until the patient calms down. (In general, the dose is not to exceed 8 mg in a 24-hour period.)
–These patients can usually be sent home with their families. If the agitation persists for more than 24 hours, hospitalization is recommended.
–Temperatures higher than 101.5 are evidence of an emergency and need to be treated aggressively in the ICU of a hospital.

Stimulants (Particularly Cocaine and Methamphetamine)

Signs and Symptoms

–Restlessness
–Euphoria
–Psychosis and Paranoia
–Tachycardia (increased heart rate) and hypertension (high blood pressure)
–Fever
–Seizures
–Coma

Management

–Make sure to evaluate in a quiet area, being mindful that the patient's paranoia may make him or her dangerous.

–If the intoxication is mild, reassurance may be all that is needed.

–Agitation should be treated with a benzodiazepine such as Lorezapam 1 or 2 mg IM or PO. This may be given every hour until the patient calms down (generally not to exceed 8 mg in a 24-hour period).

–Be mindful of other medical complications such as stroke and heart attack. These should be treated with appropriate medical and surgical management.

–Severe paranoia should be treated with neuroleptics such as haloperidol 5 mg IM or PO. This may be repeated every hour until the patient responds.

–Adrenergic symptoms, such as increased heart rate may be treated with Beta Blockers. An example is Propanalol (Inderal) 20 to 40 mg PO or 1 to 2 mg IV. This should be used with caution in patient with asthma, diabetes, or existing heart disease.

–Temperatures higher than 101.5 are evidence of an emergency and need to be treated aggressively and in the ICU.

Marijuana

Signs and Symptoms

–Euphoria, feelings of well-being
–Lack of coordination
–Hunger
–Injected conjunctiva (red eyes)
–Anxiety and paranoia
–Altered time perception

Management

–Reassurance in a calm environment is often all that is needed and is usually the most important factor in treatment.

–Agitation should be treated with a benzodiazepine such as Lorezapam 1 or 2 mg IM or PO. This may be given every hour until the patient calms down (generally, the dose is not to exceed 8 mg in a 24-hour period).

Opioids

Signs and Symptoms

–Pinpoint pupils
–Lethargy
–Depressed respiration and level of consciousness
–Bradycardia (slowed heart rate)
–Pulmonary edema

Management

–Support the patient's airway and make sure breathing continues; if necessary perform CPR.

–Treat with Naloxone 0.4 to 2.0 mg IV every 2 to 3 minutes until respiration is stable. If the patient shows no response with the first dose, and is unresponsive after 10 minutes, then it is appropriate to consider some other reason for the clinical condition. If the patient responds, remember that the half-life of Naloxone is short in comparison to that of most opioids and as the Naloxone wears off, the patient will require more. It is vital that the patient not be permitted to leave the ER, thereby running the risk of becoming comatose. It is the clinician's obligation to keep the patient under observation, using restraint if necessary.

PCP and Ketamine

Signs and Symptoms

–Ataxia (uncoordinated gait), nystagmus (rapid eye movements to the left and right upon gaze to the side—one or two beats is normal, more may be suggestive of a problem).

–Disorientation

–Hypertension and Tachycardia

–Stupor

–Decreased sensitivity to pain

–Extreme strength (these are the patients that may need many security guards to hold them down). Use caution. These patients can be very dangerous and the safety of the staff as well as the patient is a cardinal concern.

–Coma

Management

–Minimize all sensory stimulation. In contrast to other situations, reassurance may backfire and agitate the patient, therefore, the less stimulation the better.

–Severe paranoia should be treated with neuroleptics such as haloperidol 5 mg IM or PO. This may be repeated every hour until the patient responds. Haldol is the neuroleptic of choice here because these drugs are anti-cholinergic themselves and Haldol is the least anticholinergic neuroleptic.

–Agitation should be treated with a benzodiazepine such as Lorezapam 1 or 2 mg IM or PO. This may be given every hour until the patient calms down (generally in a dose not to exceed 8 mg in a 24 hour period).

–Acidify the urine with ascorbic acid, ammonium chloride, or any comparable agent. This will aid in excretion.

–Monitor these patients closely. Coma and death are not rare in these intoxications but are usually preventable with close observation and treatment.

Sedative Hypnotics

Signs and Symptoms

–Ataxia and slurred speech
–Confusion
–Lethargy
–Decreased respiration

Management

–An overdose with a sedative hypnotic is a medical emergency and needs to be addressed in an ICU setting. There is no blocking agent available, but the person should be monitored and his or her vital functions need to be supported.

–Watch for signs of withdrawal—this is a serious medical emergency which needs to be addressed by an expert.

Anxiolytics and Benzodiazepines

Signs and Symptoms

–Similar to alcohol
–Confusion

–Ataxia
–Lethargy and stupor
–Slurred speech

Management

–This type of overdose is rarely fatal unless combined with alcohol. Most of the management involves observation of vital signs and supporting vital functions if necessary.

–Flumazenil is a benzodiazepine antagonist that can be used to reverse intoxication. This needs to be administered in a hospital setting. 0.2 mg is administered IV over 30 seconds. This is repeated until the patient responds. Doses higher than 3 mg per 24 hours should be avoided.

–Caution must be used for anyone with a concomitant tricyclic antidepressant overdose, or if they are benzodiazepine dependent. In both cases, Flumazenil may induce seizures.

GHB (Gamma Hydroxy Butyrate)

Signs and Symptoms

–Similar to alcohol
–Ataxia
–Lethargy and stupor
–Slurred speech
–Decreased rate of breathing

Management

–Most of the management involves monitoring vital signs and supporting vital functions if necessary. Patients should be observed as they can fall into coma, and death is a possibility.

–GHB is rarely taken by itself, so the patient should be screened for other drugs.

16

CHAPTER

The Evolution from Addiction to Recovery: the Psychology of State Change

Since there is so much variability among human beings, it is virtually impossible to universally define the precise stages involved in both addiction and recovery. In recent years, a number of prominent researchers have developed an important theoretical model aimed at describing addiction and recovery. This has coalesced into a "stages of change" model to explain the addiction process and its treatment. This model seeks to describe, as accurately as possible, the universal elements of addiction for all individuals who abuse substances. These stages exist on a spectrum, one end of which, for example, is the casual user of cocaine who realizes that his use is becoming a problem and quits without much difficulty. On the other end is the stereotypical "strung out" heroin addict who has lost job after job, alienated friends and family, and come close to death before seeking help and treatment. In the former case, even such "natural" quitters go through an evolution and a process of thought, perhaps mostly unconscious, before giving up the substance.

A Model of Change and Recovery

Described below is a model of addiction and recovery presented in stages. As with so many phenomena, this has many variations. The following are presented as possible phenomena.

Stage 1: the Emergence of an Addictive Process

Phase 1: Initiation (the Beginning of Drug Use)

Initiation is an obvious but sometimes overlooked initial stage. To become an addict and to then enter into recovery, one must begin to use a given substance. An individual may have a significant amount of genetic loading for alcoholism and every risk factor imaginable, but if he or she never drinks, alcohol will never become a problem. The rate of alcoholism among the Amish, for example, is extraordinarily low. The reason for this is the lack of availability of alcohol in that community. For all substances of abuse, the vast majority of those people who try the drugs, and even those who use them on a regular or semi-regular basis, do not become dependent or addicted. Still, certain individuals do go on to develop severe and difficult-to-treat addictions.

Phase 2: Positive Consequences

A substance must have positive side effects for the individual to continue its use. These positive consequences can be divided into the internal and external realms. The physiological and psychological consequences of certain substances, especially at the early stages of use, can be quite pleasurable. A glass of wine can induce relaxation; a line of cocaine can make the experience of the world more acute and thinking clearer; small amounts of heroin can be quite euphorigenic. The user who experiences positive reinforcement is likely to look for it again. Individuals who use drugs may receive positive reinforcement from their peers who are themselves users. A friend who remarks how relaxed her friend seems after a glass of wine is subtly reinforcing the behavior of drinking.

> Jack was a first year associate at a law firm in Boston when he first tried cocaine. He had always eschewed drugs; he had an older cousin who died as a result of an alcohol addiction, but on this occasion, he was nervous about meeting some important clients at a large party. His friend assured him that snorting "a line of coke" would be pleasurable, inconspicuous, and that he would be more confident. A few snorts and three minutes later, Jack was indeed calmer, more self-assured, and felt more in control. Jack liked cocaine.

Phase 3: Adverse Consequences Develop But Are Kept Out of Awareness (Pre-Contemplation)

Many individuals use substances judiciously for years, sometimes for their whole lives, without experiencing negative consequences. These users would not be considered addicts. In the addictive process, the positive aspects are gradually, sometimes over years or decades, supplanted by negative sequelae which eventually become severe. Often, the addict is not aware of the negative consequences of the drug he or she is taking.

This is the phase of the addictive process when denial, a primitive psychological mechanism for dealing with reality, is first employed. If the psyche does not wish to accept it, troubling stimuli are ignored. It is as if the normal feedback channels for behavior are impaired. The destructive behavior does not elicit the appropriate enlightened response of "I'd better do something about this. My drug use is getting out of hand." Some researchers have called this type of denial a focused delusional system. At this level, addicts are capable of making sense of their world, with one very important exception: they are unable to make the causal connection between the problems in their life and their excessive drug use.

> Jack enjoyed the positive aspects of his cocaine use and found that it gave him the confidence he needed to perform in client meetings and in difficult work situations. He began to use cocaine to help him perform in other areas of his life. He found that it helped him socially and also reduced his sexual inhibitions. He began to use cocaine more and more. After a while, his work began to suffer and colleagues asked him if there was anything wrong. He often looked tired and haggard and he had lost weight. He was rarely on time for work, especially on Monday mornings. His performance evaluations plummeted. His friends were concerned and asked him about the drug use which he had tried to keep a secret. Friends and co-workers eventually began to withdraw from him. His escalating cocaine use and the disastrous toll it was taking on his work, health, and life, did not seem to register. At times, he would wake up after a binge and acknowledge the lack of control he had, but most of the time Jack believed that his problems had nothing to do with his cocaine use.

Individuals who are in this phase of addiction know on some level that they have a problem. Their energy, however, is spent avoiding and denying what is obvious to everyone else. Somewhere in what psychodynamic theorists call the "pre-conscious" or "unconscious" is the knowledge that the situation is out of control and something needs to be done. These individuals are said to be in the pre-contemplative phase of recovery. This pre-contemplative phase may either be short lived or go on for decades.

Stage 2: the Evolution of Quitting

Phase 1: Turning Points

Turning points occur when the consequences of substance abuse become impossible for the individual to ignore, and the thought of quitting pierces the dense veil of denial. This is a time of intense ambivalence. On one hand is the desire to quit and end the painful cycle, and on the other is the desire to continue. Turning points usually follow destructive behaviors and may occur at any time during the addictive process. A normally shy clerk in a supermarket may be embarrassed by her drunken behavior at the company picnic and seriously look at her alcohol use. A middle-aged woman may finally realize that she has a problem with alcohol after being convicted of her fifth DWI. These turning points parallel the Twelve Step notion of "hitting bottom" before an individual begins the recovery process.

For a turning point to occur, an individual has to accept personal responsibility for his or her actions and identify the substance abuse as the major destructive agent in his or her life. This may not lead to immediate recovery, but it is the low end-point (and there may be many end-points in this process) of a complex array of physical and psychological factors.

> Jack's boss was aware of his erratic behavior, but chose for his own complex reasons to ignore it as well. He assigned Jack an important presentation. Jack, believing that he could not complete the task without the help of cocaine, did a few lines while preparing. This resulted in an extended cocaine binge. He did not complete the task. He arrived at work to explain his delinquency in an agitated and disheveled state. His colleagues were appalled and could no longer deny the obvious. The company nurse was called, and Jack was sent home to rest. When he awoke three days later and remembered, with humiliation, his behavior, Jack was reduced to tears and contemplated the difficulties cocaine had caused him.

Phase 2: Contemplation

"Lately I've been thinking, I just might quit drinking" goes the popular Jerry Jeff Walker song. This is a country music-infused example of contemplation that occurs after a turning point. In the song, contemplation occurs after the narrator's wife has left him because of his alcohol use. It can be a terrifying time for the addict who considers life without the substance. The substance has served an important, often central, focus in the life of the addict. Giving up the substance means completly changing a lifestyle, and includes abandoning the friendships which were predicated on mutual drug and alcohol abuse.

The clinician must be sensitive to all that the patient must give up in turning away from the substance and whatever "positive" effects the drug afforded. An appreciation and acknowledgment of this will go a long way in establishing an empathic working relationship with the patient. This type of concern reminds the clinician and substance abuser that there is a vulnerable person beneath the defenses of the abuser.

> That morning Jack picked up the phone and called his Employee Assistance Program and admitted that he had a cocaine problem. A treatment plan was formulated and the necessary arrangements were made. Given the severity of his problem, it was decided that a brief inpatient stay would be most beneficial, followed by a highly structured outpatient program, after which he could return to work.

Phase 3: Relapse Prevention

For the addict, substance use will always be an issue. Individuals who have been clean and sober for many years talk about the need to constantly be on guard against picking up another drink or using drugs. It is the clinician's role at this phase to reinforce the patient's choice of sobriety. Many individuals seem to quit cocaine spontaneously but, in fact, almost always go through the phases discussed previously if they do not utilize external help. Achieving sobriety in this manner ought to be reinforced as well.

Many addicts who become sober from one substance substitute another substance or another form of compulsive behavior to kick the habit of their original problem. The perpetually full coffee pot and smoke-filled AA meetings are examples of this. However, some non-self destructive compulsive behavior can be quite beneficial: The individual who becomes heavily involved in exercise or in community service as an alternative to addiction ought to be lauded in most cases.

> Jack returned to work. The first few months were difficult. He felt humiliated by his failure to control himself and believed his fellow workers looked down upon him. At first, he followed the outpatient program rigorously. He eventually tapered down his attendance, but continued to go to regular Cocaine Anonymous (CA) Meetings. Years later, Jack continues to be abstinent from cocaine. He left his first firm and has been successful in his own firm. He enjoys a happy home life. He still goes to CA meetings on occasion. Even though he sometimes feels the pull of cocaine, especially when he is being asked to perform, he has remained abstinent.

The clinician's understanding of where the substance user falls on the continuum of pre-addiction to recovery is essential in planning timely and successful treatment efforts. The chapters which follow focus on a variety of therapeutic interventions based largely on the substance abuser's current place along the addiction-recovery spectrum.

PART

V

PSYCHOSOCIAL TREATMENT APPROACHES TO SUBSTANCE ABUSE

17

CHAPTER

The Intervention

The individual with a drug or alcohol problem may require more pressure to address his or her addiction than is provided by a clinician or family. The abuse may be an integral part of the person's coping strategies. Despite having been undoubtedly warned about the further consequences of continued use, that person is denying and avoiding the reality that a serious problem exists. The "intervention"—a systematic strategy for confronting the addict with his or her addiction—draws together a social and familial network, forces the individual to address the problem, and then offers a concrete treatment plan as an alternative to continued drug and alcohol use.

The intervention is a serious tool and is used when other methods have been tried, failed, or refused. In order to conduct a successful intervention, three elements must be in place: (1) agreement of the parties involved with the patient; (2) a concrete plan for treatment; and (3) consequences which *must* be adhered to if the patient does not accept the plan.

A classic example of someone for whom an intervention is appropriate is an individual with an alcohol problem that is increasing in severity. He or she may have had some treatment or tried attending a Twelve-Step meeting, but the behavior has continued. The individual may start to have trouble at work, not necessarily drinking on the job, but is much less productive because of his or her alcohol use. The following is a case example:

> Charles is a 45 year-old advertising executive, married to his wife Liz for twenty-one years. They have three children ages 20, 16, and 13. He has a

> history of hard work, and those that know him describe him as "driven." For the past three years, following the loss of his beloved father, who drank heavily, Charles has been drinking heavily. He spends each evening in the basement of his house, a converted bar, drinking between four and eight martinis. His doctor has warned him that his liver enzymes are elevated and that the drinking is adversely affecting his health. His wife is upset with his drinking and the fact that he never seems to be emotionally available to the family, either being drunk, or working off the effects of his hangovers. She has urged him to stop, but he accuses her of nagging. Charles's drinking has begun to taint his friendships. Normally a pleasant tempered man, he has recently gotten into fights with some long-standing friends. Charles' work performance has also suffered, and he has been notified by his usually supportive boss that his performance needs to improve. On several occasions, Charles has acknowledged that he has a problem with drinking and has vowed to do something about it; however, he quickly begins drinking shortly thereafter.

An intervention is designed for people who either refuse to accept responsibility for their treatment or do not think that they have a problem. In the above example, Charles is in denial about the amount he drinks and the consequences that it is causing him. If nothing is done, he will likely lose his job, his health, and probably his family.

The clinician is in a unique position to organize an intervention. He or she must coordinate a convenient time for the participants to meet. While getting the people in the patient's life to be involved with the intervention may sound daunting, individuals who care about the person are usually remarkably willing to come forward and help.

The participants in the intervention can come from various areas of the patient's life, but they should be adults without a substance abuse problem of their own. People with substance abuse problems of their own can undermine the therapeutic process. In fact, their own concerns and ambivalence about substance abuse can be insidious and sabotage the intervention. The individuals involved in the intervention should be important players in the individual's life: friends, colleagues, or family members. This meeting should always include the spouse or spousal equivalent. In the above example, ideal participants would be Charles' wife, his friends that he has been fighting with, his boss, and his children.

On the day of the intervention, the participants gather together and meet with the patient. The people in the intervention, in a loving and supportive way, confront the patient individually with concrete consequences of his substance abuse.

> At the urging of the clinician, Charles' wife began the session, saying that she loved him, and that for many years she felt they had had a good marriage. In the past couple of years, however, he had been drunk for so much of their time together. She no longer felt that they were in a marriage because their

intimate life and sex life had suffered so greatly. Charles' friends spoke about his changes; he had always been reliable and trustworthy, someone to be counted on, but now he was irritable and unpredictable. Charles' boss spoke about his problems at work, all attributable to his increased drinking, which was clearly out of control. Finally, his son spoke about what a great dad he had always been, but that now there was a lack of a father in his life. He believed the drinking was responsible for this change.

The tone during the intervention needs to be concerned, helpful, firm, and loving, and should never take on the nature of an attack. If humiliation and blame are emphasized, the patient who is the focus of the intervention will undoubtedly feel judged and ashamed. Following the confrontation, the patient will either accept that he or she has a problem, or protest. It is important, even if the patient immediately accepts the intervention, that the participants go through the process of describing the effects that the patient's drug use has on them. The substance abuser's immediate acceptance of the intervention may be superficial in nature; he or she needs to be helped to understand the profound impact that the problem has on the people in his or her life. This will be important in subsequent therapy and in the future for maintaining sobriety.

There has to be a specific treatment plan in place to offer to the substance abuser. Cases that are severe enough to warrant an intervention almost always require an in-patient stay. The plan should be carefully orchestrated and if, for example, the treatment facility is out of state, plane tickets should be purchased before the intervention takes place. If the individual refuses to accept the need for treatment, then the consequences of such refusal should be articulated. These can be the loss of financial support, the threat of separation, loss of contact, or loss of employment, among other things. These consequences should be severe and meaningful enough to the patient so that his or her refusal to accept the plan would be very difficult.

Charles resisted at first, saying that he appreciated their effort, but that he could handle it on his own. His wife then gently but firmly insisted that if he did not get help, she would leave him. His friends said that they would end their contact with him; his son also would cease contact until he got sober, and his boss would terminate his employment. Charles became angry but accepted and said that he would follow their plan for treatment.

The patient is generally admitted to an inpatient facility, detoxified, if necessary, and then begins a treatment appropriate for the addiction, the stage of substance use, and the patient's personality. Aftercare is arranged and most often includes Twelve-Step meetings. At that point, the individual has likely accepted his or her condition and is usually inclined to continue to work on it. Still, aftercare is extremely important even following a successful intervention. Continued treatment can be mandated by the clinician, family, or friends under the same contingencies as the initial treatment.

> After a 30-day stay at a facility out of state, Charles returned to work, his family, and his friends. He had difficulty adjusting to a sober life, and had one relapse that did not require re-hospitalization. Gradually, he began to see the benefits of staying sober, and how much better he felt about himself and his life. At a three year follow-up, Charles is an active member of his community and a devoted father and husband. He has started his own business, which was a lifelong dream. He is public about his alcoholism and an advocate of sobriety who attends A.A. meetings on a twice-weekly basis.

Not all interventions are as successful as Charles', but with coordination, organization, and effort, an intervention can accomplish the goal of helping an individual learn to live a sober and rewarding life.

Elements of a Successful Intervention

- The individual must need the dramatic step of an intervention. This is a serious step and the subject ought to have been approached before. The intervention is seen as a response to the patient's unwillingness to get treatment voluntarily.
- A good coordinator is absolutely necessary. He or she should be skilled in this kind of approach. A skilled coordinator will be able to keep the intervention on track, and the individuals involved focused upon their goal.
- Organization is paramount. The plan must be formulated beforehand and be agreed upon down to the last detail.
- Agreement: All individuals must agree that if the substance abuser does not follow through with the plan, then any steps agreed upon by the team must be enforced. This can be very difficult for some people, but members of the team can provide support for one another.

18

CHAPTER

Hospitalization

Whether or not to hospitalize an individual is a crucial and important decision that may have far-ranging implications for both the clinician and the patient. This decision must be made judiciously and thoughtfully. At times, the individual suffering from a substance abuse disorder requires hospitalization, thus the decision not to hospitalize someone who is in severe straits and in need of detoxification may lead to serious complications, including death. This is especially true in the case of withdrawal from alcohol or in the case of drug overdose. On the other hand, a plan to hospitalize an adolescent who is experimenting for the first time, and acting in an alarming manner, may label, pathologize, and stigmatize that individual.

When the individual substance abuser poses an immediate danger to himself or others, then hospitalization is absolutely necessary. An example of this might be an individual with a history of heart attacks induced by cocaine who has relapsed, and despite having severe chest pains, is unable to interrupt his binge. A person with a history of severe alcoholism, who relapses and is unable to interrupt substantial drinking, would also need to be hospitalized, especially if that person has a history of significant symptoms of withdrawal.

Another class of people at risk are those with a severe concomitant medical illness that is complicated by substance abuse. A diabetic who is also suffering from a relapse of chronic alcoholism may be in danger of experiencing a diabetic coma and may need to be put into a hospital for stabilization. A method of dealing with these individuals who need an interruption from their substance abuse cycle and need to take their medication, is involuntary hospitalization to monitor the first period of medication administration.

> Mary is a 42 year-old secretary with a long history of insulin-dependent diabetes and concomitant alcoholism. She had been sober for three years after repeated treatments. For the past three years, Mary's life and her diabetes have been stable. After learning of the death of her twin sister from a heroin overdose, Mary relapsed and began drinking. She stopped following her insulin regimen and would sometimes go days without taking any insulin. At other times, as a result of impaired judgment from alcohol, she would take much larger doses of insulin than were prescribed. Her physician and her family became alarmed and brought her to the emergency room.

The above example is one of a person who needs hospitalization. She has a serious medical illness and her relapse is severe.

There is a high degree of correlation between substance abuse disorders and psychiatric illnesses. The dually diagnosed patient may require hospitalization in order to be treated optimally for both conditions. This affords the opportunity to stabilize the patient medically and also to tease out the most salient reasons for the current symptoms. For example, an individual who is drinking excessively may be severely depressed or even suicidal. A hospitalization will provide a protective environment for detoxification and allow the clinician to determine if the depression is an underlying condition or the result of alcohol's toxicity.

The detoxification from certain substances of abuse presents variable degrees of risk. Withdrawal from alcohol can be a life-threatening condition. The individual whose withdrawal from alcohol progresses to the delirium tremens stage has a 15–20% chance of dying. Alcohol withdrawal is a medical emergency and requires hospitalization. If the individual has entered into delirium tremens, then admission to the intensive care unit is necessary.

When a person is going through withdrawal from a large opiate dependency, hospitalization may be necessary in order to keep the person comfortable. Unless there is a medical problem which makes the person otherwise unstable, withdrawal from opiates is not a medical emergency. These individuals are quite uncomfortable however, so it may seem like an emergency to the inexperienced physician. It is a crisis in that the person who does not receive some relief (i.e., those drugs which relieve the symptoms of withdrawal) is likely to relapse into substance abuse.

There are two types of immediate hospitalization. The first occurs in a general hospital and usually involves the medical treatment of an individual's problems caused by the substance and withdrawal. This can be done on any general ward of a hospital and can take place in almost any

TABLE 18.1. Possible Reasons for Hospitalization

1. Severe depression, especially with serious suicidal plans or intentions, lasting beyond 1 to 3 days after the acute effects of the drug or withdrawal have passed.
2. Psychotic features persisting 1 to 2 days after the immediate effect of the drugs.
3. Repeated outpatient failures.
4. Intractable and unremitting use of the substance.
5. A history of severe alcohol or sedative withdrawal.
6. Any severe psychiatric or medical problem which coexists with the substance abuse.
7. Lack of motivation for any form of treatment.
8. Lack of family or social support.
9. Individuals with extreme availability of the substance, such as dealers.

community hospital. Most hospitals have at least one individual who is knowledgeable about substance abuse and detoxification. This person can coordinate the efforts necessary for detoxification and subsequent treatment.

The second is the specialized detoxification unit. These can usually be found in urban areas and are hospital wards that deal specifically with those individuals who need detoxification (from alcohol, heroin, or cocaine). In the case of cocaine, withdrawal is not as physiologically apparent, but an individual who has been on an extended binge may need to be hospitalized briefly to monitor the effects of exhaustion and malnutrition.

The best hospitalization programs have attached programs that deal with subsequent treatment. An ideal time to introduce an individual to the principles of substance abuse treatment is during a hospitalization. It is hard for a person to deny that he or she has an addictive disorder when he or she has just been hospitalized for detoxification. This can be very useful to the clinician in order to break through the rigid barrier of denial defenses.

Once a hospital stay has accomplished an accurate diagnosis, stabilized the patient, and introduced them to a recovery program, the patient can be considered for discharge. Treatment is an ongoing process which continues after hospitalization in a variety of outpatient formats. It is these outpatient models which form the basis for the next few chapters.

CHAPTER 19

Individual Psychotherapy for Substance Users

The bedrock of the healing profession is an individual relationship with the person in need. Certainly, someone presenting with a primary substance abuse problem qualifies as an appropriate candidate for help. With substance abusers, all forces necessary to deal with the problem must be marshaled, and a variety of approaches need to be utilized. The clinician is often in the role of individual counselor, case manager, therapist, and sometimes social engineer. Issues of addiction are usually problematic to deal with on an exclusively individual basis, and consequently the mainstay of traditional substance abuse treatment is group therapy, inclusive of the Twelve Step models.

Of course, not every method works for every patient. Most people with a severe problem probably require more than one approach—sequentially, and often simultaneously. The substance abusing individual will often benefit from an individual relationship with one therapist. An alliance with this therapist may give the patient an understanding of his or her illness, the disease process, the toxicity of the given substance, and the tools to achieve and maintain sobriety. Individual approaches to substance abuse are quite varied. Three representative methodologies used in the treatment of substance abuse disorders are: cognitive-behavioral, psychoeducational, and psychodynamic. These are not theoretically, methodologically, or practically exclusive of one another. In fact, they share some fundamental characteristics as well as the same goal of helping an individual recover from a substance abuse disorder.

The practitioner may choose to use one or any other of these approaches or some combination of techniques. Flexibility in formulating an initial treatment plan plus periodic review and revision of the plan as clinical circumstances dictate offers the best chance for successful psychotherapeutic work.

☐ Cognitive-Behavioral Therapy

Group therapies, which will be covered in a subsequent chapter, are probably the mainstay of substance abuse treatment. Of the *individual* (that is, one-to-one) therapies most frequently recommended and employed for substance abusers, the most prominent school of therapy relies on the principles of cognition. Psychotherapies that focus primarily on behavior and cognition are usually termed "cognitive-behavioral." This model posits that experience molds the "hard-wiring" in an individual's brain. Over the course of a lifetime, thoughts and behaviors are shaped and molded; some of these are adaptive and others are quite maladaptive. These methods of coping are dependent upon the context in which they are employed.

To date, this kind of therapy has been tested with a variety of conditions, including depression, anxiety, and personality disorders. In recent times, clinicians and researchers have realized that these methods are highly applicable to the understanding and treatment of individuals with a substance abuse problem.

Relapse Prevention

Relapse prevention is perhaps the best known and best studied application of cognitive-behavioral therapy with substance abusers. It is based upon a behavioral model, with a focus on the training of interpersonal and self-management skills. The primary goal of this form of treatment is to master the skills needed to maintain abstinence from drugs and alcohol. This involves the identification of high-risk situations that may increase the likelihood of relapse. The precipitating events include things external to the patient such as situations and individuals, as well as internal events and feeling states. Once these issues are identified, the patient is taught basic mechanisms for coping with such situations without resorting to drug or alcohol use.

Theory

The brain is a dynamic structure consisting of billions of interconnected neurons. Early life experiences influence the way the brain develops, and neuroscientists believe that the physical connections of neurons are important to understanding the way organisms function. These early experiences influence the development of basic and conditioned beliefs. This is how the individual experiences the world around him or her. These cognitive constructs which are repetitively employed are termed "schema."

As an individual gets older, they are exposed to various substances of abuse. Exposure to and experimentation with addictive substances leads to the development of drug related beliefs. An example of this is an individual who recognizes that alcohol relieves the anxiety associated with socializing and then, over the course of time, develops the belief that alcohol is an absolute necessity in all social settings.

In the case of the addict, these beliefs and the more complicated schema around them are reinforcing. As the addiction grows, the individual's thought patterns form a self perpetuating cycle of automatic thoughts and impulsive behaviors that become more and more self-destructive. Cognitive therapy calls for the formation of an alliance between the therapist and the substance abuser. In a mutual collaboration, these thought patterns are explored, questioned, and if maladaptive, altered. The patient and the therapist examine the patient's automatic thoughts, illogical beliefs, and the schema together to come up with alternatives that are not self-destructive.

In summary, cognitive-behavioral therapy is based on the premise that life experiences, early or recent, inform and shape a cognitive style. This leads to certain core beliefs which can be distorted and do not correspond with reality (these are termed "cognitive distortions"). Around these core beliefs, conditional assumptions, ideas, and rules are created by which the patient lives. Some individuals are more susceptible to developing compensatory strategies which involve substances of abuse. This can then led to a substance abuse problem. A given situation which leads to automatic thoughts and sometimes painful emotions may elicit maladaptive behavior. An example of this is a person who uses marijuana for its calming effects, and comes to rely upon it as a sleep aid, then believes that he or she cannot ever sleep without smoking marijuana before going to bed.

Practice

Cognitive-behavioral therapies for substance abuse are highly interactive, collaborative, supportive, and empathic. This collaboration is vital to the therapeutic process as it creates an alliance that makes possible the difficult work of changing addictive behaviors. The therapist meets regularly with the patient (usually once or twice per week), and the format is structured, but flexible in execution.

> As a child, Jane was subject to relentless criticism by her parents. Both parents were flawed people, locked in a mutually destructive marriage. Although she possessed a high IQ, and features most would find attractive, she grew up being told she had a weight problem, had a limited intellect, and would never be successful. In her words, she grew up believing that she was "fat, stupid, and would never amount to anything." Both parents were psychologically damaging and their behavior had a serious impact on Jane. They would ridicule her on any occasion that they could. She found acceptance with the "outsider" kids who smoked cigarettes and drank alcohol at an early age. More than any drug however, marijuana helped calm her nerves and "chill out" thus numbing for her the difficult emotions associated with her painful situation at home—her reality.

In the above example, we see the reasons for the evolution of the patient's cognitive style. Any success or indeed any action on Jane's part led to criticism and rebuke. Jane, therefore, grew up with the internalized message that she had heard from her parents: "I am fat, stupid and worthless." This is an irrational thought pattern and a cognitive distortion.

> Over the years she smoked more and more marijuana and did poorly in school. She dropped out of school just before graduation. After a year in a dead end job, she took the advice of a friend and approached the local clinic where she was evaluated for her depression and her dependence on marijuana. She met with a cognitive-behavioral therapist who was supportive and warm. She listened to Jane attentively and offered no judgments. She asked Jane about her marijuana use, and what positive and negative things it did for her.

This illustrates an important principle of almost any psychotherapeutic process: the necessity for the clinician to have a non-judgmental attitude toward the substance abuser. This does not imply colluding with the patient or condoning self-defeating or self-destructive behavior, and it does not imply that the clinician has no individual opinions, just that these need to be kept in check for the therapeutic alliance to develop. The therapist operates from the premise that all behavior has meaning and motivation, and by understanding it, the patient can be helped. By adopting an unbiased stance, Jane's therapist sought to gain the trust of her potential patient. She did not condemn Jane's use of marijuana, but sought to understand what it meant for her. In taking this posture, she encouraged Jane to engage with the issues at hand.

The first sessions in this type of therapy involve developing a rapport with the substance abuser and creating a treatment strategy with him or her in order to plan a course of treatment. This approach is flexible, remains in the "here and now," and explores the origins of the kind of thoughts that the patient is having. As an example, Jane may come into a future session and say that she has used marijuana at a party the night before. The therapist's intervention at that time is to assist Jane with an exploration of the beliefs, context, conditions, strategies, automatic thoughts, and behavior which precipitated the use of marijuana.

In developing a cognitive conceptualization diagram of the above example, the therapist takes into account what he or she knows about Jane. The therapist may actually write this schema out and share it with the patient. This helps both the patient and the therapist concretely focus upon the task at hand. One of the most widely used schema of this kind contains eight elements: (a) relevant childhood data, (b) core beliefs, (c) conditional beliefs, (d) the specific situation, (e) the automatic thoughts that emerge, (f) the meaning of the automatic thought, (g) the emotions involved, and (h) the behavior which occurred. An illustration of this situation, using Jane's example, is as follows:

Schema

Relevant Childhood Data: Abusive parents, peers who are drug users

Core Beliefs: "I am fat and ugly; people do not accept me."

Conditional beliefs: "If I smoke pot, I will be less anxious and people will tolerate me."

Situation: "I am invited to a party where I will be nervous."

Automatic thought: "I can't take the pressure of a party, I need to get high."

The meaning of the automatic thought: "I cannot cope with life because I am defective, and I need marijuana to deal with life."

Emotions: Anxiety, frustration, isolation

Behavior: Smoke marijuana before the party and during it.

The first phase of the therapy in this situation involves working with the patient to identify the emotions, automatic thoughts, and behavior surrounding whatever incident the patient chooses to explore. The therapist then guides the patient and helps him or her discover other alternatives to the maladaptive behavior used. In the above example, the therapist might explore the distorted notion that Jane cannot cope with life by suggesting several examples where she did just that ("but in the last session you told me that you went to your favorite cousin's bar mitzvah, without using marijuana, and had a good time.") This is done in order to challenge the belief that she really needs marijuana to function.

It is sometimes useful to have patients write down their beliefs. This exercise is often quite revealing. The therapist and the patient can then examine the patient's beliefs and, if useful, refute them. For example,

Jane might write that "I can't stand craving, I always give in." Since there have to have been times in her life when Jane had a craving and did not use marijuana, the therapist may then explore this erroneous belief. The therapist may inject some reality to these mistaken beliefs. Alternative strategies and ideas may be written down, such as: "No one ever died of craving." As the therapy progresses, the two collaborators may come up with creative solutions for various situations and problems and alternatives to using drugs to cope with stressful life circumstances.

Course of Treatment

This type of treatment is active, prescriptive, and very often involves homework assignments outside of sessions. Maintaining abstinence is hard work and usually cannot be achieved by applying effort in only the one or two therapy sessions per week. While early sessions are devoted to establishing rapport, later sessions involve identification of high risk situations and emphasize solutions dealing with those situations. Later on, more specific individual issues are addressed, and finally the last sessions are focused on shoring up the newly learned behaviors and techniques as well as preparing for emergencies in the future.

This therapy may be of short or longer duration, depending upon the needs of the patient. It may also be adapted to a group setting. In any case, as always with substance abusing patients, patience and tolerance for fluctuations in behavior, knowledge that relapse is a part of the illness, and the maintenance of a non-judgemental (but not all accepting) attitude ought to be employed.

Mechanics

Most commonly, the mechanics and execution of relapse prevention occur between an individual therapist and patient or in a therapeutic group setting. The treatment is divided into "core sessions" and elective meetings which are tailored to the individual patient's current needs. The description below is of a few representative sessions which are intended to give the reader a general sense of the nature of the work. Each session lasts about an hour, but time factors can be modified if necessary.

Introduction to Coping Skills Training

The introductory meeting is designed to be informational and provide opportunity to develop motivation. The therapist gets to know the patient in the context of his or her life and substance abuse. The therapist explains about the nature of addiction, as well as the general treatment approach.

In the first session, the therapist contracts with the patient and explains what will be expected in terms of attendance, fees, homework, and other details of the work they will be doing together.

Coping with Cravings and Urges to "Use"

In this session the patient is taught about cravings (i.e., intense states of desire for drugs or alcohol). Although difficult to define, it is a concept immediately understood by almost everyone with an addiction. Cravings usually have triggers, many of which are obvious. An individual addicted to crack cocaine will almost always have urges when passing by the corner where the crack was originally purchased. Some triggers are much more subtle and may involve issues of self esteem and emotional states. Such subtle triggers are the subject of future sessions.

The other aspect of cravings that is important for the patient to learn is that they are "survivable." The client is taught a number of techniques for dealing with cravings, such as talking it through or "urge surfing." "Urge surfing" is a technique in which the addicted individual is taught to visualize the craving as a wave which crests and then recedes. The patient relaxes and focuses on the part of the body that experiences the physical aspects of craving. They then literally imagine riding the wave. The urge or craving almost always diminishes if it is not satisfied; it has a beginning, a middle, and an end. The purpose of "urge surfing" is not to eliminate craving, but rather it is for the addict to experience craving in a new way. Cravings do not kill people; if delayed, they diminish. The exercise gives the addict a new understanding of craving, and some mastery over it. Craving is reframed as a challenge and is experienced in a new and more tolerable way.

Problem Solving

In this session the individual patient is asked to fantasize about specific, difficult circumstances where relapse is likely. The therapist and the patient then talk about the experience and come up with ways of dealing with those instances. In preparing for these crisis situations and practicing them in the safety of the therapy situation, the patient is better prepared to deal with such situations as they occur in life outside of therapy.

At the conclusion of this therapy, the patient will have learned a number of psychological techniques; for example to recognize triggers, deal with difficult situations, and regulate cravings. These "tools" are then available in the service of sobriety for the duration of the patient's life.

Psychoeducational Therapy

This model is usually incorporated into other forms of treatment such as psychodynamic, cognitive-behavioral, or group therapies, but can also be useful to discuss in its pure form. Psychoeducation is a delicate, didactically oriented relationship with the patient in which the clinician teaches the patient about substances, their use, and their consequences. Individuals with addiction problems are usually curious to learn about the substances that they are using. The skilled clinician knows when to offer facts and information and when this will be experienced negatively as "just another lecture."

> Jane initially came to therapy with depressive symptoms. When the clinician suggested in the first interview that her symptoms might be caused by the marijuana, Jane was resistant and said "you're going to give me a lecture just like my mother aren't you?" The clinician quickly backed down. Six weeks into treatment, when the subject came up again, the therapist indicated that Jane's poor mood might be influenced by her marijuana use. At that point, Jane was receptive to finding out more about the relationship between mood and substance use and more readily accepted the knowledge provided by her therapist and the educational materials she was given.

The clinician who chooses to work with this population must be knowledgeable about the substances that their patients are using. Continuous re-education is vital in this regard. Staying current with new developments in the field is important for a variety of reasons, one of the most important being that the clinician's credibility increases in direct proportion to the breadth of his or her knowledge about substance abuse and treatment. Acknowledging ignorance about a question posed, rather than making up an answer, or dismissing the patient, is often greeted with an increase in respect on the part of the patient.

Psychodynamic Therapy

Psychodynamic therapy has a negative reputation in many substance abuse treatment circles. This is unfortunate, as the principles associated with this type of therapy can often be useful in working with this population. Unfortunately, some clinicians misinterpret psychodynamic concepts such as therapeutic neutrality to mean pasivity and nonintervention. A common story encountered is of an alcoholic, or cocaine addict, who continued to abuse substances destructively, while his or her therapist said nothing. Because of inappropriate experiences like these, many people who eventually achieve recovery have a low opinion of this form of therapy. If used judiciously, this form of therapy may have great utility. This is less a criticism of individual psychodynamically oriented psychotherapy than of its misapplication with addicted populations.

Theory

The early part of the century saw the evolution and refinement of psychoanalytic theory. This has evolved as a comprehensive model which seeks to explain motivation and behavior. The basic tenet is that most cognitive and mental processes occur out of consciousness. This is hardly a strange concept when one considers that there are over 16 billion neurons that make up the cortex of the average human brain, with an exponential number of interconnections between those neurons. The vast majority of the activity of this system is not devoted to momentary consciousness. It is these powerful unconscious forces that drive most human activity and emotion.

Sigmund Freud, the founder of psychoanalytic theory, was an original thinker and a tower of twentieth century culture. Freud was originally a neurologist but found his understanding of neurology inadequate to explain some of the presenting complaints and symptoms of his patients. This led him to develop theories of psychoanalysis and create a type of therapy that many found useful. Given the prominence and common occurrence of addictions, it is no surprise that early psychoanalysts attempted to explain and treat addiction using psychoanalysis.

One of Freud's many contributions is the observation that processes that begin in childhood have resonance and meaning in adulthood. Freud saw addictions as substitutions for infantile autoeroticism. Addicts use substances in a vicious and repetitive cycle in which the desire to satisfy a primitive wish is gratified, but only with accompanying guilt and loss of self-esteem.

There are a number of early analytic theories which attempted to explain addiction. Most of these involved sex, aggression, or both. An example of this is visible in the work of Fleisher. Fleisher was an early psychoanalyst and theorist who believed that alcoholism was the result of unconscious homosexual wishes. Fleisher was German and made this observation after viewing drunken soldiers in pubs who always acted more affectionately and demonstratively toward their comrades after consuming many beers.

The earliest psychoanalytic models placed much emphasis on regressive aspects of the human psyche and the need to gratify infantile wishes. Psychoanalytic thinkers also recognized in practical terms, how difficult these patients are to treat. Carl Jung was unable to help one of his first patients (Roland H.) become and remain sober. He eventually agreed with the founders of AA that some form of spiritual re-awakening was also necessary. Afterwards, Roland H. joined the Oxford Group, an evangelical religion interested in alcoholics, and did indeed become sober. Later, Jung became an advisor to the early growth of AA.

Even the earliest psychodynamic formulations recognized that addiction is a progressive phenomenon. These early theories have blossomed and shaped current psychodynamic thinking. More recent thinking, consistent with a dynamic unconscious model, still relies on the premise that substance abuse is a maladaptive attempt to deal with unpleasant emotional states. The substance use has two elements. The first is to relieve or medicate painful affects (the self-medication hypothesis) where the substance use is a dysfunctional defense against unwanted drives and affects. The second element concerns mastery of the substance itself. The addict is locked into a cycle of impossible omnipotence, where they continually try to master the effects of the unmasterable substance.

Practice

A key to psychodynamic theory is that uncovering the unconscious dynamic elements, enlightening the patient, and then applying these insights into active behavioral form in one's life will lead to a diminution of the symptoms. In practice, this kind of discovery is helpful for the individual who is attempting to achieve and maintain sobriety. Psychodynamic work is useful in different ways at different stages of the addictive process. In early stages of substance abuse, for example, when a young person is beginning to drink too much, psychodynamic interpretations can sometimes help the patient arrest the progression and discover a more adaptive way of dealing with painful feelings and emotions. This is only the case when the substance abuse is problematic, but the "switch has not been flipped."

> Jim is a 38 year-old advertising executive, married with two children, one age two and the other a newborn. After hearing Dr. Roth give a talk on anxiety and alcoholism, which he attended because of a proposed ad campaign for a drug company, he called Dr. Roth. His first statement over the telephone was, "I think I need to see a doctor about my anxiety, but I feel like a fourteen year-old nervous to call you." Dr. Roth did an extended evaluation and while he asked about the extent of Jim's drinking in the first session, he chose not to focus on it. He believed that a dogmatic stance would frighten the patient and cause him to flee from treatment. Over the course of a six month, once-per-week therapy, it emerged that Jim had not accomplished some of the maturational tasks associated with adolescence. His opening line on the telephone was, unbeknownst to him, his unconscious chief complaint—he did indeed feel fourteen. He was overwhelmed by his responsibilities at work,

and feared he would be an inadequate father for his two young sons. As he began to trust his therapist he revealed that he often drank 5 to 6 beers at night after getting home from work. On these occasions, Jim played music that he had loved as an adolescent. This pattern of drinking had increased since the birth of his youngest son and being given more responsibilities at work. An exploration of his feelings, about how he did not feel grown up, greatly relieved his anxiety and his drinking diminished considerably. At a three year follow-up, he was still successful in his work and home life and drinking only moderately.

It should be emphasized that the above case example describes someone who was drinking problematically at the time of presentation, but was not physiologically dependent on alcohol and did not have an extensive history of problem drinking. The elucidation that he was self-medicating his anxiety because he did not feel adult was enormously helpful to this patient. At least in the early stages of problematic substance use, an understanding of what painful emotions the patient is attempting to deal with by using a given substance is enormously useful in relieving the presenting symptoms.

For the individual who has become addicted and has lost the capacity to regulate his or her use of a given substance, psychodynamic therapy is not recommended as the initial treatment. It is often contraindicated, as the therapist may unwittingly aid the patient's denial mechanisms. Individual psychotherapy can, however, be an enormously helpful tool once the individual is stable in sobriety. A self-aware individual is better equipped to confront the difficulties presented by life and better able to maintain sobriety. The fourth step of Alcoholics Anonymous compels alcoholics to make a "searching and fearless moral inventory of ourselves." This is the basis of analytic therapy. Individuals search themselves for the clues to their emotions, motivations, and behavior. The approach is exploratory and the posture of the therapist is supportive. The exploration is about those dynamics which contributed to the painful emotions. The aim is for sobriety and any tools available which aid in that cause.

The recommended approach for someone who has a clear-cut addiction who wants dynamic therapy is a combination of supportive and exploratory therapy. Although there are no hard and fast rules, an individual who embarks on this type of therapy ought to have at least six months of sobriety before beginning. Therapy can be very difficult for some individuals and the therapist must be extremely careful not to stir up too many painful issues too soon which might overwhelm the patient and promote a relapse. "Gentle, gentle, gentle" should be the refrain for the therapist working with an individual with a history of substance abuse problems. It can be clinically useful to explain the rationale for going at the pace selected.

With careful work, substance abusing individuals can learn about themselves in order to discover what feelings they were medicating and how to prevent relapse.

> Anne is a 52 year-old single high school teacher who lived alone with her two cats. She had been sober for six years since she first sought out a therapist. Dr. Lewis did a long evaluation and agreed to treat her. Anne began what was to become a three-year relationship. Anne's father had been a cool and remote figure, and her mother, a busy career woman who had little time or affection for Anne. Her parents had an ambivalent relationship, and Anne was born late in the life of both parents. Anne was frequently left in the care of nannies and baby-sitters. As an adult, she had a terrible fear of abandonment and anxiety over attachment. As a result, her relationships were brief and tumultuous. Early on, Anne learned that alcohol calmed her anxiety in social settings. Over the years, her drinking became more and more problematic and after several attempts, she finally achieved sobriety at Hazelden in Minnesota after attending many AA meetings. In her therapy with Dr. Lewis, she was able to explore and understand her difficulties with emotional attachment. Dr. Lewis was careful to support the assistance she found in AA and interpreted that it was an environment quite different from her home. The environment at AA was non-judgmental and supportive, which the patient found comforting. As the therapy progressed, she came to understand herself better, establish the realization that she was an alcoholic, and form more intimate attachments. At follow-up, she remained sober and was involved in a caring relationship with a man who lived out of state, but whom she saw on weekends. She expressed a longing to be able to "enjoy a gin and tonic after work, like my friends can" but acknowledged that this was impossible for her.

In the previous example, the therapist was able to help the patient maintain her sobriety, while sensitively exploring those emotions which were hard for the patient to deal with. The therapeutic alliance diminished her anxiety and led to a successful compromise in terms of intimacy (a supportive boyfriend, but one who lives out of state) for the patient.

☐ Conclusion

There are quite a number of other schools of individual therapy for substance abusers, but the above examples are probably the most widely employed. None of the therapies are mutually exclusive. The therapist has to be creative and flexible in combining elements which form an individualized psychotherapeutic mosaic. Almost always, patients in individual psychotherapy are encouraged to attend Twelve Step meetings in concert with therapy. It is these Twelve Step programs which form the basis of the chapter to follow.

20

CHAPTER

Twelve Step Programs

"My name is Bob and I am an alcoholic." Thus begins a typical meeting of Alcoholics Anonymous. Although Alcoholics Anonymous was the first such group, Cocaine Anonymous, Narcotics Anonymous, and many other variations can be found in cities and rural areas throughout the country and the world. Similar phrases are heard with different substances of abuse: "I am a cocaine addict" or "I am a heroin addict." The self-revelatory admission defines one of the guiding principles of Twelve Step groups: the need for humility and identification; humility about an individual's powerlessness against these substances, and identification as an addicted person among other addicted people.

The speaker identifies himself as an alcoholic and thereby recognizes the first of the Twelve Steps. This identification is voluntary. This is another guiding principle of AA and a reason for its success. The substance abuser admits powerlessness over alcohol and that life with alcohol has become unmanageable. The psychological freedom that such honesty affords in the context of a warm and supportive group is responsible, at least in part, for the tremendous success of AA.

The "Twelve Steps" refers to twelve guiding statements created by the founders of AA. The belief is that following these "steps" leads the alcoholic to sobriety and a more balanced life. The process is deceptively simple. An analysis of the meaning of the steps reveals the reasons that they are so effective for some addicts. They actualize a number of psychological principles necessary for most people to undergo a profound change.

AA is over fifty years old and it is by far the most prominent and best known addiction treatment approach in the world. Members of AA are proud to cite the fact that the telephone number of a local chapter of AA can be found in *every* Yellow Pages in the United States. Less common are the twelve step meetings specific for other substances (e.g., Narcotics Anonymous, or Cocaine Anonymous) or other compulsive disorders (e.g., Overeaters Anonymous, or Sexual Compulsives Anonymous). For reasons of simplicity, the following discussion focuses on alcohol and AA, but most of the discusion, principles, and logistics apply to all Twelve Step programs.

☐ History

The roots of AA are long and stretch back into Puritanism and a number of evangelical movements, as well as more recently developed psychological theories. AA was "born" on a late Saturday afternoon in May 1935, the day before Mother's Day. Bill Wilson (known in the rooms of AA as Bill W.), generally considered the father of the Twelve Step movement, was on a business trip in Akron, Ohio. An important deal had fallen through and Bill was under considerable stress. He came from New York and had a long history of chronic alcoholism with a deteriorating course. Recently, he had been able to maintain sobriety for six months. During a hospitalization six months before and following a conversation with his friend about spirituality, Bill W. had what he could only describe as a religious conversion. What occurred to Bill W. was a profound recognition of spiritual dimensions and of the utter hopelessness and severity of his situation. After that, he was able to remain sober. The events of this business trip and the stress they were causing were severely testing his new found sobriety.

One afternoon, while under increasing stress, he contacted a minister from the evangelical Christian Oxford group. Bill believed he needed to talk to someone who would understand what he was going through. He was referred to a man who was receptive to the idea that he needed to talk to another alcoholic. Dr. Bob Smith was a surgeon from Akron, who was also a chronic alcoholic. The next day, the two met and over the course of a long afternoon at Dr. Smith's house, both discovered the power of simply telling their stories and sharing experiences. "Yes, that is like me, that is just like me," Bob kept reiterating. The simple act of self-revelation in an accepting setting was enormously relieving, rejuvenating, and powerful.

Bill Wilson and Bob Smith became the co-founders of AA. Wilson went on to develop the fellowship of AA and to provide a remarkably profound chapter in the social history of the twentieth century. Although cloaked in religious symbolism and relying on those same principles that guide religion, AA retains a secular rooting. Furthermore, Bill W. did not try to set up AA as "his organization," but rather allowed it to develop autonomously. Bill W. was not without his own narcissism; he left a legacy in his will for his latest mistress, whoever that happened to be, but his ego was not dependent on his keeping power in the organization. This abdication of absolute authority was, some believe, as profound as Washington's refusal to accept the mantle of King which was offered him after securing victory for the new United States. The fact that AA was able to grow independently probably accounts for its long and continued survival.

Four years after the founding of AA, its membership had increased to 100. By the end of 1941, 8,000 members could be counted. Since that time the growth has been and continues to be exponential. It is hard to define who is a "member" of AA, and indeed there are many degrees of affiliation to AA. Some people go to many meetings a week, for many years, and consider themselves very involved in "the fellowship." Others believe they have benefited from attending just one meeting. What is clear is that, no matter the degree of involvement, AA has played an important role in the lives of millions of people seeking sobriety.

> Satishe was a 34 year-old African American woman living in the southern part of the United States, in a medium size city. She began drinking in her early teens, and by her mid twenties, had progressed to drinking every day. She concealed this from her friends and family, but was aware that she had "a problem." One morning, awakening with a particularly bad hangover, she went out seeking breakfast. She noticed a group of people, hanging around the church at the corner. Curious about what was going on she asked one of the people, who explained that an AA meeting was about to start. She had heard about AA, but had never known much about it, nor had she attended a meeting. She was reluctant, but entered the basement. Hearing the stories of the people struck an enormous chord in her. She was relieved and exhilarated to hear so many stories with which she identified. She has been attending meetings twice per week since then, and has remained sober for ten years.

The Twelve Steps and the Twelve Traditions

The guiding principles of AA can be found in the well-known Twelve Steps and the lesser known Twelve Traditions, shown in the following tables:

At the heart of the Twelve Steps are a concrete and tangible program for accepting the loss of control in the addiction process. The "Big Book," a publication which explains the process, states: "Rarely have we seen a

TABLE 20.1. The Twelve Steps of Alcoholics Anonymous

1. We admitted we were powerless over alcohol and that our lives had become unmanageable.
2. Came to believe that a Power greater than ourselves could restore us to sanity.
3. Made a decision to turn our will and our lives over to the care of God as we understood Him.
4. Made a searching and fearless moral inventory of ourselves.
5. Admitted to God, to ourselves, and to another human being the exact nature of our wrongs.
6. Were entirely ready to have God remove all these defects of character.
7. Humbly asked Him to remove our shortcomings.
8. Made a list of all persons we had harmed, and became willing to make amends to them all.
9. Made direct amends to such people wherever possible, except when to do so would injure them or others.
10. Continued to take personal inventory and when we were wrong promptly admitted it.
11. Sought through prayer and meditation to improve our conscious contact with God as we understood Him, praying only for knowledge of His will for us and the power to carry that out.
12. Having had a spiritual awakening as the result of these steps, we tried to carry this message to alcoholics, and to practice these principles in all our affairs.

The Twelve Steps and Twelve Traditions are reprinted with permission of Alcoholics Anonymous World Services, Inc. Permission to reprint this material does not mean that AA has reviewed or approved the contents of this publication, nor that AA agrees with the views expressed herein. AA is a program of recovery from alcoholism. Use of the Twelve Steps and Twelve Traditions in connection with programs and activities which are patterned after AA but which address other problems does not imply otherwise.

person fail who has thoroughly followed our path." These steps work for many (but certainly not all) in large measure because they are practical, concrete, and tangible. They also may trigger cognitive processes which can be employed in staying sober and avoiding relapse.

☐ How a Meeting Works—The Mechanics

The following is designed to describe an overview of how a representative AA meeting works. Meetings may take place at any hour of the day. In more populated areas, meetings are available more frequently. In a densely populated area like Manhattan, it is literally possible to attend an AA meeting at any hour of the day, 24 hours a day, 365 days a year. In order to find out about the schedule of local meetings, the interested indi-

TABLE 20.2. The Twelve Traditions of Alcoholics Anonymous

1. Our common welfare should come first; personal recovery depends upon AA unity.
2. For our group purpose there is but one ultimate authority—a loving God as He may express himself in our group conscience. Our leaders are but trusted servants; they do not govern.
3. The only requirement for AA membership is a desire to stop drinking.
4. Each group should be autonomous except in matters affecting other groups or AA as a whole.
5. Each group has but one primary purpose—to carry its message to the alcoholic who still suffers.
6. An AA group ought never endorse, finance, or lend the AA name to any related facility or outside enterprise, lest problems of money, property, and prestige divert us from our primary purpose.
7. Every AA group ought to be fully self-supporting, declining outside contributions.
8. Alcoholics Anonymous should remain forever nonprofessional, but our service centers may employ special workers.
9. AA, as such, ought never be organized; but we may create service boards or committees directly responsible to those they serve.
10. Alcoholics Anonymous has no opinion on outside issues; hence the AA name ought never be drawn into public controversy.
11. Our public relations policy is based on attraction rather than promotion; we need always maintain personal anonymity at the level of press, radio, and films.
12. Anonymity is the spiritual foundation of all our Traditions, ever reminding us to place principles before personalities.

vidual need only consult the phone book. Meetings are free of charge, but voluntary donations are taken at the end of the meeting (for coffee, and to support the larger organization's very modest budget). Donations are completely voluntary. The locations for meetings are often church basements, but they may be anywhere, and people involved with AA are fond of saying that all it takes is two addicts to make a meeting. The physical setting is secondary to the "atmosphere" of the meeting which is intended to be relaxed, accepting, friendly, and without reproach.

There are two basic kinds of meetings: open and closed. "Open" meetings are available for any individual who is interested in finding out about the process. "Closed" meetings are for those individuals familiar with AA and who have identified themselves as having a desire to stop drinking. There are further subdivisions, such as beginner's meetings, which are geared to the novice attendee, and Step meetings, which specifically focus on one of the Twelve Steps.

A typical meeting consists of a beginning speaker who "qualifies." This qualification consists of the individual's personal story of the history of his or her alcoholism and steps to recovery. These are individual stories, but there are common threads with which others can easily identify that permeate most narratives. These consist of an initial honeymoon phase with alcohol or with the drug, when use was pleasurable and often controlled. The story often proceeds to the gradual dominance of the substance over the individual's life and ends with the recognition of loss of control and the seeking of help. After the speaker finishes, individuals are free to share their thoughts or they may remain silent and gain strength through the sense of being among kindred spirits. Everyone in the meeting is struggling with control over alcohol (and/or drugs) and participates in order to help themselves and others present at the twelve step meeting.

There is some debate about the composition of meetings and what this means for an individual interested in AA. Many addicts insist that "an addict is an addict is an addict." Still, humans have a need to affiliate with people whom they consider "like me." Most clinicians believe that the meetings probably work best if individuals in the meetings come from at least moderately similar backgrounds. Clinical experience indicates that it can be a disappointment or traumatic experience when the first encounter an individual has with AA is at a group where they may feel they have nothing in common with other members.

For a high powered businessperson, whose narcissism is already injured in the process of accepting the idea that he or she is an alcoholic, it may not be therapeutic to experience the first meeting at a shelter for the homeless. Experienced clinicians often encourage attendance at a meeting where the person will feel more comfortable. Later on, as the addicted person accepts the need for treatment, he or she may be more willing to attend heterogeneously composed AA meetings. In dealing with a person who the clinician believes will benefit from attendance at AA, it is sometimes helpful to suggest that he or she seek out a person in the next meeting they will attend, and ask him or her which meetings in the area are most helpful.

An unofficial but extremely important part of AA often comes after the meeting. Here, sober individuals share continued stories over coffee or food. This is an extension of the fellowship involved in attendance. Many people new to AA have no social outlets other than alcoholics and this is a wonderful opportunity to meet and deal with sober people. This socialization fosters the creation of a sober network of friends.

Some terms which may not be recognizable to an individual who is unfamiliar about Twelve Step programs are worth mentioning. A "home" group refers to the AA group that an individual most frequently attends, and hence is most closely allied. The "fellowship" refers to the program itself, and the spirit which infuses it. The "rooms" refer, not to a physical structure, but the process involved with a twelve step program. One who is actively working on sobriety in a twelve step program is said to be "in the rooms of AA." A sponsor is an important, though not mandatory, part of this form of recovery. Sponsors serve as aids to recovery. In theory they make themselves available to the "sponsee" at any time of the day or night, to help maintain abstinence. It is recommended that individuals "check in" with a sponsor on a daily basis. Sponsors come in two basic forms—temporary and regular. Temporary sponsors are usually individuals who have a substantial time in recovery, and who serve as sponsors to individuals who are new to the AA experience. Later on, individuals may choose a sponsor on a more permanent basis. People can change sponsors whenever they want, and some of these relationships last for many years.

☐ The Dynamics and Effectiveness of AA

The reasons for the effectiveness of AA are probably as individual as the people who seek its' fellowship. Part of the success comes from the group process at work in the meetings (see chart in Chapter 21—Group Psychotherapy). Individuals are offered hope and information at meetings. They learn from and identify with the stories of others and therefore feel a sense of cohesiveness and universality. By nature, people are social beings and feel closer when in the safety of others with whom they feel secure. AA provides this kind of group identification and the psychological stability that comes from it.

AA emphasizes the concept of loss of control which accompanies alcoholism, and the alcoholic's powerlessness over the substance. There is considerable biological evidence that addicted individuals are, in a real sense, powerless over the substance. AA allows the individual to recognize this loss of control and then accept that he or she needs a powerful counter-force in order to combat this loss of control. While this can be described in complex psychological terms, what AA simply does is allow the addicted individual to "borrow" some ego functioning from other members in the group. The observing ego, the healthy care-giving portion of the psyche, is therefore activated, strengthened, and fortified.

Empathy is a powerful tool in any therapeutic milieu. Part of the reason for AA's success is due to the high level of empathy and identification available to attendees. The environment is comfortable, and the style of interpersonal contact, non-threatening. AA provides the alcoholic with a protected environment. Furthermore, the meetings are filled with individuals who have the same set of problems, thus destigmatizing the idea of being an alcoholic or substance abuser. This feeling of identification with others is a powerful tool in achieving and maintaining abstinence.

Along with empathy is the idea of responsibility. The efforts to stop drinking and the desire to do so are the individual's responsibility. The alcoholic is not asked to admit that they are an alcoholic, only that they have a sincere desire to stop drinking. As sobriety continues, the rise in self esteem helps the addicted individual build a new life as does the social reinforcement for sobriety which comes from other AA members.

Another powerful, central part of AA is its spiritual dimension. The spirituality involved with AA is distinct from religious dogma. AA is probably as successful as it is for some individuals because it adheres to certain religious principles which are almost universal. Even avowed atheists recognize that religion fulfills profound psychological needs in people. This alone is reason for its ubiquity. The principles that AA borrows from religion and spirituality include release, gratitude, humility, forgiveness, and tolerance. These elements are important in higher religions and mysticism, and operate to foster the principles of AA. Furthermore, these principles encourage the kind of spiritual transformation which is often necessary for the severely addicted patient to change so radically and become sober.

Conclusion

What began as a meeting between two individuals in the spring of 1935 has evolved into a worldwide movement that has informed and influenced social thought in the twentieth century. AA does not work for everyone and there are certain people for whom it probably does not work at all. There are alternative therapies that are probably more helpful for such individuals. AA and the other Twelve Step programs remain an invaluable tool for those people who are addicted and those who seek to help them. Twelve Step participation is compatible with virtually all other "formal" psychotherapeutic interventions described in this text. Substance abusers in individual, group, marital, and family therapies are encouraged to simultaneously attend Twelve Step meetings.

21

CHAPTER

Group Psychotherapy

Group psychotherapy is often the centerpiece of the psychotherapeutic management of people struggling with substance abuse issues. The proliferation of groups has been exponential and the composition, setting, and leadership of experiences which take place in the group milieu is both impressive and potentially confusing. In order to differentiate among the array of group interventions, the authors have chosen to discuss different representative models of small and large, in-patient and out-patient groups as separate entities despite the fact that in actual clinical practice many of these group formats overlap.

This chapter makes a distinction between psychotherapy groups for addiction and other experiences which transpire in a group setting but possess significant differences in goals, style, and conduct of the group meetings. A prime example of the interface between groups is visible in the comparison between the two most frequently employed group models: the self-help group and the psychotherapy group.

Very often, self-help group and psychotherapy groups are simultaneous parts of a treatment plan for an addicted individual. When properly understood by clinician and patient, these two group experiences complement one another and function in a non-competitive way. Some common examples illustrate this point. Mutual-help groups advocate "sharing" of experiences and feelings but are not designed to supply peer interaction or confrontation by a leader or other members, as is the case in the psychotherapy group. Similarly, traditional psychodynamic constructs such

TABLE 21.1. Cocaine group formats

	Self-Help Group	Psychotherapy Group
Size	Large (size often unlimited)	Small (8–15 members)
Leadership	1. Peer leader or recovered cocaine user	1. Mental health professional with or without recovered user
	2. Leadership is earned status over time	2. Self-appointed leadership
	3. Implicit hierarchical leadership structure	3. Formal hierarchical leadership structure
Membership Participation	Voluntary	Voluntary and involuntary
Group Governed	Self-governing	Leader governed
Content	1. Environmental factors, no examination of group interaction	1. Examination of intragroup behavior and extragroup factors
	2. Emphasis on similarities among members	2. Emphasis on differentiation among members over time
	3. "Here and now" focus	3. "Here and now" plus historical focus
Screening Interview	None	Always
Group Processes	Universalization, empathy, affective sharing education, public statement of problem (self-disclosure), mutual affirmation, morale building, catharsis, immediate positive feedback, high degrees of persuasiveness	Cohesion, mutual identification confrontation, education, catharsis, use of group pressure re-abstinence and retention of group membership
Outside Socialization	1. Encouraged strongly	1. Cautious re-extragroup contact
	2. Construction of social network is actively sought	2. Intermember networking is optimal

TABLE 21.1. Continued

Goals	1. Positive goal setting, behaviorally oriented 2. Focus on the group as a whole and the similarities among members	1. Ambitious goals: cocaine problems plus individual personality issues 2. Individual as well as group focus
Leader Activity	1. Educator/role model catalyst for learning 2. Less member-to-leader distance	1. Responsible for therapeutic group experience 2. More member-to-leader distance
Use of Interpretation or Psychodynamic Techniques	No	Yes
Confidentially	Anonymity preserved	Strongly emphasized
Sponsorship Program	Yes (usually same sex)	No
Deselection	1. Member may leave group at their own choosing 2. Members may avoid self-disclosure or discussion of any subject	1. Predetermined minimal term of commitment to group membership 2. Avoidance of discussion seen as "resistance"
Involvement in Other Groups/Programs	Yes	Yes—eclectic models No—psychodynamic models
Time Factors	Unlimited group participation possible over years	Often time-limited experiences
Frequency of Meetings	Active encouragement of daily participation	Meets less frequently (often once or twice weekly)

as the analysis of resistance to self-exploration or group participation, the exploration of peer and authority feelings or transferences, and the restriction of social contact outside of group sessions are more commonly the province of psychotherapy groups.

Conversely, self-help groups have an extensive networking and sponsorship program which extends beyond the confines of meetings. They permit groups of greater size than a psychotherapy group, charge no fee for participation, and provide members with the experience of democratic peer leadership. Self-help groups provide greater access to meetings than therapy groups which often meet once or twice per week. People who feel in need of interpersonal contact or who are at risk to resume substance use may avail themselves of a Twelve Step meeting at virtually any time of day or several times a day if need be.

While there are inevitable comparisons between mutual-help groups and psychotherapy groups, these distinctions are not drawn as criticism of either but rather as illustrations of what each group experience does best and how they can be successfully combined to offer comprehensive resources to people dealing with drug and alcohol problems.

Since the focus of this chapter is the psychotherapy group, a closer look at the construction and conduct of these groups is in order.

☐ Pre-group Issues

Many decisions which influence the eventual outcome of group therapy with substance abusers are made prior to the first group session. The goals of the pre-group phase are to carefully screen, select, and prepare prospective group members. The importance of the pre-group preparation is visible as early as the initial group session. Members who are well-oriented come into group with realistic goals and expectations.

The tasks for the group leader in the pre-group phase are threefold: (a) to evaluate potential group members; (b) to decide which group best suits a person at this point in time; and (c) to provide a verbal orientation for each incoming group member. The use of a pre-group checklist is a simple and time-efficient way of presenting key aspects of group therapy to new members.

A representative sampling of specific items which comprise the checklist include:

1. the length and location of each group session;
2. whether the group is time-limited or open-ended;
3. if the group is designed to accept new members during its course;
4. what the role of the leader will be;
5. issues related to contact outside of group and confidentiality;

6. the policy about "slips" or relapses back into drug and alcohol abuse;
7. plans for hospitalizing members when indicated;
8. arrangements about billing and fees;
9. the pros and cons of the use of therapeutically prescribed drugs such as anti-depressants; and
10. a discussion about the goals of the group.

In all groups, the group "ground rules" are presented prior to the first session. This subject takes on added meaning when the problem for which a group is homogeneously composed is substance abuse. Members are instructed in advance that minimal behavioral guidelines must be met in order to maximize group benefit and not to undermine the work of the group. Abstinence from all mind and mood-altering substances is a basic group requirement. There is strong agreement in addiction treatment circles that unless the addiction is under control, no therapeutic efforts will be effective. People who enter group therapy while in a state of transition from active drug use to abstinence are expected to have difficult times during the course of their recovery. Incoming members are encouraged to utilize the group as an alternative to handling dysphoric or anxiety-laden episodes by resorting to drug and alcohol use.

In many group therapy models, patients are asked to participate in voluntary random urine screening for the presence of drugs of abuse as a condition of group membership. This serves as both a test of a person's readiness or lack thereof to give up his or her addiction, and also is used as a way of tangibly validating healthy recovery efforts in members who can be proud of having "clean" urine test results. The adjunctive use of urine testing has been overemphasized from the perspective of shaming and blaming members and underemphasized as a therapeutic tool for promoting positive self-esteem and credibility for sober members.

☐ Group Goals

When individuals break their ties to the drug and alcohol-using subcultures in order to achieve sobriety, they often are simultaneously rupturing their interpersonal attachment bonds. Group therapy is particularly useful at this early stage of recovery in substituting a drug-free peer network composed of fellow group members to offset the sense of loss experienced by the new member. The group leaders and the group members function as an interpersonal anchor during stormy personal times. Group membership helps counter feelings of loneliness, isolation, and alienation.

Once detoxification and early sobriety have been reached, the central group goal becomes one of helping the substance abuser achieve a state of emotional equilibrium. Disabling emotional states such as anxiety, panic, and depression typify the immediate emotional sequellae which follow initial abstinence. Group participation aids in restoring a feeling of balance through peer support, advice giving and the sense of acceptance which comes from being a valued member of a therapeutic group.

Commonalties among group members not only form the basis for group cohesion and support, but also facilitate the recognition of common life issues which are at the heart of the themes to be dealt with in the ongoing group experience. The leader chooses to focus on relevant group themes which reflect areas of unresolved conflict in the lives of group members. Examples of recurrent group discussions include the appropriate expression of strong affect, mainly anger and feelings of intimacy; problems with self-esteem and self-awareness; competitive feelings; "loose ends" or unresolved problems stemming from the families of origin of group members; issues related to personal and professional success and failure; concerns about aspects of sexuality; and the theme of how to incorporate pleasure and excitement into one's life without having to resort to drug use.

Another central goal of any substance abuse group is to teach self-monitoring techniques to the group members. Educational and confrontational elements present in effective substance abuse groups contribute to the enhanced ability of members to prevent relapses by understanding those triggers which place substance abusers at risk to resume drug and alcohol use.

> In a men's cocaine group, Tom, a man with eight months sobriety, reported feeling very "shaky" when he listened to others in the group talk about past drug experiences. Tom realized that romanticized renditions of life on cocaine were stimulating to him and made him aware of a desire to "try using the drug again in a limited way," a feeling which he thought had long disappeared. His acknowledgment of his anxiety was met with a positive reception by all group members who, in turn, noted similar urges in themselves and described the varied ways in which they were currently handling these urges.

The development of problem-solving skills and the acquisition of new, drug-free methods of coping with life issues forms an integral part of every substance abuse group's agenda. As part of the group norm of engaging with, rather than denying, aspects of reality, members help one another with pragmatic problems which have arisen in the course of their addictions. Group members with longer-term sobriety can help new members make plans to repay accumulated debts; decide when would be the most opportune time to return to work; teach them how to account for large portions of their lives which were governed by substance abuse, to prospective employers, friends, and potential romantic partners;

and how best to repair and resuscitate damaged family relationships and friendships.

Leading a Substance Abuse Group

Leaders of drug and alcohol groups begin the group with an early emphasis on similarities, support, and encouragement. This sets the stage for the rapid development of group cohesion, an essential building block in the foundation of any therapeutic group. While motivation for change must originate with the addicted group member, peer support and reinforcement of the patient's positive motivation for change by the group leader are essential elements in the construction of therapeutic group norms.

Support is not unconditional in substance abuse groups. Members and therapists do not condone counter-therapeutic behavior such as lying, irregular attendance, sabotaging maneuvers, questionable sincerity about readiness for change, and frequent lapses back into drug use. All these behaviors are detrimental to the recovery process and to the goals of the substance abuse group and, as such, cannot be rewarded in group. Unconditional acceptance of all behavior by members of substance abuse groups can require the therapist's collusion in a pattern of denial. If this happens, the leader's credibility suffers and dysfunctional defense mechanisms such as excessive use of denial are inadvertently reinforced.

One of the ways in which the group is kept on track toward its goals is by the system of checks and balances which occur through the process of confrontation in the group. Group therapists have to be careful to monitor confrontation to insure that it serves a therapeutic end. Scapegoating of members and character assassination of others are to be scrupulously avoided. Gentle or caring confrontations by leaders and members blend confrontation with genuine concern and allow for a more workable group climate. In this atmosphere, members learn how to express negative feelings in an appropriate and non-damaging way. In addition, the leader who monitors the form and timing of confrontations protects the group from the risk of purging unpopular members or using defenses of projection to avoid dealing with individual issues by attacking them in other group members.

Members of substance abuse groups gain valuable insights as part of the psychotherapeutic experience. The learning which takes place in group therapy occurs on several levels. Experientially, members learn a great deal from being in an ongoing relationship with people in the safe and controlled setting of the group. Feelings of attachment, competition, favoritism, and jealousy are regular experiences for members of these groups.

The subjective recognition and accurate labeling of emotional states is a focus in these groups. As simple as this may appear, it is of critical import in the treatment of people with drug and alcohol problems. Most, if not all, members of the group have had lives governed by the avoidance of dealing with a range of affective states by resorting to substance use to mask the feelings. In early sobriety, substance abusers are no longer in a state of emotional anesthesia and are flooded with emotions which they have historically suppressed, denied or medicated. The astute group leader can help supply an emotional vocabulary for identifying important emotions and then proceed to design alternative ways of handling these feelings without involving the use of substances.

The following striking example occurred in an adult out-patient addiction group:

> Jim, a self-employed businessman, early in recovery from an alcohol and cocaine addiction problem, came to a group session stating that, "I don't know why, but I feel really weird this week. I'm nervous, I can't concentrate, and I just feel out of it." He denied that there was anything he was aware of which could be causing this set of feelings. The group leader asked him to discuss what was going on in his daily life, whereupon Jim said, "Nothing much. Business is good. I saw my internist Tuesday and I'm in good health. I'm getting married on Saturday. I think my brother is coming to visit next month and that's about it."
>
> Upon hearing Jim's presentation, the group burst into laughter. To others, it was obvious that Jim's impending marriage was at the center of what was bothering him. Jim however, was unaware of something as basic as premarital anxiety until the group focused their feedback to him on this specific issue. He was initially unconvinced but when the leader kept the group focus on this issue, Jim was able to realize that many of his fears were mobilized by the prospect of marriage.
>
> He was reminded of his earlier marriage which ended in an ugly divorce which hurt him financially as well as emotionally. He reflected on what a poor marriage his parents had and how he vowed never to reproduce that experience for himself. He was nearing fifty and marrying a woman fifteen years younger who was interested in having children. Jim had two grown daughters from his first marriage and had a strained and distant relationship with them. Consequently, he had strong ambivalent feelings about the prospect of starting a new family even though he loved his fiancée very much.

This vignette illustrates how a group therapy experience can simultaneously supply insight about motivation, personal history, and maladaptive coping mechanisms to a person who is literally unaware of basic factors. In point of fact, despite Jim's initial reluctance to stick with the topic, he described feeling greatly relieved at the end of the session and had a sense that, "Dealing with things directly is not so bad. I feel like a burden is off my shoulders." He left the group meeting with a renewed sense of enthusiasm for his upcoming wedding and asked the group to "Please help me stay on track with this problem and don't let me get away with my old tricks."

While substance abuse groups are excellent vehicles for learning on the affective level, they are not confined to this domain. Cognitive work is a regular part of all addiction groups. Members are helped to deal with irrational beliefs, fears, and unrealistic expectations by learning alternative skills for dealing with the same issues. In addiction groups, poor self-image and low self-esteem are frequent symptoms among group members. The leader can interrupt self-deprecatory statements and re-frame, re-label or supply an alternative way of thinking about oneself. Group members who are serious about sobriety are taught to replace malignant self-labels such as "junkie", "sleaze-ball", "drug dealer", or "degenerate" with the positive and more accurate image of themselves as people with substance abuse problems who are actively working in a recovery program.

Insight-oriented substance abuse groups supply another level of learning for members. Psychodynamically based groups value self-awareness, and structure experiences in ways which maximize the possibility of attaining insight for the members. Both the "here and now," interactions which occur between members in group meetings, and the "there and then," historical events are the substrates upon which the leader bases his or her interventions. In traditional psychodynamically oriented groups, the group parallel of individual psychoanalytically derived principles is in evidence. The liberal use of interpretation, linking present behavior with past experience, and the analysis of transference phenomena as they emerge in the group are generally regular elements of these approaches. In general, psychodynamic work, if done at all, is best done after a stable period of long-term sobriety has been in place and with that sub-group of the addiction-prone population who, like their individual therapy counterparts, are deemed high-functioning enough to benefit from psychodynamic work. While this period of abstinence is variable, a good rule of thumb is that an individual ought to have at least a year of sobriety before potentially stirring up emotions that may endanger sobriety.

Before leaving the subject of goals in group work with substance abusing patients, a word is in order about the special value these groups hold as vehicles for managing affect in members. Intense feelings of anger, rage, depression, fear, despair and desperation frequently propel people into patterns of chronic substance abuse to ease the pain of these intense emotional states. A central goal of any substance abuse intervention is to help people who are struggling with these feelings. Groups offer many options to therapist and patient in the service of this goal.

Group therapy is known for its ability to facilitate the combining of several elements into a technically eclectic treatment model. This is very much in evidence when the group agenda is the appropriate expression and management of affect. Through the incorporation of behavioral techniques such as role playing, assertiveness training, and communication skills training, members can develop an emotional language which helps them understand feelings which would have formerly propelled them to drug and alcohol use.

Since depression, bipolar disorder, and other abnormalities of the regulation of affect are so prevalent among substance users, the capacity of groups for countering demoralization and despair makes them an ideal milieu for people in the throes of extreme states of emotion. Group interaction and identification with others who share similar feelings counters a sense of interpersonal isolation experienced by most people in such states. The tangible demonstration of the universal nature of feelings and the acceptance by others, even when one is not at his or her best, is a powerful force against sinking into deeper depression. For many people, merely being in a group and being respected and valued by peers is a unique experience. Group norms which value self-disclosure, humility, and honesty, and teach that most people are trying to cope with similar psychological and environmental stressors go a long way toward reducing the emotional burden on any substance abusing individual.

Membership in a psychotherapeutically oriented substance abuse group provides a reality-based, positively cast climate of mutuality and collaboration. This stands in sharp contrast to the life experiences of the majority of people whose lives have evolved into a pattern of chronic alcohol and drug abuse. Merely staying in this new climate over time, through participation in psychotherapy and self-help group membership, provides an unparalleled corrective emotional experience for people prone to substance abuse problems.

☐ Stages of the Group Process

All psychotherapy groups pass through definable, often overlapping, stages in their development. A working knowledge of where the group is in its clinical flight path is indispensable information for the leader. Awareness of a group's level of development facilitates the introduction of stage-specific or stage-appropriate interventions by the therapist. The converse is also true. A leader's lack of understanding of where a group is in its course can cause him or her to run the risk of making ill-timed interventions which will have bad repercussions. For example, the leader who encourages forceful member-to-member confrontations before a group has attained a solid sense of group cohesion invites negative psychological sequellae from this experience. Without the emotional "shock absorber" of peer support, which only comes after a group has reached a stage of true cohesiveness, members are essentially unprotected from attack by others. The unfortunate results of leadership errors in failing to recognize the stage of a group's life are seen in increased drop-out rates from treatment, recurrence of psychiatric symptoms, hospitalization of members, and resumption of drug and alcohol use.

The stages through which substance abuse groups progress can be categorized as follows:

1. Crisis management
2. Stabilization
3. Induction into group
4. Establishment of group cohesion
5. Middle or working group stage
6. Transition, termination, and relapse prevention

Each group stage has its own characteristic features. Crisis management forms the initial stage of the substance abuse group because so many people are motivated to seek help during or immediately after a personal crisis. Escalating drug use to the point where hospitalization may be necessary, job loss, breakup of a significant romantic relationship, financial troubles are all crisis states requiring immediate attention. Entry into group helps decelerate escalating patterns of substance abuse and helps fill in for losses recently experienced by the substance dependent person. Once the crisis has passed, the group functions as a stabilizing influence in the lives of its members formerly in crisis. During this stabilization phase, the group therapist relies upon the peer support aspects of the group in order to engage members in therapy and to construct a welcoming group atmosphere. Issues related to the induction into the group relate to establishing trusting relationships, dealing with competition, and maneuvering for favored positions with respect to the group leader.

Group cohesion develops as a result of the interaction among members in the two earlier stages. Greater personal disclosure and higher levels of affect are hallmarks of this stage. Cohesion forms the backdrop against which the working group phase can develop. In many time-unlimited substance abuse groups, the working group phase is the longest and parallels the working-through phase of psychoanalytically oriented individual therapies. It is during this stage that insights gained in the group are applied to life situations outside the group.

Eventually, group participation concludes with a transition and termination stage. Plans for relapse prevention and a review of accomplishments made in the group are two major foci of this stage. Dealing with feelings of loss of the group, separation, and fears of being on one's own are common group themes. Aftercare planning begins with a review of individual members' goals, an assessment of what remains to be done, and concludes with a specific plan to address these issues for each departing member.

The clinician's awareness of the stages of development of substance abuse groups affords a unique channel for the rapid differentiation between normal group and individual "growing pains" and hazardous trends which threaten the viability of the group.

☐ Leadership Considerations in Substance Abuse Groups

Many decisions which influence the success or failure of substance abuse groups face the leader during the course of the group's existence. Group leaders must be clear on the rationale for their choice of approach to any of these clinical management considerations. The following is a representative cross-section of core decisions regarding leadership and membership which arise regularly in the conduct of group therapy for addiction.

Structure and Limit Setting

The group therapist sets the stage for a constructive group experience by supplying a group structure and setting limits for the members. This is particularly important in substance abuse work since so many people with problems of addiction come from families in which appropriate limits were not set and inter-generational boundary lines were not successfully delineated.

The watchwords for group structure are *firmness* and *fairness*. The group norm must be one of total abstinence from all drugs and alcohol. This is a non-negotiable condition for group membership. Failure to have a tight group framework for substance abusers runs the risk of consuming valuable group time with avoidable discussions about recreational or limited drug and alcohol use. Setting the total abstinence ground rule from the outset keeps the group on track and circumvents detours which are merely disguised resistances to the drug-free model.

Group Composition

Many factors have to be taken into account in composing a therapeutic group experience for addicted members. The most important factors are:

Open or Closed Group Membership?

The question to be decided is whether the group goals are best facilitated by having a small nucleus of members and adding members over time or to start and finish the group with the original members only.

The advantage of open membership is that adding members as the group goes along allows for a group that is always of sufficient size if members leave the group because they get better or drop out of therapy. The customary size for out-patient groups is approximately eight members for therapists who work alone and 10 to 12 members for co-led groups. Rapid turnover of membership is a problem in many substance abuse groups. The addictive properties of the drugs themselves, legal problems such as arrest and incarceration which accompany illegal drug use and drug sales, and the tendency of substance abusing patients to use flight and avoidance as defense mechanisms, contribute to a potentially unstable group membership. Advocates of the open membership model feel that these drop-out risks are sufficient to warrant inclusion of new members at any point in the group.

Two caveats to be taken into account when planning to add new members are that the timing must be when there are no acute individual or group crisis situations and not too soon after the departure of a group member. In the former instance, the group is too preoccupied with its internal business to adequately integrate a new member who may feel unwelcome in this climate. The latter circumstance is one where the group needs to work through the feelings connected to the loss of a member, a process which would be obscured by the rapid addition of a replacement member.

Fixed or closed group membership avoids the inevitable disruption of the established group process in order to orient and incorporate a new member. This can be a source of considerable resentment among group members if this experience occurs too frequently. Groups that are far along in their lifespan may reach a point where the addition of new members would require enormous effort by the leader and the group to help the new member understand what has transpired before he or she entered the group. Exponents of the closed group model feel that the expenditure of group time, the fact that a new member has not lived through the stages of group development with the charter members, and the interruption of the progress of the group are all reasons for prohibiting the addition of new members.

Age-related Factors

Age is often a consideration in composing substance abuse groups. Not only is the group homogeneous for drug and alcohol problems but matching the participants by age may facilitate therapeutic goals in selected circumstances. The adolescent substance abuse group is a prototype of the age-specific school of group composition. Restricting the group to adolescents makes it more likely that the issues which come up in group sessions will most closely approximate the external life circumstances of the members.

Since peer-group relationships are central to the experience of all adolescents, an adolescent group provides a therapeutic arena which will mobilize this issue. Groups are helpful in consolidating the normal developmental processes of ego and identity formation in young men and women. Teen-agers are often more receptive to participate in a therapy plan in which they are not the sole focus as in individual or some forms of family therapy. The school and social experiences of adolescents are group experiences, and hence, adolescents have some precedent for being in a group of their contemporaries.

The social aspects of therapy groups overlap with the age-related social concerns which often motivate adolescent substance abuse. Groups allow for healthy experimentation with new behaviors. Adolescents can try out drug-free ways of relating interpersonally and can borrow from the styles, attitudes, and actions of the leader and other group members.

The reasoning just outlined forms the basis for the preference for groups matched for age among members.

Gender Considerations

Homogeneity of group composition also comes into play when thinking about the advisability of having men and women in the same group, particularly in the early stages of the recovery process. Virtually everyone who has a drug problem has also experienced difficulty in forming and maintaining intimate relationships. Mixed (male and female) groups pose the threat of mobilizing social and sexual anxieties which can be overwhelming to a person who is not very far from his or her last drinking or drug episode. In order to concentrate on attaining a stable state of sobriety, it may be advantageous to place substance abusers with high levels of relationship anxiety in a same-sex group.

Same-sex groups remove the added layer of stress which comes from having to interact with opposite sex members and thereby foster the retention of members who might otherwise flee from therapy. Same-sex groups are often protective of members who are early in sobriety. Deprecatory attitudes towards men and women, expressed regularly by members who have unresolved issues in this area, are edited out of the initial group experience by restricting it to an all male or all female model.

A clinical case in point occurred in a men's dual diagnosis group. The majority of men reported that the bulk of their experience with women during their periods of drinking and drugging were with women drug abusers and prostitutes. The prevailing group belief towards women was stated graphically by one man who said he believed, "most women are either drug whores or air-headed alcoholics." This extreme, skewed, and deprecatory attitude was shared by most of the men in the group. It was clear that bringing women into the irrational and hostile group climate with this group of men would be a destructive choice by the group leader.

Alternatively, keeping the group homogeneous for gender allowed the male therapist to address the members' profound discomfort in the presence of women, their excessive concerns about their own sexual inadequacies, and their strong competitive feelings for positions of dominance in the group. None of these issues would have been accessible if women were regular members of the group.

Later in therapy, when long-term sobriety has been attained and members are actually dealing with relationship issues in their lives outside of group, is the point at which mixed-sex groups make more sense.

Solo or Co-Leadership

Leaders of substance abuse groups are charged with many simultaneous tasks. There are many extra-group issues which require the therapist's attention. The family of the group patient also requires periodic attention. Telephone calls, legal problems, letters to agencies or employers, and coordinating group treatment with other therapeutic efforts all make strong demands on the group leader. A leader has to be confrontational and supportive at the same time. The workload can be great and the potential for therapist "burn out" is high. For these reasons, many practitioners of substance abuse groups advocate co-therapy as the preferred leadership form.

Team leadership permits a division of labor in the leading of the group. The presence of two therapists increases the options for identification, interaction, and the exploration of intra-group relationships. In order for co-leadership to maximize its potential, the leaders must function collaboratively. Potential sources of competition such as theoretical orientation, level of experience, age, sex, and professional discipline have to be integrated so that they function synergistically. Co-leaders who respect each other and work cooperatively provide an excellent role model of healthy collaboration between adults.

A form of co-therapy which is uniquely the province of substance abuse is the use of a recovering alcoholic or drug abuser as part of the therapy team. The recovering user/leader occupies a position midway between that of a leader and that of a member. His or her member-like qualities, not the least of which is first-hand experience with life on substances, adds a dimension to the group experience that cannot be supplied by the professional mental health staff.

In order to qualify for this "elder statesperson" role in the group, former substance abusers must have a documented history of at least two years of sobriety. They must also consent to participate in random urine testing. As a further safeguard for the group and for the recovering leader, brief post-group discussions and de-briefings are held with the other therapist after every meeting. This meeting involves a review of the new leader's reaction to the content of the session, plans for future sessions, and a check to see if anything in the group poses a potential threat to the sobriety of the recovering leader.

Conventional leadership by one therapist is certainly a more common mode of leadership in substance abuse groups. The foregoing discussion of the advantages of co-leadership is not meant to imply that drug and alcohol groups cannot be successfully led by one person. The issues identified as prompting a choice of working with a colleague serve as a preventive measure for the leader who works alone. An awareness of the pressures on the leader can help a leader choose a style of leadership which is least likely to result in demoralization or burn-out, owing to the above-noted factors.

Family Involvement

Group therapists must be aware of the family circumstances of every group member. Families are critical to the therapeutic endeavor both for the positive contributions they can make which support sobriety and for the potential some families harbor for undermining the therapeutic alliance and the overall therapeutic effort.

A family interview at a very early point in treatment planning is invaluable in many ways. Substance abusing patients may be poor historians, owing either to lapses in memory, brain damage, or through the habit of engaging in manipulative behavior which distorts the reporting of experience. Seeing the addict with his or her family provides direct observational data about interpersonal and family functioning, both of which are essential to treatment planning for substance abuse problems.

The family is not only an excellent source of historical material but it is a natural group in which the patient has had to function. Understanding the dynamics and patterns in families is directly transferable to making a treatment decision about which group best suits a particular person. Family interviews can often serve as vehicles for enlisting relatives in the service of recruiting resistant drug and alcohol abusers into sorely needed treatment. As noted elsewhere in this text, guided family interventions and the construction of kin networks mobilize powerful intra-familial forces which push the reluctant family member into a rehabilitation program, a core component of which will be a psychotherapy group.

Of course, many addicts and their families will be appropriate for family therapy as well. This subject will be a chapter unto itself later in this text (Chapter 22). For group purposes, the therapist who leads an addiction group also needs to be "family knowledgeable" whether or not family therapy is eventually incorporated into the treatment program. Family dynamics will inevitably unfold in the therapy group and the leader who has had first-hand experience with the families of group members is in a better position to recognize and intervene promptly when family-based issues complicate the recovery process.

Medication Issues

The use of therapeutically prescribed psychotropic medication in conjunction with a psychotherapeutically based plan for recovery has been the source of some controversy historically. The judicious use of specific medication, conservatively prescribed and carefully monitored, has found a place in the treatment of people who not only develop problems of addiction but who are also depressed, have a bipolar disorder, or are psychotic. In addition, medication may be useful in the detoxification/withdrawal phase of treatment for many substances of abuse.

Medication, when employed, is never presented as a substitute for dealing with life's problems or for substance abuse. It is an adjunct to treatment or to help traverse a critical impasse in the recovery process. Medications are prescribed for as brief a time as is clinically warranted and are discussed openly in group sessions. Members who are new to sobriety and those who are engaged in Twelve Step programs frequently question "using one drug to treat another."

This apparent paradox or contradiction has to be clarified immediately. A distinction has to be made between drugs with abuse potential and those designed to treat a targeted psychological symptom or condition. Themes related to medication are present in virtually every group session of groups composed of members whose primary adaptation to handling stressful life events was to resort to the use of chemical substances. Group members are encouraged to express all feelings about medication, including the fact that many may see it as an unnecessary crutch or abdication of personal responsibility for one's recovery.

Coordination of Therapy

The concurrent use of group therapy along with AA meetings, individual, family or couples therapy is commonplace. When group therapy is the hub of the therapeutic wheel, the group leader is responsible for coordinating all treatment efforts to see that there is minimal duplication of services and to insure that each intervention reinforces the overall treatment goals.

Observation of a patient's functioning in a therapy group is very useful in determining what other needs have to be addressed which are beyond the scope of the therapy group. Contacts or conversations with others involved in a group member's program is essential. This can be done on an infrequent basis if the patient is doing relatively well or can be increased during times of crisis. Communication between therapists guards against splitting defenses used by substance abusers who have personality disorders and attempt to disempower their therapists by playing one off against the other.

On occasion, group members may require an in-patient stay in a rehabilitation center or in a psychiatric hospital. The group leader discusses this possibility with group members in the pre-group orientation and has a plan in place should the occasion arise where a member has to be hospitalized directly from the group.

Hospitalization of group members is considered when there is a pattern of recurrent "slips" which are unresponsive to management in the group alone; in cases where the familial and social circumstances of the user are highly reinforcing of continued drug use and when the possibility of a severe withdrawal state exists. Groups can be very supportive and instrumental in convincing a member of the need for an in-patient stay. When geographical circumstances permit, the hospitalized member is told that he or she is welcome to come to group meetings while in the hospital and that he or she may re-join the group upon discharge.

Extra-group Contact Among Members

One form of peer networking possible in the early stage of group development is the establishment of a telephone network among members.

The purpose of exchanging phone numbers is so that members who feel tempted to resume drug use can call a fellow group member as an alternative. These phone contacts are discussed openly in the next group session and their significance is explored.

The issue of actual personal contact outside of group meetings is more complex. Traditional wisdom in psychodynamic group psychotherapy has been for the leader to prohibit extra-mural socializing among group members. Historically, the rationale for this approach has been to force the interactions between members into the group where it is available for observation and analysis and to prevent "acting out" by members of the same group. Getting together for social, sexual, or drug-taking purposes runs counter to the norms of the group.

While this stance of prohibiting outside contact may work for traditional exploratory psychotherapy groups, it probably is not directly applicable to substance abuse groups for many reasons. First, because most group members attend self-help groups, they may already be used to seeing one another outside of group in a context that promotes sobriety. Telling them to stop this contact gives a very confusing message. Second, the notion that if the group leader prohibits contact, then members actually do not see each other outside of group is also naive. Many people who enter group, whether substance abusers or not, have significant problems with authority. These members are likely to test or break the rules of the group as a way of enacting their conflicts. What the authoritarian or parental leader who "forbids" contact outside of group actually gets is not compliance but secrecy or silence. Members who are so inclined do what they want and edit out the reporting of these experiences in group sessions. This is certainly an untenable therapeutic situation.

As an alternative, it has proven more productive in adult groups to base the therapeutic contract and therapist-patient relationship on trust and honesty rather than on the prohibition or sanctioning of specific behavior. In this way, everything from the group member's life is open for examination in group. This includes contacts outside the group, lapses back into substance use, or anything else which might be embarrassing or uncomfortable.

When the group leader adopts a respectful, non-judgmental stance, it is easier both for the patient to voluntarily disclose difficult material and for the therapist to take an understanding and collaborative posture in dealing with the information disclosed. The leader aligns with that part of the member which is making healthy efforts to change and is wrestling with firmly entrenched habits to the contrary. The therapist's agenda is to understand the patient and to share his or her insights with the patient in order to help the patient gain self-awareness.

Confidentiality

Confidentiality is a cornerstone of all therapies but takes on added meaning in group therapy since a patient reveals himself or herself not only to a therapist but to other group members. Members of substance abuse groups come from all walks of life and are united in group therapy only because they share a common problem of addiction. It is impossible to know the breadth and intricacies of the interpersonal connections of members of the same therapy group. Because many of the drugs of abuse are illegal, confidentiality in groups is all the more essential.

Participants in substance abuse groups need to be encouraged to put a premium on confidentiality. Negative impact on a member's employment, public image, and family relationships can all be initiated by breaches of confidential information shared in the therapy group. In addiction groups, failure to adhere to the group contract regarding confidentiality is grounds for dismissal from the group.

The group leader has to make clear the difference between taking lessons learned in group and applying them to life outside the group, and "gossip" about what well-known person is a member of the group. Anonymity of members must be preserved if group members discuss anything related to their group experience with friends, co-workers, or family members. Stating to a spouse that, "A lot of people in my group want to drink as a way of squelching their angry feelings. I think I do that too" is a constructive transfer of information learned in group. It is not a violation of confidentiality. Whereas, "Guess which actor is in my group?" is a breach of confidentiality.

It is not possible to expect essential self-disclosure from members unless the group climate is safe. Insuring tight confidentiality standards is one of the measures leaders take to construct a trusting group atmosphere.

☐ Alternative Group Therapies

Twelve Step programs have been enormously successful since their inception. AA is not, however, a "cure all" for every patient with an addiction. The dropout and failure rate is quite high. Research suggests that those who successfully affiliate with AA are in general middle-class, cognitively rigid, prone to guilt, and socially stable. Their alcoholism is more likely to be chronic and episodes of loss of control are frequent. Although the spiritual dimension of AA is often downplayed, in many instances, some of the emphasis on loss of control and higher power may not sit well with certain individuals. The adage used by clinicians that AA "works for those for whom it works" is true.

A group format is a very useful one—especially in dealing with something as pervasive as an addiction. Fortunately, there are alternatives available for those who wish to deal with their addiction in a group setting, but do not want to attend twelve step meetings, or have not found them helpful.

The following are intended to be a description of five common and easily available alternative groups. This list is by no means exhaustive and is intended to provide a description of at least some of the options available. These groups are less available on a national basis than the older, better established, and more common Twelve Step groups. At least one prominent researcher suggests to her addicted patients that if they are really motivated, they may start their own self-help group. This demonstrates the principle that the best way to really learn something is to teach it. While daunting, founding such a group might in fact be enormously helpful to an individual suffering from addictions.

The following are brief descriptions of the origin, philosophy, and mechanics of a number of alternative groups. Again this is not intended to be an exhaustive list of all alternative groups, but rather a sampling of the origin, mechanics and philosophy of a number of alternatives to Twelve Step meetings. Contact information is given after each brief description. These are the most up to date telephone numbers and web site adresses at the time of writing. Given the frequent changes in some of these groups, the numbers may not be up to date in the near future. The reader is advised to consult any web search engine for more up to date information.

Rational Recovery

This group was founded in 1985 by Jack Trimpey, LCSW, to provide a rational, not spiritual, approach to recovery. Trimpey was dissatisfied with the emphasis on giving up the autonomy he found at AA, so he wanted to create an alternative. The principles of Rational Recovery (RR) were originally based upon Albert Ellis's Rational Emotive Therapy (RET). These ideas evolved into Addictive Voice Recognition Technique (AVRT). The goal of RR is lifetime abstinence. In essence, AVTR is the recognition that certain cognitive processes lead to relapse. Recognizing this voice (the "beast" as it is called in RR terms) allows the participant to change his or her thought patterns. RR philosophy emphasizes the control an individual possesses over certain functions related to substance abuse and relapse. For example "I may not have control over every urge or desire to drink, but I do have control over whether or not I pick up the drink, put it to my lips, and swallow."

The original RR format consisted of meetings which were sometimes held several times a week. In recent years, this copyrighted and privately owned enterprise has shifted its emphasis towards publishing educational materials. Meetings can still be found throughout the country, and some empirical data exist to demonstrate that this is an effective therapeutic tool. However, in recent years, the group has suffered some internal dissention. A distinct but similar group (SMART Recovery, described below) has adopted many of the original principles of RR.

Contact:
Rational Recovery Systems (RR)
Box 800
Lotus, CA 95651
916-621-4374, 800-303-CURE (voice)
916-621-2667 (voice and fax)
rr@rational.org
http://www.rational.org/recovery

Self Management and Recovery Training: SMART Recovery

This is an outgrowth of what was once known as Rational Recovery. It has changed its name since the middle 1990s because of some well-documented disagreements with the founder but has attempted to maintain the original focus of RR, emphasizing the importance of groups. The SMART program is consistent with a cognitive-behavioral model which describes addiction as an example of maladaptive behavior. SMART's philosophy is that addictive behaviors exist along a spectrum of severity. For some individuals for whom the substance or activity has achieved a maladaptive pattern, abstinence, or at least a trial of abstinence, is warranted.

There are four guiding principles to the SMART program: (a) motivational maintenance and enhancement, (b) effective urge coping, (c) rational thinking, and (d) lifestyle balance. Different coping techniques, based upon cognitive behavioral research, are taught. Meetings can be open (anyone is welcome) or closed (only those involved with the program are involved), and typically occur once per week. The beginning of the meeting involves a presentation and discussion revolving around the cognitive distortions or mistaken ideas that lead to a continuation of the addiction. An informal discussion among all attendees follows. These groups seem to be most successful for those individuals who use "higher" level psychological defenses, especially intellectualization, in their lives. Individuals who have difficulty with authority or who may be opposed to the twelve-step concept of powerlessness are also likely to do well in these groups.

Contact:
S.M.A.R.T. Recovery (SMART)
24000 Mercantile Road, Suite 11
Beachwood, Ohio 44122
216-292-0220 (voice)
216-831-3776 (fax)
SRMail1@aol.com

Women For Sobriety (WFS)

Jean Kirkpatrick, Ph.D. founded this group in 1976. She had a long history of problematic drinking and found it very difficult to maintain sobriety, despite numerous attempts at treatment and faithful AA attendance. She believed that AA was effective for men with drinking problems, and the recounting of the sometimes horrific stories provided incentive not to relapse. However, for some women the experience was different and less helpful, because recounting the humiliations which occurred while drinking only lead to further problems in self-esteem regulation. Kirkpatrick was influenced by the self-reliance literature of Emerson, Thoreau, and the Unity Church. The philosophy of WFS is based on self-reliance, and the recognition that the building of self-esteem is extremely difficult for women in our society.

Meetings are coordinated by a facilitator who has been certified and is familiar with the group's literature and philosophy. Meetings are open to all women alcoholics. Newcomers are given a packet of information about the group and its philosophy. The tone of the meetings is supportive and non-judgemental. The groups emphasize the difficulties of dealing with sexism and the particular concerns of women who recognize the need to maintain sobriety. Discussions are usually centered around the 13 items in the "New life Acceptance Program." This group is probably most appropriate for women who have been successful in initial stages of sobriety but need help in building self-esteem to prevent relapse.

Contact:
Women for Sobriety (WFS)
P.O. Box 618
Quakertown, PA 18951-0618
215-536-8026 (voice and fax)
WFSobriety@aol.com
http://www.mediapulse.com/wfs

Men For Sobriety (MFS)

This is a relatively new group, also founded by Dr. Kirkpatrick. Its creation was a result of repeated requests to form an organization for men similar to WFS. Since 1994, it has been growing, though membership is still limited. The basic principles are also based on self-reliance and self-esteem, with a focus on those issues that are particularly pertinent to men.

Contact:
See contact information for WFS.

Moderation Management (MM)

MM was founded in 1993 by Audrey Kishline to support individuals who wish to limit their alcohol consumption. She reported that at times her use of alcohol was out of control but in her later years, she was able to moderate it. Finding almost no support for this belief but resolute in her own experience, she founded MM for those individuals who are having difficulty maintaining sobriety.

The program of MM consists of nine steps which basically include a resolve to examine the individual's drinking pattern, its effects, and its consequences. The program also includes a commitment to abstain from alcohol for the first 30 days of the program. The most problematic drinkers, those who cannot keep from alcohol for a month, are weeded out. Meetings are led by a monitor and are kept at an educational, open-minded, and supportive level.

Contact:
Moderation Management (MM)
P.O. Box 6005
Ann Arbor, MI 48106
612-512-1484

Secular Organization for Sobriety/Save Ourselves (SOS)

James R. Christopher is a self-identified alcoholic who had been sober since 1978. He found that because of his skepticism of religion and spirituality, he went from being a guilty and fearful alcoholic to a guilty and fearful sober person in AA. His experiences coalesced into an article published in Free Inquiry, a secular humanist journal, in which he detailed his experiences and his path to sobriety. Christopher was uncomfortable with the AA approach and preferred to maintain his sobriety through personal responsibility and self-reliance. The article was met with a tremendous response. This popular reaction prompted Christopher to found SOS. Its first meeting was held in 1986, and the organization has grown exponentially since then. Like AA, it is anonymous and accepts no outside sponsorship or donations, but relies on modest support from members. Unlike AA, it eschews sponsorship, believing people are responsible for their own sobriety and that members should all approach each other as equals.

Meetings are full of discussion and education promoting scientific knowledge about alcoholism and emphasizing personal responsibility for abstinence. The SOS program is offered as a suggested strategy which may be useful for some people in achieving and maintaining abstinence, its primary goal. Studies done on the SOS program indicate that it is well received by attendees, and most find it helpful. The chief complaint is, like many of the other alternative groups, meetings are not as frequent or as easy to find as AA.

Contact:
Secular Organizations for Sobriety/Save Ourselves (SOS)
5521 Grosvenor Blvd
Los Angeles, CA 90066
310-821-8430 (voice)
310-821-2610 (fax)
http://www.codesh.org/sos/

☐ Summary

Groups have enjoyed a position of prominence in the field of substance abuse. The broad applicability of groups and the ease of adaptation of many different treatment philosophies into the group milieu has led to an expansion of group work with alcohol and drug problems. What is emerging from these efforts is a greater understanding of the role groups can play and what contributes to the unique benefits offered by groups which are soundly composed, thoughtfully led, and clear in their sense of direction.

Every indication points to the fact that this trend is expanding and that groups will continue to play a central part in the comprehensive treatment of substance abuse. With increasing numbers of people seeking treatment for drug and alcohol related problems, groups are even more likely to be called upon to meet the special needs and address the clinical challenges posed by this segment of the population.

22

CHAPTER

Family Therapy

Often the treatment of the family, one or more members of which may have a substance abuse problem is desirable. Such treatment allows the clinician to see the entire family as a unit, and the substance abuse problem as serving a "function," albeit a destructive one, within the family unit. The first stage of this type of treatment is suggesting, and then covincing, the essential members of the unit to come to treatment in the first place. Such engagement, and scheduling, can be considered part of the initial phase.

Family influences have long been valued by psychotherapists of diverse theoretical persuasions. Therapists who work with issues related to drug and alcohol abuse are keenly aware of the central role played by families in the genesis and maintenance of substance abuse problems in their members. Family therapists subscribe to the premise that in order to create a successful plan for recovery, the family must be actively involved in the process.

The focus of this chapter will be to provide an overview of how the therapist evaluates a family and decides when family therapy is indicated, and to discuss some of the pragmatic issues involved in the actual conduct of family therapy when addiction is the presenting symptom in a family member.

General Principles of Family Intervention

The concept that alcohol and drug abuse are symptoms that express the final common pathway derived from the interplay of genetic, behavioral, familial, environmental, socio-cultural, ethnic, economic and other variables, is the most popular view of these conditions from a family therapy standpoint. The emphasis given to any of these factors shapes the form of family intervention chosen and relates directly to the theoretical orientation of the practitioner.

In general terms, the prevailing approaches in contemporary family therapy are systems-derived techniques. The family is seen as a closed system and the current behavioral manifestations or "problems" in the family are a result of the interaction of all members of the family system. Although styles of intervention may vary, all family therapists regard the whole family system as "the patient." In this orientation, substance abuse is viewed as one of many symptoms of family disruption.

An appreciation of the substance abuse symptom, its point of emergence in the family life cycle, and its "function" in terms of maintaining the family homeostasis are considered most important to the family therapist. The pharmacological and physiological properties of the substances involved, while important, are relegated to secondary roles in creating a treatment plan that involves the family.

Generally speaking, the treatment philosophy of clinicians who work with families where substance abuse is the current family symptom is to design a treatment model that is brief, pragmatically oriented, emphasizes family process more than content; looks for adaptive and maladaptive behavioral patterns in the family system; and requires that the therapist be active in formulating diagnoses, setting treatment contracts, hypothesizing about relevant family interactions, and assigning out-of-session tasks that address relevant family dynamics which hinder change in a positive direction.

Initial-Phase Issues

The overriding goals of the first phase of family work are to make a comprehensive evaluation of a family system and to formulate a treatment plan that considers all family members. Family therapy aims to make a plan of abstinence that the family can support the addict in maintaining consistently. In order to accomplish this, the clinician has to adhere to several general guidelines.

Communication with the family has to be clear and direct. This serves not only as a role model for effective communication but also helps to achieve family compliance in the treatment plan. The clearer the clinician's formulation of a method of evaluation and treatment, the greater the likelihood for success in both these areas. The ability to be active in providing structure and setting limits for the therapeutic experience is essential. A therapist who is flexible and has an integrated point of view about substance abuse therapies stands the best chance of engaging families in therapy.

The clinician's knowledge of the family over time serves as a road map for deciding which family members to include in sessions as therapy progresses. A general therapeutic climate of support, clarity, firmness, fairness and availability on the therapist's part sets the stage for a positive working alliance with the family. When these essential ingredients are present, the realistic pre-therapy expectations for success are heightened in both the clinician and family members.

Evaluation of the Family

The initial stage of family therapy for drug and alcohol abuse begins with the evaluation of the family. Although observation is the cornerstone of this process, it is an observational stance borne out of active interaction and exchange with the family. Starting with the initial interview, the therapist is both participant in and witness to the family's mode of relating to the world. A wealth of data emerges from this process and has to be quickly synthesized by the therapist. It is essential, therefore, to have an organized evaluation plan that concentrates on aspects of family structure and function relating to the substance abuse problem.

A useful evaluation phase model assesses the family along the following parameters: (a) family structure, (b) diagnostic issues, (c) family strengths, and (d) drug issues per se.

Family Structure

Evaluating the family structure refers to an appreciation of how the particular family deals with universal aspects of family life. Boundary issues, role assignments, coalitions, enmeshment, triangulation, limit setting, and communication patterns are some of the central components of family structure that relate to treatment planning. Most families where substance abuse is the presenting problem have trouble with one or more of these aspects of family structure.

For practical purposes, some family therapists seek information about family structure by assigning the in-session task of constructing a genogram (McGoldrick & Gerson, 1985). This family map provides information across at least three generations of the family and adds an historical perspective to the evaluation of the family in the present. Genograms concretize the dimensions of family structure and identify important alliances, splits, or boundary blurring in families, all of which will be relevant in setting treatment goals which are most specific to the family being evaluated.

Whether through a process of gathering direct observational data or combining it with specific techniques such as the genogram, the effective family evaluation results in a three-dimensional family picture which lends itself to immediate translation into a treatment plan.

Kaufman (1985) has developed a typology of family structure with substance abuse which facilitates the transfer of information gained in the evaluation into actual treatment. Using his schema, families are classified using the yardstick of their degree of reactivity to the substance abuse problem. The categories of family structure as defined in this system include: functional, enmeshed, disintegrated and absent families. The first group, which Kaufman termed "functional," has a state of equilibrium which is based on avoidance of open family conflict. For these families, short-term family therapy with an educational, cognitive, and behavioral slant is recommended. An emphasis on family roles and rules, coupled with an avoidance of uncovering or insight-oriented techniques rounds out the treatment philosophy. Established family defenses of denial and emotional isolation are respected rather than challenged once the substance abuse has ceased.

Enmeshed families form the major group for whom family therapy is the treatment of choice. These families are highly reactive, levels of affect are more dramatic than with functional families, and the tendency for relapse is high. Consequently, family therapy strives for rapid control over substance use but expects that the intra-familial structure and dynamics are such that repetitive, dysfunctional patterns are likely to reappear during the course of therapy.

Flexibility in forming a treatment plan is a sine qua non with enmeshed families. Aspects of cognitive and behavioral methods are useful first-stage efforts geared to attaining drug abstinence, but definitive treatment requires attention to systemic issues in the family through structural or strategic family therapy approaches. The inclusion of external support through attendance at Twelve Step meetings aids in the disengagement phase of therapy with enmeshed families.

Disintegrated families show the scars of deteriorated family functioning over time. These apparently disconnected families and marriages have often been assisted in their downfall by the catastrophic interpersonal side effects of chronic substance abuse. It is hard to evaluate the degree of involvement in families that act as though there are no remaining family ties. Family approaches with this group begin with rehabilitative efforts directed toward the individual substance abuser, followed by exploration and appraisal of family structure. Reconstitution of the family is not a goal of the first phase of therapy. Once the family evaluation is complete, treatment decisions center on family therapy to attempt reconnection among disengaged members, or other agendas such as brief family therapy designed to consolidate effective separation among family members.

Absent families show no overt connection between the substance abuser and the original family, and an absence of major relationships of an emotional sort outside the family. Supportive and social therapies utilizing non-family networks (AA, church groups, etc.) have both rehabilitative and affiliative goals simultaneously. This approach may ultimately pave the way for a renewed basis for resumption of marital and family relationships in the future.

"Diagnostic" Issues

Family therapists do not use individual diagnostic terms as in the traditional model represented by the DSM-IV. The focus in therapy is on the *identified problem* rather than the *identified patient*. In other words, family therapists are more concerned with answering the question "what is the nature of the problem?" as opposed to "who has the problem?" As an example, the phenomenon of scapegoating of a family member serves to show the different use of diagnosis in family therapy as contrasted to other therapies.

In families where conflict is detoured through a symptomatic family member who becomes the family scapegoat, the family therapist has a specific set of diagnostic concerns. Therapists are interested in the significance of detouring as it reflects aspects of family functioning. (Detouring is the family therapy equivalent of displacement. It refers to "assigning" a given suggestion to another members of the family unit.) For instance, is the detouring protective of family members or is it used to attack others in the family? Detouring which is "protective" of family members as an avoidance of dealing directly with family issues is more commonly seen in families where one member has psychosomatic symptoms. Detouring through scapegoating in an attacking and hostile fashion is more often observed among families where substance abuse problems such as heroin addiction is present. Family therapists do not regard scapegoating as evidence of the presence of masochistic personality disorder in the scapegoated member as individually oriented therapists might.

Other important variables which augment a diagnostic understanding of families have to do with culture, race, ethnicity, and socioeconomic status. Family life-cycle issues need to be taken into account to see if the present family addiction crisis is in response to an event in the life of the family such as a death of a family member, a period where young adult children are leaving home, or concerns about the viability of the parental marriage. Any or all of these elements can be stimuli for the emergence or recrudescence of drug and alcohol problems.

In principle, diagnostic assessment of families with a substance-dependent member is multi-factorial, placing the largest emphasis on systemic issues and decentralizing aspects of individual phenomenology. Family-based treatments follow this diagnostic paradigm and intervene at the level of the family as a system with a teleological view that drug and alcohol abuse are symptoms of family dysfunction.

Family Strengths

One risk of holding a diagnostic focus too heavily weighted toward the evaluation of dysfunction in families is the tendency to ignore or undervalue family assets. Elucidation and recognition of family strengths can be a difficult task. In families where there has been significant drug and alcohol abuse there is usually co-existing a strain or rupture of family ties. Parents often tire of bailing their children out of the legal, social, educational and financial problems accumulated by chronic substance abuse patterns. Similarly, adult children resent being lectured to about their behavior in a way which they feel belies their chronological age and demeans them. The common result is a family in need of therapy, but very disconnected from what positive attributes of the family remain intact.

The therapist has to actively pursue evidence of constructive forces within the family. Many families with an addicted member have their first therapeutic contact during a point where the user has "hit bottom" or gone public with a confession of drug use to one or more members of the family. Anger, demoralization, mistrust, fear, and frustration are first-line responses in most families. Emotional depletion characterizes the entry posture of families in these circumstances. This is a most difficult climate within which to try to gain a sense of the strengths of a family.

Nevertheless, the therapist has to evaluate the natural resources present in the family, for they are the elements which the family brings to bear in trying to solve problems in areas where they are currently at an impasse. One easy way to obtain this information to take the focus of the meeting out of the present and ask the family how things used to be before the substance abuse issue was a problem for them. Casting the question in historical rather than current terms allows family members to be less consumed with strong emotions of the moment and, instead, be more reflective in thinking about better times when family strengths were not camouflaged by substance abuse.

The discovery and delineation of true family strengths allows the therapist to take an enthusiastic and positive approach to a treatment which will rely heavily on the family's shared resources. Identification and labeling of strengths helps counter feelings of depression and despair and gives the family a firm basis for the expectation that change for the better is possible through family treatment.

Drug Issues

Evaluation of the family is best done in an atmosphere where common sense and clinical judgment prevail. Despite a preference for a systems-oriented approach to family problems, astute clinicians realize that there are properties of the drugs themselves and their patterns of use which must also be understood and incorporated into any plan of family therapy. In the case of a family that is being evaluated where an adult child is admitting to excessive cocaine use, several specific questions must be asked as part of the initial family assessment. Much, if not all, of this information can be obtained in the initial interview with the family.

In this particular case, the relevant drug issues are: the route of cocaine administration (e.g., snorting, free-basing, or intravenous use); the duration of drug use; the physical effects (positive and negative) on the user; prior treatment efforts; major mood changes while on cocaine; and the means by which cocaine use was financed. Whether cocaine was used by itself or in combination with other substances, most notably marijuana, alcohol, or heroin, is another core drug-evaluation issue.

Taking a drug history with the family present requires tact and skill on the part of the therapist. Feelings of guilt, embarrassment, anger, and shame influence the type of drug information furnished by the abuser in front of his or her family. The therapist must be sensitive but persistent in pursuing information related to drug use. An accurate approximation of the extent and type of drug use is essential to any plan for family therapy.

The Initial Treatment Contract in Family Therapy

The desired end of a first family interview is the formulation and presentation of an initial contract for treatment. Creation of the therapeutic contract involves several important elements. An initial plan for gaining control over the use of drugs and alcohol is the cornerstone of a universal initial contract. In attempting to achieve an early abstinence plan, the therapist must make sure to include all family members in the process in order to circumvent the pitfall of inadvertently supporting the family's view that only the substance abusing member is in need of therapy. This dovetails with another initial contract goal: redefining the problem as a family issue. Redefinition of the problem puts it into a therapeutically workable form. It permits the family to be proactive in determining their treatment course by inviting their suggestions and participation in goal-setting discussions. The initial contract works well when it acknowledges the family's priorities and incorporates them into any plan for therapy. Goals have to be agreed upon by family members, and if disputes about goals arise, these become the focus of the early phase of family therapy.

Just as initial goals are negotiated through family discussion, the ongoing treatment contract is also viewed as flexible and open to modification as family therapy progresses. The use of outside support groups is an example of a decision that must be made when initial family therapy sessions indicate a need for additional resources outside the family.

The initial treatment contract should include a brief orientation segment which helps the family understand the basic premise of family therapy and outlines the ground rules for family sessions. The former emphasizes the need for all family members to contribute to the treatment process, to make themselves available for meetings, and to participate in a productive manner. The latter concerns itself with the logistics of treatment. Matters of format, including length and frequency of sessions, fees, location of meetings, and any other procedural issues are presented to the family at this time.

A well-conducted initial treatment contracting session results in a family that is prepared to understand and participate in family therapy. They view the therapy as practical and problem-focused, occurring in a relatively short-term format which requires active family involvement for the realization of mutually agreed upon, positive, and achievable goals.

Sequencing the Events in Family Therapy

Determining appropriate treatment priorities is pivotal in family work with problems of substance abuse. Sequencing of treatment events can enhance or destroy a treatment plan. Clinical experience suggests some rules of thumb which are applicable to the family therapy of drug and alcohol abuse and are acceptable to families in treatment.

As previously noted, delineating a plan for abstinence is the first event in therapy. Next, the early treatment focus involves some aspect of the family's chief complaint in the "here and now." This can be accomplished by starting treatment with the whole family of origin present in the first session. Attention is centered on the identified problem, which is worked on until its resolution is complete. Plans to work on marital or other family issues are deferred until the presenting problem is well under control.

This format suggests working on family issues related to substance abuse first. Once abstinence is achieved and maintained over some time, then other non-drug related family issues which have arisen in sessions can be fruitfully addressed. In an enmeshed family with a heroin-abusing child, the therapy is doomed if the sequence does not start with addressing the family of origin before tackling the marital problems which inevitably ensue in families where the heroin abuser is incompletely separated from his or her parents.

Treatment of this type stresses treating the family first, and viewing the substance abuser's father and mother primarily as parents and secondarily as spouses. Family therapy addresses the extra-familial relationships of the substance abuser after the family has resolved the issue of "releasing" him or her from the primary family attachments. In families where the substance abuser lives at home, the sequence of treatment priorities proceeds from abstinence, to construction of an independent work or educational plan, and perhaps to the eventual quest for an autonomous living situation outside of the familial home.

Treatment priorities and sequencing of therapeutic events must be constantly monitored by the therapist in order to keep the family engaged in therapy and to provide a meaningful treatment.

Composition of the Family Session

A common concern for the family therapist is which members to include in sessions. One way to simplify this task is to meet as many of the extended family members as possible, as soon as possible. In this way, the therapist has a glimpse of the full range of players who might participate in family therapy. The choice of who actually attends ongoing meetings should be made by the therapist, not the family.

The current family circumstances and the nature of the problem being addressed in therapy are two determining factors in choosing the participants at any point in family therapy. Family circumstances such as a child who is away at school or works in another state may preclude their participation on an immediate basis. If, however, the presence of this family member is essential to the therapeutic endeavor then sessions can be scheduled at time when that family member will be able to attend. The nature of the problem often dictates the people needed in the session to resolve it. In a family with young children, parents who are experiencing sexual difficulties should be seen alone as long as sexuality is the focus of therapy. When issues of parenting, collaboration, or limit setting come to the fore, then it makes sense to see the parents "in action" with their children.

In surveying the family landscape of the substance abuser, the clinician looks at the extended family and the influential subsystems within it. Siblings, for example, a commonly under-addressed segment of the family of a person with a substance abuse problem, can be extremely influential in supporting or sabotaging family therapy plans. Care must be taken in considering whether or not the presence of a sibling is necessary for the realization of treatment goals. Siblings who are also enmeshed within the family and who may themselves be drug users differ from those who are supportive of the substance user and can shore up initial treatment gains in other family members.

The presentation of therapy to the family is of critical significance in their ultimate recruitment. The therapist who delivers a non-blaming, impartial message to the family, coupled with the recognition that the focus of early sessions will be on the substance abuse problem, stands the best chance of successfully involving most family members.

☐ Middle-Phase Issues

Gaining Entry into the Family System

When efforts to involve the family are successful, the therapist must contend with their struggle between the forces for sameness and familiarity versus a co-existing desire for change. A common manifestation of this ambivalence arises in therapy when the therapist attempts to affiliate with the family. This effort is aimed at gaining entry into the family system in order to have the therapeutic leverage needed for therapy to progress.

At first, the therapist respects family defenses and avoids excessive confrontation. The family therapist looks for an opening in the family system which will allow him or her to join with the family. Joining with the family in this context means supporting the existing family structure and trying to enlist it in the service of change in a therapeutic direction. The therapist will use his or her alliances with different family members to effect change by shifting the balance in the family system. Lending support to a weak or peripheral father helps bolster him and reinstate his position in the family. In a similar vein, the therapist rapidly attempts to work with the parents to get them to align with each other in helping their drug-dependent child. In so doing, efforts to restore weakened generational boundaries are reinforced and the seeds of healthier family structure are planted.

The therapist has to be in charge of family sessions in order to give the therapy a direction and to keep it on course. Destructive family exchanges must be limited and viable alternative models of communication must be supplied. This process takes many forms. Reframing changes the labels put on objectionable behavior and converts it to a more acceptable and workable form. For example, blame, complaining, and criticism are relabeled as manifestations of concern and apprehension by family members. The therapist's insistence that family members confine their discussion to the present is another means of interrupting unproductive family communication in which a litany of past complaints are used to build a case against another family member. These kinds of simple interventions block the perpetuation of habitual dysfunctional family communication patterns which only serve to alienate others.

Management of Resistance

Resistance in family therapy refers to those emotions and actions which serve to prevent change. Resistances vary in the forms they take and the times at which they appear in therapy. Identifying resistant forces and creating effective plans for their management constitutes the bulk of the work in the middle phase of family therapy with substance abusing patients.

The most basic resistance encountered in families with a drug- or alcohol-dependent member is the outright refusal on the part of the user to participate in any therapy. Under these conditions, the most productive use of family resources is to employ these resources in the construction of an organized family or network intervention.

The extreme use of denial emerges as a central resistance in family therapy with substance abusers. A family's need to appear "normal" in the eyes of others, coupled with their sense of shame and failure in having an addicted person in their group, increases the tendency to use minimization and denial as coping mechanisms. Recognizable forms of denial can be seen when the family is involved in excessive intellectualization, rationalization, and incessant social chatter which prevents the focus of the session from moving into anxiety-laden areas. Editing the reporting of events and deliberately concealing information is another form of resistance. The net effect of these resistances is to slow down or sabotage therapeutic efforts.

In response, the family therapist can utilize several avenues to make inroads in managing resistance to change. Educational efforts designed to increase awareness about substance abuse issues and to de-stigmatize drug and alcohol problems is a useful first step. In families where denial is more intractable, more active intervention is necessary. Deliberate intensification of family patterns by in-session amplification covers an array of techniques used by family therapists who work from strategic and structural family therapy models. The maneuvers push family defenses to dramatic, often absurd levels which make them so visible in sessions that they are no longer deniable by the family.

Experiential and actualization techniques, such as family sculpting, psychodrama, the use of metaphors and paradox, and the assignment of tasks, are central to the process of overcoming denial resistances in families. All these techniques are selected on the basis of their capacity to create states of emotional intensity, heightened affect, and experiential learning in family members who avoid such states.

Excessive blaming, scapegoating, and attempts to disempower the therapist by either questioning his or her competence or trying to hook the therapist into established family patterns where the family, not the therapist, is in control, are other avenues of resistance which require vigilant monitoring throughout the course of therapy.

Since depressive symptoms are common among drug and alcohol users, the therapist has to be alert to the misuse of these symptoms in the service of resistance to sobriety. Defeating the therapeutic effort by resorting to postures of extreme hopelessness, pessimism, despair, and open hostility are instances of amplified "garden variety" resistances which are prominent in substance abusing families.

Management of Crisis Situations

Crises in the families of drug and alcohol abusers are of two kinds: spontaneous or planned. Spontaneous crisis situations are a virtual certainty in substance abuse work, and family therapy is not exempt from this phenomenon. Most often the crisis centers around lapses into resumption of drug and alcohol use. It is essential for the therapist to understand the familial context within which the relapse takes place. In the middle phase of family therapy, a crisis often develops in reaction to changes which are evolving through therapy. Using this premise, the therapist can view a crisis situation as a set of behaviors whose aim is to restore the family balance back to an earlier, more familiar state. The therapist's goal is to decode the meaning of the crisis and harness its power as a force for learning and change for the family. In order to reach this goal, it is essential to keep the crisis confined to the immediate family so that it can be worked on in sessions.

Crisis situations are well-known to families of substance abusers and for many families they are a way of life. The job for the therapist is to design a plan which uses the crisis situation as a catalyst for change. This is a time when a family can be activated and can be mobilized toward the goal of resolving the current crisis. When the therapist takes this position, then several ordinary steps which are often resorted to during times of crisis have to be deferred for the moment to enable the family to have the necessary time together to work on crisis resolution. If the family is separated by hospitalizing the member in crisis, or if angry parents banish the user from their home, they lose the opportunity to experience their own competence as a family working toward a common goal. When possible, it is better to try to help the family use their strengths to develop the skills they need not only to resolve the current crisis but to be better prepared to deal with critical situations after therapy is over.

Relapses into substance abuse are not the only crises that regularly occur in treatment. Other behaviors that require attention are threats by family members to discontinue therapy; suicidal threats, gestures, or actual attempts; job-threatening crises; and some form of trouble with the law.

A planned or therapist-induced crisis may be necessary as an extreme intervention with rigid, treatment-resistant families where the risk of continued substance abuse outweighs the risk taken by introducing a crisis designed to shake up the family system. When a therapeutically induced crisis is indicated, it is achieved by judicious, but very active interventions designed by the therapist. Techniques of unbalancing family alignments include assigning tasks that intensify emotions in members, reframing the meaning given to events, and other techniques aimed at stimulating the responsivity of an unresponsive family system. The use of paradoxical interventions, other than prescribing increased substance use, is most often used in this middle stage of family therapy. A paradoxical intervention is one where advice is given that would seemingly be at odds with the therapeutic intent. An example of this might be the therapist who suggests "Mr. X, your need to keep drinking—I know it affects your health, but right now your drinking, and your subsequent behavior are the things that are keeping your family together." Such interventions point out the role of the substance abuse within the family system. Then intervention must, obviously, behave very judiciously.

Managing Confidentiality in Family Therapy

One useful maxim when working with families of substance abusers is to support the notion of privacy, except when the reluctance to share information functions as an ongoing resistance to therapeutic progress. This stance respects and supports appropriate boundary lines in the family, encourages healthy individuation with its attendant rights of privacy, yet does not naively assume that secrets in families are to be honored and unchallenged. The therapist has to avoid entering into a collusive alliance of secrecy with any family member masquerading as preserving confidentiality. Pressures to fall into this trap are enormous with substance abusers and their families.

The therapist is constantly tempted by individual members of the family to learn new information, unbeknownst to other family members. One-to-one attempts to engage the therapist in collusive alliances take the form of out-of-session phone calls, letters, or the creation of "pseudo emergencies" that require exclusive, individual attention from the therapist. These events have to be rerouted into the regularly scheduled family therapy sessions with the full family present in order to make constructive use of the information. In so doing, the therapist is making a position statement by his or her actions that he or she is not available to assist in perpetuating dysfunctional family habits by rewarding individual attempts at contact outside of sessions.

Confidentiality in family therapy with substance abusers comes into play around the issue of so-called "family secrets." The way in which families use secrets elucidates many issues of family structure and function. The frightened adolescent who confides information about his alcohol use to his mother, the person to whom he feels closest in the family, yields data about alliances and affiliations. If, upon hearing the son's disclosure, the mother suggests or encourages keeping this information secret from the father and/or other family members, then a more dysfunctional collusive family pattern is suspected. Utilization of private information in a form that excludes others in the family invariably signals a family pattern which promotes continued substance abuse. The therapist has to draw a clear distinction for the family about what is confidential material and what is a misuse of confidentiality which only serves to perpetuate the problems for which the family is seeking help.

Substance-dependent individuals and their families frequently share in the collective myth concerning secrets specifically related to concealing drug and alcohol use. Often what is presented as a secret is merely the lack of open verbal acknowledgment of some behavior or information that is already known to family members on some level. The therapist has to search for respectful, yet aggressive means of determining how and when to "expose" concealed information. He or she has to assist the family in appreciating the mechanics of their participation in conspiracies of silence which only delay or prelude the resolution of a drug or alcohol problem.

☐ Later-Phase Issues

Management of Termination

When the family reaches a point of success that is maintained for a consistent period of time, the issue of ending therapy sessions naturally arises. The termination phase of family therapy with substance abusers and their families has three components: (a) reviewing the therapy experience, (b) reinforcing gains made over time, and (c) planning for return to therapy if indicated in the future.

Conducting a review of the family therapy experience accomplishes several things. The family can concretely see how their participation has been vital to the sense of resolution they experience at the end of therapy. Identifying risk areas and developing an ability to diagnose their own symptoms can be learned by the family during the latter phase of treatment and incorporated into a plan for preventing similar problems in the future. In the process of reviewing the therapy experience, the therapist tries to simultaneously effect disengagement from the family by acknowledging their independent ability to handle many of the circumstances for which they originally sought help.

An active effort is made to positively reinforce gains made by individuals and by the whole family. A delineation must be made between validating the family's perception of progress and supplying false reassurance. Maintenance of abstinence patterns and substitution of adaptive family interaction are emphasized during the termination phase. Plans for returning for future sessions are discussed explicitly prior to formal termination. When the substance abuse symptoms are under control, other family issues may be the basis for a new stage in family work. Problems may crop up which involve family members other than the substance abuser. Parental marital problems, the emergence of a new symptom in another family member, and the shift in family focus onto a different child are all manifestations of this aspect of termination. Some families may continue to meet but the agenda in therapy is no longer a substance abuse agenda.

Aftercare Planning

It is important to end the family therapy on a positive note to increase the probability that families will return for scheduled follow-up appointments or in the event that they encounter temporary setbacks. Aftercare planning includes provision for monitoring progress and providing the family with a periodic "battery charge" at regulated intervals after the conclusion of family therapy.

In the termination phase, it is wise to build in a comfortable way for the family to return for sessions if needed. Although it is desirable to place the responsibility for change on the family, the therapist must realize that relapses can occur even after successful treatment. A contingency plan for management of setbacks is presented to the family for their approval prior to terminating sessions. The orientation to termination as the end of a productive phase of family work permits therapist and family to comfortably resume work at a future date if circumstances in the family so dictate.

Popular family misconceptions that returning to therapy equals failure and that the family must be "cured forever" work against the view of the family as an ever-changing group with different needs at different points in its life cycle. Family therapy in general, and particularly family work with a symptom as unpredictable and volatile as substance abuse, has to be flexible enough to adapt to the family's needs at different points in time.

Multi-family Groups

Before leaving the subject of the varied ways of working with substance abuse problems in a family context, mention should be made of another popular format: The multiple family group (MFG). This technique which reflects a blending of group and family therapies has proven to be useful when substance abuse is the presenting problem in a family.

The current clinical enthusiasm for MFGs can be explained by the broad potential these experiences offer to families. Multiple family groups rely heavily on psychoeducational elements to achieve their ends. To assume that these groups are merely educational and informational does not recognize the myriad ways in which MFGs can be helpful to families struggling with substance abuse issues. Along with the MFG's ability as a vehicle for the dissemination of accurate information about drugs and alcohol, it also can be used for any or all of the following reasons: desolation; support and socialization; emotional catharsis; problem solving; inter-family learning; instilling hope; role modeling; advice giving; experiential learning; supplying surrogate family members for families which are single-parent or non-intact families; and as a source of data by watching members of families interact with others in a therapeutic setting.

In the MFG, families with a drug- or alcohol-dependent member are oriented to a view which stresses the relationship between family factors and substance overuse or abstinence. Family, as well as individual, denial defenses and resistances are confronted in sessions. Family patterns such as co-dependency, enabling behaviors, enmeshment, and scapegoating are identified and alternative behaviors are sought which do not facilitate substance abuse.

Such family groups consist of several families and are led by at least two staff members. MFGs composed of more then three or four families can be very large in size and approximate a network model where leaders of the group have specific designated roles and functions to carry out. Because of the large size of these groups, therapists have many therapeutic options at their disposal. Initially, the identification of similarities among families with a substance abuser is emphasized in order to build group support and cohesiveness. The impact on a family living with a drug-dependent person is a common early session theme around which the group can coalesce.

Cross-family learning is dramatic in these groups. Participants are able to recognize in members of other families in the group, the very things they vigorously deny or avoid in their own families. As a result, inter-member and family-to-family levels of the group become prominent channels for both support and confrontation. This adds therapeutic leverage to the task of trying to change established patterns in families which foster drug and alcohol use.

The multiple family group also functions as a resource for its membership. Many families have been through repeated bouts of substance abuse, incarceration, dealing with agencies and organizations to obtain concrete services for family members, and can provide invaluable advice to others who are facing these issues for the first time. Family members are made aware of and are encouraged to join support groups of an Al-Anon type. The emphasis on addiction as a family affair helps mobilize important family members who would otherwise resist efforts to involve them in a therapeutic process.

MFGs try to maintain an optimistic tone while at the same time are dealing with some very harsh realities of life. The positive group climate is designed to offset excessive feelings of depression and any desire to "give up" on the part of group members. It is important to anticipate these and other disruptive states which might prompt a family to withdraw from the group. From the point of view of group leadership, drop-outs from MFGs involve many people at a time, leaving a large gap in the group. Individual drop-outs in non-family groups pose a problem with maintaining a sense of continuity of treatment, a problem which is only magnified if there is too much of a turnover in membership in family groups.

As another therapeutic tool and a safeguard against families dropping out of group, a strong effort is made to focus on emotions. The identification of strong feelings and their expression in group sessions is a key toward this end. Members are encouraged to use the sessions to practice effective communication of affect with members of their own family, across family lines, and with the group leaders.

Groups composed of couples is a variation on the theme of the multifamily group. Couples groups where one or both members are alcohol- or drug-dependent focus not only on sobriety but mostly on the role substances have played in the relationship. Many couples learn through the group that they have introduced substances into their lives as a way of dealing with their anxieties about being in a long-term, intimate relationship.

Themes which occur regularly in couples group for substance abuse include: (a) role definition in relationships; (b) power and control; (c) aspects of sexuality; (d) money; (e) attachment to each partner's family of origin; (f) trust and mistrust; (g) fidelity; (h) independence and dependence; (i) parenting; and (j) drug-related issues such as the role each partner plays in supporting or sabotaging sobriety in the other.

Communication skills training, learning how to express loving and angry feelings in an appropriate way, and adjusting to the differences in living together when substances are no longer part of the couple relationship are readily identifiable focal points in couples groups. Structurally, these groups are smaller than MFGs, consisting of three to four couples. Where possible, in heterosexual groups, an opposite sex co-therapy team leads the group. The choice of co-leadership helps in modeling effective collaboration between adults; respecting differences; demonstrating flexibility in gender roles; and presenting non-competitive ways of dealing with unresolved issues. These groups are usually short-term and meet once weekly with the assignment of homework tasks as a regular part of the program. The length of membership in the group is reviewed periodically to insure that members do not become too dependent on therapy as a substitute for being self-reliant.

On balance, the ways in which family and group techniques have been "married" have resulted in new forms of treatment which give the clinician, the substance abuser, and the family powerful and palatable tools which are specific for the interpersonal aspects of drug and alcohol problems.

☐ Summary

Family therapy provides a necessary dimension to the treatment of substance abuse. Systems-derived family techniques are emerging as the most promising format to date. The combination of aspects of group and family therapies has added the option to work on specific aspects of family life at different stages in the recovery process. Families play a key role in relapse prevention and need to be involved in the overall therapeutic plan in ways which acknowledge their power and channel it in the direction of drug-free living.

Preventive and educational programs for families are currently being expanded in the hopes of utilizing the family as a first line of defense against the vulnerability of its members to drug and alcohol dependency. The awareness that families and substance abuse are inextricably linked can now be operationalized into a clinically useful set of family-based therapies which specifically address both the family and the drug issues simultaneously.

23

CHAPTER

Network Therapy

The complex nature of addiction calls for the resourceful clinician to employ innovative means in determining a meaningful treatment strategy. Dr. Marc Galanter, a pioneering researcher in the treatment of substance abuse, has developed a method of dealing with individuals with moderate to severe addictions on an outpatient basis. He has named this technique *Network Therapy*. The Network refers primarily to the social and familial connections of the addicted individual. It also refers to the subtler internal array of resources available to that individual. For the suitable patient and the motivated clinician, this therapy is a practical and effective means for addressing both the addiction and the individual in an outpatient setting.

The goal of Network Therapy is twofold: (1) to deal with the addiction, and (2) to achieve and maintain abstinence. It is often the case that the newly sober individual, as part of a larger family unit, may need substantial help in adjusting to his or her newfound sobriety. Network therapy can be helpful in this process.

While the goal, direction, and single-minded resources of this type of therapy aim toward abstinence, the subtleties of the human psyche are not lost. The careful clinician pays attention to family, network, and individual dynamics and uses all of this information in the most effective means to achieve the goal of abstinence.

The clinician helps the patient gather those individuals who are in the patient's life in the united effort of dealing with the addiction. The network comes together and, along with the patient, comes up with solutions for becoming sober and maintaining abstinence. Network Therapy then uses the patient's social network to monitor and reinforce adaptive, drug-free behavior.

Selection of Patients

Patients need to be selected carefully. Network Therapy is suitable for individuals who cannot reliably control their intake of drugs and alcohol. They do not have to be able to stop; in fact, those attempting to give up substances with only limited success may be ideal candidates for this form of treatment. Those individuals who are ambivalent about stopping are also suitable. Most addicts are deeply conflicted about drug or alcohol cessation. The conflict surrounding whether to stop or not is a constant question for the active addict, and appropriate fodder for Network Therapy.

It is also important for Network Therapy that the individuals have at least one person in their network who will be willing to help them stop using drugs and alcohol. Substance abusers may be highly reluctant to involve others in their treatment for a number of reasons. Addicts may believe that no one in their circle of friends and family is aware of the extent of their problem. Denial is a powerful defense mechanism, both on the part of the patient and frequently in the people in their life, but complete ignorance of the problem is rarely the case. The clinician can assure substance-abusing patients that by the time they come to treatment, their substance abuse is not only known, but is also a cause of great concern for those around them. Most of their friends and families will be greatly relieved that help is finally being sought.

Another excuse for not involving others in treatment is that there is no one in the patient's life who can help. This is almost always a perceived social isolation in the service of denial. Nearly everyone has someone who will help out in a time of need. The resourceful clinician helps the patient find someone who will participate. Once an individual has been identified and enlisted as a network member, he or she can be invaluable in finding additional helpful members.

> Joan is an 34 year-old aspiring actress, living in New York. She has had some success on the stage and has worked intermittently on television. She currently lives alone and has not had a serious romantic relationship in over two years. She has a wide circle of friends and her parents live in a nearby community. She used a substantial amount of drugs in college, but drug use not been an issue in recent years. Joan's drinking has become a problem. A social drinker since her late teens, she has substantially increased her daily intake of wine and cocktails in the past eighteen months. She does not drink

> every day, but on more days than not, finishes four to six cocktails, sometimes more. On a semi-frequent basis, she drinks to the point of blacking out and has wound up in some bedrooms, not exactly sure of how she got there, or whether she practiced safe sex. The drinking has caused her to put on weight and has left her feeling lethargic and depressed. In rare moments of honest introspection, she acknowledges that her alcohol use has cost her at least two coveted roles, maybe more. On two occasions, she missed an important audition because she was hung-over. She has attempted to stop on her own, but after an abstinent week or so, she begins again. For the past several months, her friends, especially her best friend Sally, and her family, have expressed concern about "what is going on."

Joan is an ideal candidate for Network Therapy. She has a moderate to severe problem with alcohol that she is unable to control on her own. Her numerous attempts to quit drinking confirm this. She has a great deal of motivation to stop. Apparently on the verge of career success, her drinking has significantly interfered with the realization of her goals. In addition, she has a ready network that is concerned about her. They undoubtedly suspect that her drinking is the problem, but have not wanted to confront her directly.

☐ Exclusion Criteria

The clinician should exclude those patients who are episodic abusers and are able to return to moderation with relative ease. People who can stop their destructive substance use easily may need education and counseling, but they rarely need such an intensive treatment as Network Therapy. Similarly excluded should be the patient who has had only a single episode of severe drug or alcohol use that was time-limited (usually less than two weeks). An example of this is the individual who after being fired from a job uncharacteristically gets drunk and uses cocaine for several days, but then stops and realizes that this behavior was foolish and self-destructive. Individuals who cannot moderate their drug or alcohol use for even one day are also considered to be poor candidates. They may eventually, after detoxification and an inpatient stay, be suitable for Network Therapy, but they need a more structured environment to achieve initial abstinence. Outpatient detoxification followed by Network Therapy is an option for such a person, but an individual needs to be highly motivated for this type to therapy to be successful.

The person and his network must be stable both internally and externally in order to have success with this form of treatment. Someone who is on the run from drug dealers threatening to kill them will not be a reliable candidate. Since the physical environment the person lives in must be solid, the homeless are also inappropriate candidates. Internal stability refers to the psychological resources necessary to use the basic tools of sobriety. The patient with severe borderline personality disorder whose personal life is extremely chaotic and self-destructive will not be able to muster the consistency needed for this treatment. Individuals with severe comorbid psychological illness are usually a mismatch for network interventions as well. This is also the case for a person with severe bipolar disorder who has not been adequately treated pharmacologically. Therapy with a person with manic symptoms will likely be unproductive until the mania is addressed. A mildly depressed patient need not be excluded but should be treated for whatever biological ailment is present, before beginning the network therapy.

Starting a Network

It is important that a method of treatment be implemented rather quickly after the clinician first speaks with the patient. The window of opportunity for beginning treatment is often very narrow. It may and usually does recur, but only briefly. The guiding principle is "strike while the iron is hot." A call from a substance abuser or an associate should be answered as soon as possible. The day after tomorrow is often too late, and there patients return to dysfunctional substance use. If the clinician can not see the person in a timely fashion, then the patient should be referred to a colleague.

With many patients, the initial call often comes from a significant other, such as a spouse or spousal equivalent. This individual invariably needs to be part of the network. If the spouse is reluctant to participate, then the chances of success are greatly diminished; the clinician should point out that the addiction affects everyone in a family and will need to be handled in that arena. Spouses can be helpful in ensuring that the patient arrives to the first session sober. A representative example is found in the following vignette:

Therapist: Hello, may I help you?

Linda: I hope so. Dr. Frank gave me your name and said that you deal with people with alcohol problems, is that so?

Therapist: That is right. Can you tell me a bit more?

Linda: It's not me, it is my husband, Donald. I've known that he's had a problem for a long time now, but his boss just told him that his work has been slacking off because of his drinking, and he better get help or he'll be fired.

Therapist: Is Donald there? If he is, please put him on the phone and stay on the line.

Donald: I'm here doc. Hey, I don't know what your'e thinking, but I am no alcoholic. My damn boss is just on my ass. I think he is the one that has the problem.
Therapist: But you do drink?
Donald: Sure, I have a couple of pops now and then, but I don't think it is a problem. They say I am drinking at work, but I hardly ever do that, and only when a client comes in and we go out for a couple of beers.
Therapist: I gather from reading between the lines that you may have a real problem with alcohol.
Linda: As sure as the Pope is Catholic.
Therapist: I have an appointment for both of you available at 4:00 PM tomorrow. Donald, make sure you stay sober until then. Linda, can you pick him up from work so he is not tempted to miss the meeting and go into a bar?
Linda: I will try my best. I understand the game plan.
Donald: I will see you there at four. I'll be sober as a judge.

In this example, the therapist has made an assessment that the patient has a clear problem with alcohol, is not a reliable informant, and probably cannot be counted on to show up on time for an appointment. In the case of patients who do not have partners, the person who makes the initial call, if not the addict may be treated as the significant other.

Sally called Dr. Brooks, an expert on addictions, and spoke of her concerns about her friend, Barbara. Dr. Brooks asked if she thought that Sally could convince her friend to come in for an evaluation. She said she thought she should be able to do it. They made an appointment and Dr. Brooks said that if Barbara was reluctant, Sally should keep the appointment and they could discuss their options.

In this instance, Barbara's network will undoubtedly include Sally and probably Barbara's parents. The inclusion of others will be discussed at the first meeting.

☐ The Initial Meeting

In the first meeting, it is essential to emphasize that the goal of the treatment will be sobriety and abstinence. Not emphasizing abstinence can lead to avoidable problems later on when, for instance after two months of being sober, the patient may test the therapist and network by using drugs or alcohol again. The therapist has to make sure that abstinence is an agreed upon priority goal of treatment. Abstinence itself is not a necessary condition of treatment since addiction is a chronic and relapsing condition, but every attempt needs to be made to work toward that end.

Total abstinence from all substances is advised as the focus for the initial treatment period. Often questions arise as to the use of other substances different from the one leading to this presentation. For example, a cocaine-dependent individual may wonder if he or she can drink alcohol. It is best to explain that alcohol, though perhaps not a primary problem, can often lead to relapse with cocaine and ought to be avoided for a significant period of time. The initial abstention is from *all* mind and mood altering substances.

At the initial meeting, discussion should begin about who *needs* to be in the network—and who would be useful. The patient can be helpful here, as can the accompanying friend or significant other. If detoxification is not an issue, then the next matter should be a strategy for remaining sober until the next meeting. This can include additional support groups, such as AA or Rational Recovery, and may involve the use of medication. For the alcohol or heroin user, disulfiram and naltrexone can be useful tools for maintaining abstinence. (These individual medications are covered in much more detail in a subsequent section, but drinking alcohol on disulfiram induces a very unpleasant physical reaction, naltrexone blocks the effects of opiates, so that taking heroin, for example, produces no effect.) If a particularly stressful situation is anticipated, a friend or colleague may be called upon to be with the patient during that difficult time.

Inclusion in the Network

The people included should be those individuals who are close to the patient and concerned about the patient's condition and welfare. Members should be people whom the patient trusts and knows well. Inclusion criteria can be quite flexible. Creativity should be employed, and anyone who knows the patient is a potential member.

It is best to have a balanced group in terms of age, generation, sex, and relationship to the patient. For example, a group consisting of all family members from the patient's parents' generation would be heavily weighted in terms of attitude and viewpoint and would not create the environment of balance and support necessary to optimize this type of treatment. Four to six members is the ideal network size; however, the principles may be used with as few as one other member or as many as can fit into the clinician's office. The inclusion of too many individuals, though, is likely to make the agenda unfocused and unwieldy.

There are some people who ought not to be considered for the network. The most obvious among these are people with their own unresolved substance abuse problems. These people may be threatened by the patient's new sobriety and may undermine the process. Others who should be considered with great caution are rivalrous colleagues, subordinates, or superiors at work. In other words, other substance abusers, and people who have a potential interest in keeping the patient ill (even if they believe themselves to be well-intentioned) ought to be avoided.

> Barbara and Sally met with Dr. Brooks and Barbara admitted that she did indeed have a problem with alcohol, although she did not label herself an alcoholic. She did agree that she needed to achieve abstinence. She felt that disulfiram might be helpful, and at Dr. Brooks' assistance agreed that Sally, who lived just down the hall, would watch her take it each morning and report to Dr. Brooks if she did not. Group membership was discussed. Barbara's father was a good candidate. Her mother, however, was too sick to travel. Barbara's beloved Uncle Frank was mentioned, but as soon as tales of his penchant for martinis and frequent public intoxication emerged, Dr. Brooks suggested he was not an appropriate candidate. Barbara's arch-rival, Agatha, although close to Barbara, was deemed too competitive to be a member. Since they frequently competed for the same roles, she had as much vested interest in Barbara being drunk as her being sober. Barbara's brother, Darren, was considered a good candidate. He was frequently out of town, but could always be reached by phone. Her old friend, Tom, a middle-aged businessman with whom she is close, rounded out the group. All members were called that afternoon and Barbara was given the responsibility for reminding them of next week's meetings.

☐ Meetings

The meetings should be warm and welcoming. It is the therapist's job to maintain this atmosphere. There is a tendency in the treatment of substance abusers for otherwise well-intentioned individuals to express their anger at the individual. Attacks, scapegoating, and recrimination must be avoided at these meetings. The goal is to help the patient maintain abstinence, not to dredge up the past, or for the therapist to unwittingly host a session consisting of character assassination of the addict.

Network therapy differs from family therapy insofar as the exclusive focus is on abstinence. The group "brainstorms" about stressful or difficult situations and comes up with strategies for dealing with them. In the case of monitored medication, the network members keep the therapist informed about compliance. It is not the network members' responsibility to make the patient take his or her medicine, it is only their role to inform the therapist when the medication is not being taken. The therapist, who has a contract with the patient about medication compliance, thus informed, can then deal with the patient's resistance or non-compliance.

> Barbara had an out-of-town audition, and although she minimized the concerns of the network members that this would be stressful, she listened to them. Arrangements had been made for her to talk to Sally on the third day of the trip. When Sally asked about the disulfiram, Barbara admitted that she

had "forgotten" to pack it, but assured her she would be fine. Sally called Dr. Brooks, who got in touch with Barbara, confronted her, and phoned in a prescription at an all-night pharmacy next to her hotel. Later on, Barbara confessed that she had been tempted to go to a bar to "have just one little drink" the night before her audition, when Sally had called.

The network should meet as frequently as necessary. A good rule of thumb is twice per week during the first few weeks, then once per week as long as sobriety remains tenuous. In general, network meetings run between one hour and one hour and a half. These meetings should be supplemented by individual therapy for the patient (which can have more traditional 45-minute sessions) as well as any outside groups or meetings that may be helpful.

☐ Individual Therapy

Individual therapy for the patient is a vital part of this treatment modality. Patients are seen in individual treatment once or twice per week where issues brought up in the network meetings can be processed. Acquisition of insight and emotional expression should be encouraged in individual meetings. Defenses that are in the service of denial or threaten sobriety are explored more intensely in the individual session. Individual therapy is especially helpful for the person making the difficult adjustment to living soberly. Cognitive-behavioral techniques may be taught. All substance-abusing patients are encouraged to attend self-help groups. At the outset, it is recommended that they be mandatory since attendance at Twelve Step meetings helps reinforce abstinence. If the principles of a self-help group have been embraced by the patient, the clinician should not attempt to contradict or interpret the patient's reliance upon them.

☐ Termination of the Network

It is agreed upon from the start that the network never terminates. In the course of therapy, when the patient's sobriety becomes second nature and the original purpose for forming the group no longer seems necessary, the patient, therapist, and network members need to agree that if a future slip occurs or sobriety is threatened after formal network meetings have stopped, the therapist will be called and the network reconvened. Individual therapy can and perhaps ought to continue after network meetings cease.

Barbara was sober for one year and deeply committed to her home AA group. She was thankful to the network for helping her get and remain sober. She and Dr. Brooks both agreed that disulfiram was not necessary on a daily basis, and could be used only on stressful occasions. Barbara's career had taken off and she had begun a new relationship. Her boyfriend was aware of and supportive of the network (he had joined a few sessions). All members concurred that, if necessary, they would come together for Barbara in the future. Barbara agreed she would continue her therapy with Dr. Brooks to work out some of her remaining anxieties, self-defeating behaviors, and her intimacy issues. She was now willing and able to deal with her problems resolutely and soberly.

Network therapy is one creative addition to the therapeutic repertoire in treating problems of addiction. By bringing the real-life interpersonal network into the psychotherapeutic setting, the clinician gets a more rapid and realistic view of the "players" in the patient's life. Similarly, the use of the social, vocational, and familial resources present in the network of the addict affords increased opportunities for making patient-specific treatment planning.

Network Therapy is pragmatic, interactive, and supportive. It is readily employed even by clinicians without enormous experience in the use of the technique. The presence of many network members serves as an internal and self-regulating system of "checks and balances" against any ill-advised or ineffective treatment interventions.

24

CHAPTER

The Therapeutic Community

The Therapeutic Community (TC) is an important mode of treatment for the severely impaired chemically dependent individual. TCs are residential programs lasting as long as two years, where individuals live and work together, and try to develop drug-free coping mechanisms. These are self-contained communities with rigid rules that seek to rehabilitate, or in some cases, habilitate people. TCs have been termed a kind of "boot camp" for addicts. They are usually publicly funded, often by Medicaid. Through the successful experiences of living through an intense, structured, small community, the "graduate" of a TC is better prepared to re-enter and function in the world.

The residential TC is probably the most intense form of treatment for substance abuse. While not a last resort, it is very demanding and ought to be reserved for the most severely abusing patients. In recent years, the largest and best known TCs, such as Phoenix House and Daytop Villiage, have expanded their programs to include aspects much less rigorous than the original residential treatment programs that are the core element of these communities. This chapter will include a history of the TC movement, a description of how specialized residential treatment programs work programmatically, and the rationale for why they work.

History

Charles Dederich founded the first TC called Synanon in California in 1958. It was an innovative and effective treatment approach for those with severe addictive disorders. Dederich was interested in how a group setting could contribute to healing and treatment. Dederich himself had a serious history of alcoholism and found that regular attendance at AA was not sufficient to help him overcome his addictions but that living with sober people was more conducive to maintaining recovery.

Dederich sought to create a self-contained and self-governing comprehensive community with non-negotiable rules that was somewhat cut off from the outside world. As part of their commitment to becoming sober, individuals who joined Synanon turned over their assets to the organization. This enabled the group to purchase large tracts of land in Northern California. For the first decade, the group had tremendous success and many of the principles that guide today's TCs were developed and fostered at Synanon.

Community living and responsibility toward other members were underscored. Principles of group sharing and adherence to rules were also emphasized. Over time, the group became more and more isolated and Dederich developed the characteristics of a cult leader. The group armed itself and agents of the Federal government finally took over the organization and imprisoned its founder.

Despite the disastrous outcome of Synanon, many of the principles from the original group model were later adapted by others who have incorporated them into the treatment programs available in contemporary TCs.

TC Philosophy

TCs have a specific philosophy about substance abuse and treatment. Substance abuse is viewed as a disorder of the whole person, affecting all areas of functioning. Rehabilitation focuses on living a drug-free existence. Substance abuse is but one aspect of a dysfunctional method of living. The substance abusing individual may have been raised in a chaotic family environment and never learned the rules necessary for orderly living. Such an individual needs to learn these life skills and become appropriately socialized and habilitated. Another individual from a more privileged and nurturing environment may have responded for whatever reason by rejecting the rules he or she learned, and turned to drugs. This person needs to be *re*habilitated. Both types of individuals can be treated the same way, with immersion into the culture and environment of the TC.

TCs rely on a therapeutic environment and the psychological leverage which comes from the hierarchical structure of the community. While the goal is therapeutic, the community climate is not always comfortable. Group pressure is actively employed as a force for behavior change. The community and its philosophy promote self-help and motivation for change.

In the view of the TC, there is a "right way" to live. That way is filled with order, responsibility, positive values, and is free of disorganization and drugs. While a stay of up to two years might be considered a long time by some, in comparison to the length of peoples' drug histories, it is often relatively brief. This relative brevity is in part justification for the intensity of the treatment. Since habits which have been learned over a lifetime must be "unlearned" or changed over a short space of time (and during adulthood which lacks the plasticity of childhood learning), community living facilitates the psychological repair process.

The basic philosophy of the TC can be summarized in the rehabilitative approach: work as education and therapy, mutual self-help, peers as role models, and staff as rational, predictable, and consistent authorities.

The Process

The Admission Interview

An admission interview establishes the appropriateness of an individual for TC admission. There are two major guidelines for admission: suitability and risk. Suitability refers to the appropriateness of the patient for this type of treatment. The individuals must be able to participate in the program. This means they must be amenable and have the ability to attend groups, engage meaningfully with others, and be able to function in the community. Risk refers to the potential hazard the candidate will be to the community. The community itself must be protected from corrupting influences, those that pose a threat to its work and identity. Thus a suitable candidate must not present too severe a burden on the management of the TC. An example of a person who presents an undue risk is someone whose severe psychiatric comorbidity makes him or her unable to engage in treatment and makes continued drug use likely, and corruption of the healthy environment of the TC a distinct possibility.

Structure

The TC structure is composed of relatively few staff and a hierarchy of residents which include peers—junior, intermediate, and senior who constitute the community in the residence. This community is often referred to as a family. Hierarchically above the peer community is the professional staff who make sure that the structure is ordered and provide a sense of mutual responsibility.

The new patient enters a setting of upward mobility and responsibility. The social standing of an initiate is menial and the work tasks assigned are commensurate with that status in the program. For example, a new recruit may be required to wash pots or scrub the toilets. Behavior that is responsible and in keeping with the philosophy of the community is rewarded, and the member who performs his or her tasks "the right way" moves up in seniority. In response to the elevation of status, the tasks assigned become progressively more organizational and responsible. Work is considered extremely important and functions as a personal and communal reinforcer of desirable behavior and self-worth. "Right behavior" is rewarded with increasing status and responsibility and "wrong behavior" may result in demotion and loss of status and privilege.

Most TCs operate in stages. Stage 1 lasts from days zero to sixty. This is a period of orientation. The main objective is to familiarize the individual with the philosophy and operation of a TC. Contact with the outside world is strictly forbidden in order to foster dependence on the TC "family." Professional staff maintain contact with the outside world for the patient. The individual member participates fully in the program and the running of the operation, but is conferred a lowly status. TC membership is voluntary and an individual is free to leave whenever he or she wants. Success in the first stage is generally reflected by retention in the program. Stage 2 consists of primary treatment and lasts from months two to twelve. During this time, the individual who adapts to the community gradually accrues increased responsibility. Stage 3 refers to the second year of the TC experience where the participant gradually works toward re-entering the world at large.

Schedule

The typical day in a TC begins at 7 AM and ends at 11 PM. It includes a variety of job-related activities, meetings, individual counseling, and recreation. There are four main forms of group activity in the TC: encounters, probes, marathons, and tutorials.

Encounters are the cornerstone of the group process in the TC. The basic encounter is a peer-led group of up to 20 individuals which usually lasts for 2 hours. The main objective of each encounter is modest and limited: it is to heighten individual awareness of specific attitudes or behavioral patterns that need to be modified in order to reduce the risk of continued substance abuse.

Probes are staff-led group sessions composed of 10 to 15 residents and are scheduled when needed. These last between four and eight hours and are conducted to increase staff understanding of an individual's background for the purpose of tailoring the treatment plan.

Tutorials are just that. They are designed to train and teach, as opposed to correcting behavior or facilitating emotional catharsis.

Marathons are extended group sessions, the objective of which is to explore and delineate more adaptive resolutions to painful aspects in the patient's life. These last approximately 18 to 36 hours and are extremely intense emotional experiences designed to break down maladaptive psychological defenses. The processing of traumatic events such as abandonment or sexual abuse in the context of a supportive community, though often grueling, can be extremely therapeutic.

"Graduating" for a TC member is a misnomer. Individuals do eventually re-enter the larger world, but if they do, never truly leave the TC "family." In recent years, different TCs have developed aftercare programs. It is very common for "graduates" to assume staff positions with these agencies and continue their relationship with the community in a new capacity.

The residential TC is a rigorous and extreme form of treatment; however, it can be an extremely useful method for users who have been refractory to other interventions. Years of substance abuse and chaotic living often need a strong antidote to achieve reversal. The best evidence is that those substance abusers that stick with a program for a long enough period of time do the best. A stay of six months or longer is a positive predictor of an abstinent future. The most obvious reason that length of treatment correlates with success is that the longer an individual stays in a TC, the longer the exposure to the rehabilitative process. Another important reason is that the longer a person stays in, the more time there is for his or her former drug-using community to dissolve. Drug-using communities are, by their nature, transient. Anyone who stays away from their severe drug-using "friends" for any reason will likely not find that community in existence when they return. The TC may be viewed by some as a radical intervention, but, for many substance abusers, it can be lifesaving.

PHARMACOLOGY AND MEDICAL-MODEL TREATMENTS

Substance abuse is often thought of as a "disease." In many ways this is a useful concept, both in terms of understanding addiction, and in formulating treatment. This is the "medical model" of addiction. Given that substance abuse can be understood as a disease, it is logical that medications might be of help in treating some substance abuse disorders. This is indeed the case. Medications can be quite useful, both some substance abuse conditions alone, and in other cases with those other medical, psychological, and psychiatric conditions (co-morbid) which are associated with substance abuse.

Medications are not usually considered the first line of treatment. Most investigation indicates that these tools are underutilized. This is true both for the medications that treat substance abuse conditions, and those medications that treat the associated symptoms.

25

CHAPTER

Pharmacological Treatments for Substance Abuse

It cannot be emphasized strongly enough how important it is that therapeutically prescribed medication be a part of a comprehensive treatment plan. If medications are to be prescribed, this needs to be in the context of a strong psychotherapeutic and behavioral treatment program. Addiction is a disorder of motivation and behavior which almost always requires specific psychological interventions, whatever medications are used. In this chapter, specific pharmacotherapies are described.

Pharmacotherapies for substance-use disorders can be divided into four broad categories: (1) treatment of acute intoxication, (2) treatment of withdrawal, (3) promotion of abstinence or prevention of relapse, and (4) treatment of comorbid psychiatric conditions. Agents used for treating the first three categories work by either blocking the reinforcing effects of drugs (antagonists), creating or enhancing aversive effects of drugs, or replacing the abused drug with a less toxic version that works on the same receptor/mechanism (agonist). Each of these treatments has been discussed earlier in the text in the sections devoted to specific substances of abuse. The following is a review of the highlights of the pharmacotherapies currently available to the clinician.

☐ The Treatment of Acute Intoxications

In general, these states are not treated unless the acute intoxication reaches a level that is medically dangerous. If the intoxication is severe enough to warrant medical attention, then the symptoms which are causing distress need to be treated. As an example, while there is no medication specific for the treatment of intoxication with LSD, an individual in the throes of an LSD "trip" who is extremely agitated may need treatment for panic and anxiety. In such a case, benzodiazepines such as 10 mg of Diazepam, or 2 mg of Lorazepam are often useful in treating the agitation.

An exception to the principle that there are not specific medicines for the acute intoxication is found in the opiates. If an individual is only mildly intoxicated, then it is likely that the patient does not need any pharmacotherapy. Overdose of opiates can lead to a suppression of respiration and is a medical emergency. Naloxone is a rapidly-acting opiate antagonist that can be administered intravenously. Any person who presents to the emergency room and is obtunded for an unknown reason is routinely given naloxone. If the reason for the clinical state is opiate overdose, the result is dramatic and rapid. People will come to life very quickly and likely be in physical pain from withdrawal. (These are the patients that sometimes scream at staff for "messing with my high".) Naloxone's effects only last about 20 minutes, so it is important to keep the person in the emergency room while the opiate is still in his or her system. This type of patient must wait in a safe place where he or she can be observed.

☐ Detoxification and Withdrawal

Descriptions and protocols for the withdrawal phases of each specific substance can be found in its respective chapter, and in the chapter on detoxification within this book. The more severe the dependence, the more the need for observation during withdrawal. In certain instances, as when a patient is out of control or has a severe medical problem, hospital admission is appropriate so that detoxification can take place more safely and under professional supervision. As noted earlier, all substances which induce dependence have withdrawal phases. Some may be less physiologically apparent than others, but all of them have distinct characteristics.

☐ Pharmacotherapies for Alcohol-Use Disorders

Alcohol abuse is a major public health problem, and among alcoholics, psychiatric comorbidity is common and associated with poor prognosis. Fifty-five percent of Americans drink three or more ounces of alcohol per week. Alcohol-related health problems are estimated to be the third largest health problem, after heart disease and cancer. Alcohol is considered to be a factor in 50% of violent crimes and 25% to 30% of suicides and accidental deaths. Psychiatric comorbidity, particularly depression, has been associated with increased severity of drinking. These factors provide a strong impetus for identifying and treating alcoholism and any psychiatric comorbidity.

Disulfiram

Disulfiram (Antabuse®) is a powerful tool in the management of alcoholism. In some quarters it has a negative reputation. This is unfortunate, since for some patients it is a very effective and helpful tool in maintaining sobriety. Taken orally (the usual dose is 250 mg to 500 mg in the morning), disulfiram inhibits the liver enzyme acetaldehyde dehydrogenase, resulting in a rapid buildup of acetaldehyde upon ingestion of alcohol. This creates a very unpleasant physiological reaction, which includes flushing, nausea, headaches, and hypotension. Disulfiram needs to be used with caution even though severe hypotension or shock is rare. It is contraindicated in patients with pre-existing cardiopulmonary compromise.

Side effects of daily dosing of disulfiram, in the absence of alcohol intake, are rare. Disulfiram reactions sometimes result from alcohol contained in medications such as over-the-counter cough syrups, alcohol used in cooking, or topical perfumes. Patients should be made aware of these hazards.

Disulfiram-induced hepatotoxicity is dangerous, but extremely rare. Only about 25 cases have been reported in the world literature. Nevertheless, it is prudent to follow liver transaminase levels in the blood periodically (every three to six months) during disulfiram treatment, and to warn patients that if symptoms of hepatitis occur, the disulfiram could be involved and a physician should be contacted immediately.

Disulfiram should be considered for any alcoholic patient having difficulty maintaining sobriety during outpatient treatment. One major problem, though, is that patients can easily stop taking the medication and begin to drink a few days later. Two weeks of alcohol cessation is recommended, but, in reality, the person may usually be able to resume drinking long before that deadline. Supervision of disulfiram intake by medical staff or significant others is strongly recommended. Disulfiram compliance may be monitored by inspecting the urine for its metabolite, diethylamide. Participation by spouses or cohabitants who give the alcoholic positive reinforcement for compliance results in even more therapeutic gains than those receiving it without positive reinforcement.

If used effectively, disulfiram is not only an aversive agent, but is also a symbol of commitment to abstinence and treatment. Patients can be instructed to take their daily dose in front of their spouse or loved one, saying "I am taking this as a symbol of my desire to remain abstinent and healthy." If the patient refuses to take the medication, the spouse is instructed not to argue with the patient but to contact the prescribing physician. At that time, the physician can deal with the patient's resistance.

Patients are instructed to take their daily dose in the morning when the desire to drink is usually low. Patients frequently voice the concern that taking disulfiram will remove their control and they will never be able to drink again. These individuals are relieved if informed that it only takes away their ability to drink for the next week or so. This simple clarification can be quite reassuring. Although this has not been well studied, recommendations for treatment duration is for at least six months. This allows time for patients to learn the coping skills necessary to maintain sobriety without disulfiram.

Disulfiram taken on an "as needed" basis is not recommended, yet there are certain rare instances where this might be applicable. A patient who has been abstinent for a long time, but is faced with a particularly stressful situation which may increase the likelihood of relapse, may be instructed to take a dose prior to entering this situation. An example of this is a businesswoman who has been sober without the aid of disulfiram for several years, but is faced with a particularly stressful business retreat where her colleagues and superiors will likely be drinking heavily and, because they are unaware of her alcoholism, will encourage her to drink.

> Ellen is a long-abstinent woman with over ten years of sobriety. In those ten years, she has developed a successful international business. Her most recent professional activities have focused on the former Soviet republics. While the prospects are quite lucrative, Ellen has been troubled by the prominence of alcohol-use in these societies. She is routinely offered vodka. Lately, she has been troubled by her own desire to perhaps try some vodka. She recognizes that this would be a disaster. After consulting with her therapist, they both agreed that taking disulfiram during those times that she is in Eastern Europe will take away the temptation and relieve her anxiety. Three years later, this has proven to be an effective and painless solution to her concerns.

Although there has been little systematic study on the use of disulfiram by alcoholics with psychiatric comorbidity, clinical experience suggests that it is effective in combination with antidepressant medications for alcoholics with mood or anxiety disorders. Since depressive and anxiety symptoms are often created or worsened by alcohol, establishment of abstinence with disulfiram can help clarify the diagnosis or boost the effectiveness of antidepressant medications.

One caveat is that disulfiram has been implicated, in rare cases, in the acute onset of psychosis, perhaps because it inhibits dopamine β-hydroxylase activity thus raising central dopamine levels. Disulfiram should be used with caution in patients with comorbid schizophrenia or mood disorders with a history of psychosis. Chronically psychotic patients may require an increase in their neuroleptics dosage if disulfiram is used in their treatment.

Naltrexone

A number of clinical studies in alcohol-dependent patients have suggested that compared to placebo, the opioid antagonist naltrexone significantly reduced drinking. Naltrexone appeared to reduce the severity of relapses (i.e., number of drinks) rather than their frequency. It may work by attenuating the subjective euphorigenic effects of initial alcohol consumption. Psychotherapy administered in the clinical trials had an interesting and synergistic relationship to naltrexone treatment. Naltrexone needs to be part of a larger and more comprehensive treatment. Merely prescribing the drug to patients without other counseling and treatment is likely to be unsuccessful.

Naltrexone is currently recommended at a dosage of 50 mg per day, taken under supervision. Although not sufficiently studied, higher doses may be helpful in some patients. The drug is usually well tolerated and side effects are minimal. Periodic monitoring of liver enzymes is recommended due to rare cases of hepatotoxicity which resolves if the drug is discontinued. Dysphoria was not a problem in the controlled trials, and naltrexone does not appear to reduce the pleasure associated with such normally pleasurable activities such as running (the "runners high") or sex.

The following data support the hypothesis that opioid antagonists would be useful in treating alcoholism: (a) Opiates and alcohol have similar sedative and euphorigenic effects; (b) there is cross-tolerance between opiates and alcohol in the relief of withdrawal symptoms; (c) in animals, opiate antagonists attenuate alcohol-induced effects; (d) small doses of opiates increase alcohol consumption in laboratory animals; (e) opioid antagonists in these same animals will reduce alcohol consumption, and (f) some alcoholics have shown decreased baseline levels of endogenous opiates, and the initial euphoria associated with alcohol is thought to be more reinforcing in this population.

Other Agents

It is likely that, in the next several years, a number of other medications will become available to the clinician for treating alcoholism. These include newer preparations of the established medications such as long-acting naltrexone, as well as newer classes of agents. An example of this is acamprosate, an NMDA antagonist, which appears to have few side effects, and in a number of clinical trials has been demonstrated to reduce craving for alcohol, drinking episodes, and the amount drunk.

Antidepressant Medications

Various antidepressant medications have been tested to see if they reduce the level of drinking in active alcoholics. While all of these trials have had problems, none have shown a reduction in drinking in individuals who are not depressed.

In contrast, there is an emerging body of evidence that for alcoholics with carefully diagnosed depressive syndromes, antidepressant medications are effective in improving mood and in reducing (but usually not eliminating) alcohol consumption. Tricyclic antidepressants (TCAs) have substantial side effects, one of which is sedation, which may be of concern in an alcoholic. TCAs are lethal in overdose, and many dually diagnosed patients are at high risk for suicide. These agents should, therefore, be used only with caution.

Although more trials of selective serotonin reuptake inhibitors (SSRIs) are needed, these antidepressants are becoming the treatment of choice, not only in depressed patients without comorbidity, but also in dually diagnosed alcoholics. This is due to their more benign side effect and safety profile. SSRIs should be started at low doses to prevent anxiety reactions or "jitteriness" and then gradually titrated up to normally recommended doses. The most common mistakes in the use of any antidepressant are prescribing too low a dose for too short a period of time. The other serious error in the use of these agents is premature discontinuation of the medication once an adequate therapeutic response has occurred.

Anxiolytic Medications

The first priority with an anxious alcoholic is to rule out, or, if necessary, treat alcohol withdrawal. It is important to establish the time since the last drink, examine the patient, and take vital signs. Any history of severe alcohol withdrawal, seizures, or delirium tremens should be established since this increases the risk for more severe manifestations in the current episode. Any such history would warrant more vigorous treatment of withdrawal which is considered a medical emergency.

Benzodiazepines, such as lorazepam (Ativan) or diazepam (Valium) are a mainstay of the treatment of alcohol withdrawal. They reduce minor withdrawal symptoms and protect against the development of seizures and DTs. However, other than during withdrawal, benzodiazepines should be avoided in alcoholics or used only in special circumstances because of the risk of iatrogenic cross-addiction. Antidepressants, mainly tricyclics or SSRIs, are more effective for most anxiety disorders such as generalized anxiety disorder, panic disorder, or social phobia than are benzodiazepines. If a person has a particularly difficult time sleeping, the choice of an antidepressant with sedating properties may be in order.

Despite caveats, there are alcoholic patients with anxiety disorders who require benzodiazepines, and judicious use of these agents may be highly effective. This is acceptable if the patient remains sober, but becomes contraindicated in the setting of heavy drinking.

☐ Pharmacotherapies for Opiate Dependence

To review, opioids are those compounds that bind to the family of opiate receptors and include both naturally occurring alkaloids such as opium, morphine, and codeine, and synthetic and semi-synthetic agents, including diacetylmorphine (heroin), hydromorphone (dilaudid), oxycodone (Percodan), propoxyphene (Darvon), meperidine (Demerol), methadone, and fentanyl. Physical effects include suppression of the cough reflex, constipation, analgesia, and, in higher doses, respiratory depression. Subjective effects include indifference to distress and feelings of euphoria and well-being. Although opiates are generally thought to be soporific, some addicts paradoxically report feeling energized. Opiate withdrawal is not medically dangerous, but can be very unpleasant; as mentioned in Chapter 12, common symptoms include anxiety, dysphoria, flu-like aches and pains, and symptoms of autonomic arousal.

Therapeutically prescribed opioids are invaluable tools in the treatment of numerous medical conditions, including the management of acute and chronic pain. The vast majority of medical patients exposed to opiates do not become addicted. Only a fraction of heroin-exposed GIs during the Vietnam War showed evidence of addiction after returning to the U.S. They went through withdrawal, but did not return to addictive use of heroin. Opiates are highly addictive for susceptible individuals but the factors involved in that vulnerability are not well understood. It is currently estimated that at least 750,000 Americans are addicted to heroin, although that figure may be much higher. Opiate addiction is highly debilitating. A street habit is expensive, causing addicts to drain their financial resources or resort to crime to support their habits. Intravenous drug use is associated with a host of serious medical problems, including HIV, hepatitis, and other blood-borne infections.

Methadone and Other Agonist-Substitution Therapies

For many patients with chronic, relapsing opioid dependence, the treatment of choice has been maintenance on the long-acting opioid methadone. Methadone taken orally is slowly absorbed and appears to work by occupying opiate receptors and inducing tolerance, such that the euphoric and reinforcing effects of street opiates are blocked. Its long half-life, 12 to 36 hours, permits once daily administration without the development of withdrawal. If a patient misses a day's dose, significant withdrawal symptoms develop, the presence of which often helps to reinforce compliance with treatment. Methadone maintenance has been shown to be highly effective for opioid dependence, with improvements in health status, decreased mortality, decreased criminal activity, and improved social functioning in those taking it.

Methadone maintenance is available only in specially licensed clinics. Federal guidelines limit its use to patients with at least a one-year history of opioid dependence and demonstrated physiological manifestations of dependence. Daily attendance is usually required to ingest methadone under supervision until a patient has established a persistent pattern of drug-free (other than methadone) urine toxicologies. Because it is so highly regulated, the methadone delivery system can be quite burdensome to patients. Negative attitudes toward methadone, usually based on the misconception that it is "just a substitute addiction," must also be overcome, both on the part of patients, as well as clinicians (and some public health officials and politicians). It is the opinion of many clinicians that methadone is a very effective treatment with an often inadequate delivery system.

Effectiveness of methadone maintenance requires adequate dosage and concurrent counseling. Doses greater than 80 mg are often needed to resolve withdrawal symptoms and induce abstinence. The average daily dose across the United States is 40 mg. The lesson is simple: Methadone is woefully under-dosed in this country. Discontinuation of methadone once treatment has begun is unfortunately followed by relapse in the vast majority of patients. In order to be effective, methadone must be understood as a long-term, perhaps life-long, treatment. A comparison with a diabetic's need for insulin is often useful in discussing methadone with patients.

L-a-acetylmethadol (LAAM) is a long-acting opiate with action similar to methadone which can be taken three times per week, reducing the patient's burden of clinical visits. It has only recently been approved for marketing in the U.S. and has yet to see wide clinical application. Results of pre-marketing trials suggest it is effective, but may be more difficult to regulate at the outset of treatment due to extremely slow absorption and resultant delayed relief of withdrawal symptoms. Because of its pharmacology, LAAM is not as immediately reinforcing and patients do not like it as much.

Buprenorphine is a partial opioid agonist which binds opiate receptors with high affinity, but only partially activates them. At low doses it acts as an agonist, at higher doses it acts as an antagonist. It is not yet marketed, but results of preliminary trials suggest it will be a useful alternative to methadone for agonist maintenance. It also appears to produce only a relatively mild withdrawal syndrome and thus may be a superior agent for management of opiate withdrawal.

Antagonist Maintenance—Naltrexone

Naltrexone is an orally administered, long-acting opioid antagonist which binds with high affinity to opiate receptors, blocking the euphoric and reinforcing effects of other opiates. Originally marketed as Trexan®, it now carries the trade name Revia®. It also displaces opiates already present on receptors, and will therefore precipitate withdrawal in dependent individuals. It is very important to make sure that prospective patients have been adequately detoxified from opiates before initiating this form of treatment. The usual dose, 50 mg, blocks the effects of opiates for about 24 hours. It may be taken as 50 mg daily, but is also effective on a three day per week schedule (100 mg on Monday and Wednesday, and 150 mg on Fridays).

A major problem with naltrexone is that it is easily stopped (no withdrawal), and once illicit opiates are resumed, naltrexone cannot be restarted because it will precipitate withdrawal. Concurrent psychosocial treatment, including having significant others or clinic staff supervise naltrexone ingestion is important in increasing the odds of success. A depot or long-acting injectable form of the drug is under development and should be helpful as an adjunct or alternative to supervised dosing.

Antidepressant Medications and Anxiolytics

Among opioid addicts, the lifetime prevalence of major depression has been reported at 20% to 60%, a figure which far exceeds the prevalence in the general population. Depression is associated with a poor prognosis in opiate addicts. Tricyclic antidepressants are effective in treating depression among methadone maintenance patients. Opiates are not highly depression-inducing or anxiety-inducing except during withdrawal. There is less concern about substance-induced psychopathology with patients on stable methadone treatment, unless the patient is using large quantities of street drugs. Tricyclic antidepressants have been well tolerated in methadone patients, although clinical experience indicates that anticholinergic effects may be problematic. Methadone slows the metabolism of tricyclics so that lower doses may be needed and the monitoring of blood levels is strongly advised.

There has been little study of anxiety in opiate-dependent patients. Clinical experience suggests benzodiazepines should be avoided in opioid-dependent patients because of their abuse potential in this population. It is sometimes useful to consider that a given methadone clinic has only one patient, but that patient has 150 to 300 heads. Giving benzodiazepines to one invariably stimulates the same desire in everyone else.

☐ Pharmacotherapies for Cocaine Dependence

Cocaine is a stimulant which acts by blocking re-uptake of norepinephrine, serotonin, and dopamine. It also has local anesthetic and vasoconstrictive as well as euphorigenic effects. Recreational or occasional use has decreased over the past 10 years, although heavy use has been stable. Estimates from the National Institute on Drug Abuse are that 10% to 15% of those who initially use cocaine will become problem users. The differences between those who become addicted and those who do not is not understood.

To review, subjective effects of cocaine intoxication and use include feelings of confidence, well-being, and magnification of the intensity of normal pleasures. Anxiety is initially decreased and social inhibitions are reduced. Physiological effects include tachycardia, pupillary dilation, hypertension, and hyperactivity. In higher doses, paranoia can occur with a presentation identical to the acute psychosis associated with schizophrenia and mania. There is a post-intoxication or withdrawal syndrome which includes exhaustion, hypersomnia, hyperphagia, depressed mood, and intermittent periods of craving for cocaine. This is more extensively discussed in the earlier chapter on cocaine.

A large number of agents, mainly antidepressants and dopamine agonists, have been tested as treatments for cocaine abuse, but none have demonstrated clear efficacy. Tricyclic antidepressants, primarily desipramine, have been the most thoroughly studied, and have shown some limited promise. Trials of most other pharmacological agents for cocaine abuse have been more flatly negative.

Tricyclics cannot be recommended as a routine treatment for cocaine abuse, although they might be considered in patients who have failed other approaches or who have clear-cut depressive symptoms. As with alcohol, cocaine induces many depressive symptoms, making an accurate diagnosis difficult. However, several clinical trials have suggested that depressed cocaine abusers, that is those with "true" depression, not just the effects of cocaine withdrawal, may benefit selectively from tricyclic antidepressants.

The evaluation of anxiety disorders is difficult in cocaine abusers because cocaine is anxiogenic and its use is associated with the induction of panic attacks. In many instances, the anxiety will lessen when the cocaine or stimulant abuse remits. The clinical principles for differential diagnosis of substance-induced versus independent psychopathology, discussed more thoroughly in the following chapter on comorbidity, can be applied. If an independent anxiety disorder is suspected, then treatment with an antidepressant, either a TCA or an SSRI, is warranted. Buspirone also appears to be safe. Caution, as with all substance abusers, should be employed in the consideration of benzodiazepines with this population.

At least part of the symptomatology of the acute psychotic phase of schizophrenia is a manifestation of excessive dopamine neurotransmission. Cocaine increases dopamine neurotransmission and can mimic psychosis or exacerbate an underlying psychotic condition seen in schizophrenia. Experience suggests that neuroleptics are useful for psychosis, whatever the cause in this population. Equally important is prompt attention to the substance dependence. These patients need a great deal of social and therapeutic support, and may require hospitalization to manage periods of increased cocaine use and psychosis.

There are several experimental models of treatment that appear promising in the treatment of cocaine dependence. Perhaps the most intriguing are two vaccines which are at the stage of animal testing. The first induces an antibody which is catalytic to the cocaine molecule; as soon as the cocaine molecule enters the blood stream, it is cleaved before reaching the brain. The second model induces the body to create its own catalytic antibodies which cleave the cocaine molecule. Both models are still in such an early phase of testing that it is impossible to predict if they will be effective. They are, however, quite promising and worthy of serious research.

□ Pharmacotherapies for Nicotine Dependence

Nicotine has come into focus over the last 15 years as a classically addictive drug. It has subtle stimulant-like effects and is highly reinforcing, apparently due to its action on nicotine receptors in the brain-reward system, as well as its ability to raise dopamine levels in the nucleus accumbens. Fifty-one million people in the U.S. are nicotine dependent, mostly through cigarette smoking. The adverse public health impact of smoking is enormous, contributing to increased incidence of coronary, cerebral and peripheral vascular disease, chronic obstructive pulmonary disease (COPD), and cancer. The nicotine withdrawal syndrome is now well characterized, and appears to contribute to difficulty quitting smoking for many individuals.

What follows is a brief overview of the pharmacological treatments of nicotine dependence. A more extensive description can be found in Chapter II of the book, which specifically addresses nicotine dependence.

Nicotine Substitution

Nicotine substitution therapies, either through nicotine-containing chewing gum or skin patches, have been extensively evaluated in clinical trials. They are effective in assisting initial smoking cessation, although subsequent relapse rates are quite high once nicotine replacement is tapered and discontinued. Long-term nicotine replacement is not currently practiced because of concern about its potential health consequences, although further research on this is warranted.

Antidepressant Medications

The nicotine withdrawal syndrome produces anxiety and depressive symptoms which resolve when smoking is resumed. A history of depression correlates with the inability to quit smoking. One antidepressant, buproprion (Zyban) has recently been approved in the treatment of smoking cessation without comorbid depression. It is recommended to be prescribed in the same doses used in the treatment of depression, 200–300 mg per day in a twice-daily fashion. Clinicians should be aware that in a small subset of these patients, the use of antidepressants can cause agitation, or unmask an underlying bipolar condition. It is clearly reasonable to initiate antidepressant medication in smokers with a history of becoming depressed during quit-attempts, or who become depressed during a current attempt. In addition it is likely useful for anyone who is having difficulty stopping smoking.

Conclusions

In summary, the relationship between substance use and psychiatric comorbidity is complicated. It is often very difficult to differentiate cause and effect. The treating clinician needs to be extremely careful in evaluating these dual problems. It is usually appropriate to treat both the substance abuse and the psychiatric condition concurrently. It should be emphasized that these disorders always need to be addressed in the context of a comprehensive treatment plan. In our opinion, pharmacology is underutilized. It has a major place in the treatment of both substance abuse and psychiatric conditions, and is often a vital adjunct to an individual's treatment and recovery. As a result of newer medication treatments with relatively benign side effects, it is often prudent to treat substance abuse using pharmacotherapy.

26

CHAPTER

Comorbidity

As noted earlier in the text, substances of abuse mimic naturally occurring elements in an individual's central nervous system. They produce effects that occur naturally, but these effects, when promoted by substances of abuse, tend to heighten or distort those naturally occurring processes. It makes intuitive sense that certain individuals will seek out elements or experiences that relieve or mimic a desired biological state. An individual who suffers from a particular condition may use substances that relieve that condition. At least in low doses, alcohol acts to relieve anxiety. Individuals with anxiety may therefore use alcohol for relief. In fact, it has long been thought, and epidemiological research has demonstrated, that individuals with anxiety disorders seem to be more prone to the use of alcohol. These individuals are therefore more likely to abuse and to become dependent upon alcohol.

Many patients with drug or alcohol problems have concomitant psychiatric conditions. Conversely, patients with significant psychopathology often have serious problems with drugs and alcohol. In recent years the subject of comorbidity has received increased attention. This has resulted in complex and nuanced investigations about the causes, effects, relationships, and possible treatments of comorbid conditions. This can be a source of clinical confusion because the symptoms of both conditions often mimic one another. For example, an individual may have schizophrenia and use cocaine. Both schizophrenia and cocaine are primary causes of paranoia. In the case of an individual with schizophrenia who presents with paranoia, it is likely that both conditions are exacerbating one another. At times the treatment is the same, other times it is quite different.

Comorbidity refers to an individual with two or more conditions, one of them being substance related. In more academically oriented and research settings, the term "dual diagnosis" has been developed to describe those individuals with one or more psychiatric conditions as well as substance abuse. The phrase "mentally ill chemical abuser" (MICA) is more commonly used in settings where the principle focus is on psychopathology. Both terms refer to the same thing and merely represent a difference in labeling.

☐ Possible Relationships

The relationship between substance use, abuse, and dependence is complex and intertwined. For the issue of treatment, the cause and effect of the substance abuse would certainly seem important. Knowing which condition came first is important for a variety of reasons, as that condition is usually the one that ought to be treated first. An individual may come to a clinician with the complaint of having difficulty sleeping. Such an individual may be using alcohol with the mistaken idea that this will help him or her to sleep. This notion is a popular misconception, as alcohol use can lead to a sleep disturbance (alcohol suppresses REM sleep). Which came first—the sleep disturbance or the alcohol use—is an important distinction both diagnostically and in treatment planning.

For the purpose of discussion, the connection between substance use and treatment may be simplified into three potential types:

1. Primary psychopathology with subsequent substance abuse; this occurs when an individual has a condition and begins to use substances to try and relieve the psychopathology ("self-medication"). An individual may be anxious and discuss this complaint with his or her internist. He or she will be prescribed benzodiazepines for this anxiety, but in some instances, the individual may use increasing amounts of benzodiazepines.
2. Primary substance abuse with subsequent psychopathology ("substance-induced"). An example of this is the individual who complains of tiredness and lethargy, but who uses cocaine. While doses of cocaine cause elation at first, they can also cause someone subsequent symptoms of depression and lack of energy. In this case, it is the cocaine that is causing the problem.

3. Both may be simultaneous and independent conditions. In this final relationship between substance use and psychiatric conditions, there may be no relationship at all other than the observation that both conditions exist simultaneously.

Primary Psychopathology

This therapy derives from the psychoanalytic belief that substances are used as a means to cope with painful affects. An individual may turn to substances with the belief or feeling that they will relieve his or her condition. The "self medication hypothesis" was pioneered by Dr. Edward Khantzian, an addiction psychiatrist and analyst who postulated that underlying psychiatric problems contribute to the development and continuation of substance abuse disorders. Substances can be used to treat certain conditions and, in some instances, will not cause problems. In low doses, alcohol can act as mild anxiolytic. It is, if used responsibly, useful in certain social situations. Cocaine is stimulating and, for some users, decreases inhibitions. Most often, the individual who has a documented psychiatric condition and uses abusable substances to self-treat this condition, gets into trouble with it.

The corollary of this model implies that treating the underlying disorder in an individual who is "self medicating" should decrease the substance abuse as well. In some cases this corollary is probably true. If taken too literally, this position results in the risk of the therapist never adequately addressing the substance abuse as a separate issue. An individual may have depression which can be treated, but the treating therapist ought not to condone continued abuse of alcohol in that person. The familiar vicious cycle where a person comes to treatment week after week complaining about the pain of existence; however, he/she continues to take heroin, and the effects of the drug, and the lifestyle that surround heroin use, wreak havoc around that person thus perpetuating instead of solving the problem.

A more sound approach is to view substance use either as a form of resistance, or as ineffective self-treatment, which must be given up in order to allow for more definitive treatment of the underlying co-morbid condition. The person in question may indeed have a significant condition that merits treatment, either pharmacologically, or in a psychosocial manner (or both), but this ought not to be used as an excuse to continue destructive and damaging behavior. In some instances the individual, once treated, may be able to go back to responsible use; however, in most instances he or she will not be able to do so.

Clues to Primary Psychopathology

1. Psychopathology which began before serious substance abuse.
2. Psychopathology which persists during past periods of abstinence.
3. Chronic, as opposed to intermittent or transient, psychopathology.
4. Emergence of psychopathology during periods of stable substance use.
5. Positive family history of similar psychopathology.
6. Uniqueness of the psychiatric symptoms.
7. Extreme severity of psychiatric conditions in relation to moderate levels of abuse.

Secondary Psychopathology

Many of the substances that are topics of this text, used in even small amounts cause damage and toxicity. Psychopathology may be induced by the toxic effects of substances. Even small amounts of alcohol interfere with sleep. Large amounts of alcohol cause the well-known effects of a hangover, and even larger amounts, over extended amounts of time may induce cognitive decline, or in the case of acute delirium tremens, may cause psychosis and other mental status changes. Psychopathology does often remit shortly after abstinence is achieved. The individual who stops using alcohol often returns to restful sleep, and in the matter of just a few days may feel refreshed and renewed.

If this model is correct, then adequate treatment of the substance abuse should cure the presenting psychopathology. Locking someone up in a place where they do not have access to cocaine, for example, may result in the remittance of agitation and paranoia. This is probably true for many cases of substance dependence and many clinicians insist that stopping the substance use is always the first approach that should be taken. These clinicians argue that attempting to treat the psychopathology and not first addressing the substance issue may divert attention from the substance abuse, thus inviting a dangerous resistance that can contribute to denial. The view articulated in the concept of secondary psychopathology is part of the tradition of many self-help groups, most notably Alcoholics Anonymous.

Unfortunately, this view may be taken to extremes leading to advice not to take medications for potentially dangerous conditions such as major depression, bipolar, or schizoaffective disorders. Conditions such as bipolar disorder have a high rate of comorbid substance abuse, but are independent biological conditions which need somatic treatment. A patient with bipolar disorder and alcoholism, who is advised to refuse prescription medications for a mood disorder, is receiving bad advice.

While this topic of models can engender considerable controversy among both clinicians and patients, there appears to be support for both models articulated above (primary psychopathology versus primary substance abuse). The best approach for a given patient will often lie somewhere in between the two. The fact that these models are not mutually exclusive is helpful for providing this combination approach. Often the most effective clinical result occurs when both the co-morbid condition and the substance abuse are addressed at the same time. If a person is trying to stop their alcohol use but keeps complaining of an inability to fall asleep, it may be advisable to treat that individual with a short course of a soporific, especially at the beginning of treatment. The inability to fall asleep may no longer be used as an excuse to continue drinking; however, in this case, the need for a sleep aid will eventually need to be addressed as part of the overall substance abuse treatment.

The most important consideration for the clinician dealing with an individual substance abuser who has symptoms of comorbidity is "What is clinically most useful and timely in the treatment of the individual?" Ignoring the psychopathology, and ascribing all complaints to the toxicity of the substance is often simplistic, thereby allowing the continued destructive use of a substance by the rationalization that the individual is in pain. Alternatively, allowing such "self-medication" to continue may be highly damaging to a given patient.

Rigid adherence to either view is not in the best interest of patients, and instead a flexible approach is recommended, open to the possibilities that either disorder may be primary, or that both may co-exist independently.

☐ Approach to the Patient

History

Assessment of patients who suffer from substance abuse and a psychiatric condition begins with a complete history and physical examination. The history should be as comprehensive as possible. Often this involves the involvement of people who know the patient. Substance abusers are notoriously bad historians and often cannot be relied upon alone to provide an accurate accounting of their conditions.

A good history for a patient for whom there is a question of dual diagnosis includes the following four areas: (a) precipitating events leading to presentation; (b) onset and pattern of drug use over the patient's lifetime; (c) positive and negative consequences of drug use for the patient (Does substance use temporarily relieve psychiatric symptoms?); and (d) onset and course of psychiatric comorbidity in relation to course of substance use. (Which began first, substance abuse or the psychiatric disorder? Does the psychiatric disorder remit or persist during periods of sobriety?) All of the questions in these four areas must be addressed in order to understand the relationship between the substance use and psychopathology.

It is also important to consider the social context in which drugs are used. An adult with social phobia may use drugs or alcohol to tolerate social gatherings; however, an adolescent may take drugs impulsively, to enrage his or her parents, or to gain peer acceptance. In the assessment of comorbidity, it is useful to include members of a patient's social network to obtain an adequate history and to develop a treatment plan. Spouses, family members, friends, employers, social workers, or parole officers can all be productively involved in this process. Collateral historians will aid in clarifying the circumstances surrounding a patient's substance use and psychological state. A therapeutic climate where there are no adverse consequences of accurate reporting increases the probability of getting useful information from patient self-reports of their substance abuse. An open and accepting interview posture, rather than a moralistic or disapproving stance, on the part of the clinician is most likely to elicit the kind of data most relevant to questions of comorbidity.

Physical and Laboratory Examination

A thorough medical history, in addition to a physical and laboratory evaluation, is essential in the patient with a dual diagnosis. There are numerous physical consequences of substance use, both from the substances' direct toxicity (e.g., substance-induced cognitive impairment, nicotine or cocaine-related cardiovascular disease, and alcoholic liver disease), and high-risk behaviors associated with intoxication (sexually and parenterally transmitted diseases such as viral hepatitis, HIV, AIDS, and AIDS Dementia Complex). Other problems occur as a result of the harmful consequences of route of administration, particularly injection drug use, smoking, and freebasing (e.g., chronic lung disease and bacterial endocarditis). In addition to requiring direct evaluation and treatment, many of these substances may produce fatigue, apathy, cognitive impairment, or anxiety. These symptoms may obscure or mimic psychiatric disorders so that their consideration becomes a critical part of the psychiatric differential diagnosis.

☐ Differential Diagnosis

The diagnosis of psychopathology in active substance abusers is a clinical challenge. The most prudent approach, recommended in DSM-IV, requires persistence of psychopathology during at least a one-month abstinence period before the diagnosis of a comorbid disorder such as depression can be made. In actual practice, this is not always possible, and an individual clinician may need to make an educated guess weighing a variety of factors in order to determine the priority of any etiology.

Since psychopathology worsens the severity of substance abuse, it is often those patients with comorbid psychiatric symptoms who are the most difficult to keep abstinent. This creates an unfortunate dilemma. For example, when depression is not diagnosed or treated because of lack of abstinence, maintaining abstinence may hinge upon treating the depression. While the first effort in diagnostic evaluation should be to treat the substance abuse and achieve abstinence, in practice abstinence is often difficult to achieve on an outpatient basis, and patients frequently cannot or will not be hospitalized. In some cases patients can only be hospitalized for a matter of days due to insurance constraints or pressures to continue to make a living.

The alternative approach is to attempt the differential diagnosis in an outpatient who may still be actively using substances. There are a number of features of the history and presentation of an individual that can indicate if a comorbid condition is primary or independent of substance use and warrants specific treatment. Several elements may be helpful in differentiating whether the current presentation is more the result of the psychiatric condition, or the toxicity of the substance itself. Among these clues are:

1. Psychopathology which is chronologically primary (that it began before the onset of substance abuse). An example of this is the person with alcoholism and depression who has a clear history of depressive episodes dating back to his or her teens, well before heavy drinking began. Such an individual with a significant history of depression is more likely to have recurrent depressive episodes that would likely occur whether or not the person was using substances. Similarly an individual with, childhood history of attention deficit hyperactivity disorder (ADHD) may be abusing cocaine as an adult (there is emerging evidence that individuals with ADHD are more likely to become dependent upon cocaine). Both the substance abuse and the ADHD symptoms will need to be addressed in such an individual.
2. Psychopathology which persists during past periods of abstinence. If the patient gives a reliable (or preferably verifiable) history of abstinence in which the psychological symptoms continue to persist, this indicates that the person may have a primary condition. A person with a substance induced depression, for example, who becomes sober can expect to have those depressive symptoms remit within a relatively short period of their stopping drinking (most likely within a week)

If the symptoms continue, this would suggest that depression as the more likely etiology rather than the substance abuse.

3. Chronic, as opposed to intermittent or transient, psychopathology. Psychopathology caused by substances most often waxes and wanes with the severity of the substance abuse. If it does not, this points away from the substance as the cause. An example of this condition is someone who has unremitting hypomanic symptoms for years and who uses cocaine. Cocaine may induce these symptoms but they should not last for that great a time. If the psychiatric symptoms continue without a fluctuating course, it is likely that something other than the substance abuse is the primary cause of the depression.
4. Emergence of psychopathology during periods of stable substance use, rather than periods of rapidly escalating (or diminishing) use. An example of this condition is the person who once per week for the past five years has used a consistent amount of intranasal cocaine in a social setting (e.g., only when dancing on Saturday nights) and now has developed panic symptoms. In such a case although the clinician has a responsibility to warn about the potential dangers of cocaine, it is unlikely that substance abuse is the cause of the patient's development of panic attacks. An individual might be a "heavy social drinker," who develops depression. For instance, someone may drink two to three cocktails every evening, and have done so for the past 20 years, and now presents with the full panoply of depression symptoms. In such a case at least temporary abstinence is advisable, and is probably the initial clinical step to take. However, because the depression occured within the context of long standing but stable substance use, abstinence alone is unlikely to relieve the full severity and dimension of the symptoms described.
5. Positive family history of similar psychopathology (since many psychiatric disorders are, in part, due to inherited factors). An example of this inherited condition would be a person, abusing marijuana, who has irritability and restlessness, in addition to having several family members with a history of variations of bipolar disorder. The irritability may be exacerbated by repeated withdrawal from marijuana, but it is more likely that this symptom may well be the manifestation of an underlying mood disorder.
6. Uniqueness and severity of the psychiatric symptoms. Examples of this include agoraphobia, social phobia, and obsessions or compulsions. These are more typically related to anxiety disorders and do not routinely occur as part of drug toxicity or withdrawal. Likewise, profound suicidal ideation should increase suspicion that a true mood disorder is present. It is important that the professional conducting the assessment exercise clinical judgment after weighing all of the evidence. This

orientation is most likely to result in a comprehensive evaluation and an appropriate combination of therapies can be recommended.

7. Extreme severity of psychiatric conditions in relation to moderate levels of abuse. Moderate amounts of substance abuse can create significant problems in drug and alcohol users. In general it is unusual for them to cause severe, dramatic and sustained psychiatric symptoms (in the case of hallucinogens, these may cause severe symptoms, but they are typically short lived.) Someone who presents with severe panic disorder of several weeks duration, and who (verifiably) used a small amount of cocaine several weeks before, is unlikely to benefit from substance abuse treatment alone, which excludes therapy for what is likely an independent panic disorder.

Comorbidity and Specific Substances

Certain comorbid conditions are more likely to co-exist with certain types of substance abuse and dependence. The corollary is also true that certain substances are likely to induce and to be associated with certain conditions. The following discussion is intended to familiarize the reader with some of those conditions that are more likely to be associated with one another. Most substances of abuse can cause a variety of effects and these effects are often unpredictable. Nevertheless there are some associations that are more common than others. If substance abuse is diagnosed or suspected, the clinician may think about the existence of such a disorder.

Alcohol

Alcohol is associated with a variety of comorbid conditions. Chronic use of alcohol is often the cause of, or associated with, mood disorders. The most common of these is depression. Anxiety symptoms and panic often co-exist with alcohol abuse.

Cocaine

Cocaine is also associated with mood disorders and may be the cause of, or an inappropriate "self treatment" for, anxiety or depression. Another association with cocaine is attention deficit hyperactivity disorder. People with ADHD are more likely than others to become dependent upon cocaine. One possible explanation for this association is individuals with ADHD probably have low dopamine "tone" (tone in this sense is an unscientific way of describing the usual levels of a neurotransmitter in an individuals CNS). Cocaine and other stimulants raise the levels of dopamine and help such individuals become more focused and organized. Thus, they are more attracted to cocaine's ability to organize them, they may continue to use it, and they are therefore more likely to become dependent upon cocaine. Schizophrenia is also associated with cocaine use, and may be particularly destructive in this population, since cocaine can severely exacerbate the underlying condition.

Marijuana

There is emerging evidence that marijuana use is associated with mood disorders, especially those that involve irritability and explosive mood. The marijuana user may be trying to "self medicate" an underlying mood disorder, perhaps even bipolar disorder. Marijuana's (not THC's) anticonvulsant properties may be providing the impetus for this use.

Nicotine

Nicotine use is more common with several psychiatric conditions, in particular mood disorders and schizophrenia. Many depressed individuals use nicotine, and nicotine withdrawal may cause depression. Similarly, it is extremely rare to find an individual with schizophrenia who is not a smoker. This relationship has provided ample fodder for recent research.

Heroin

Heroin use is associated with chronic anxiety and other mood disorders. There is some evidence that individuals prone to opiate use and abuse may be chronically deficient in their own pleasure–reward systems, and are thus more likely to be drawn to use and abuse heroin.

Alertness to the possibility of comorbid psychiatric and substance abuse problems coupled with a systematized plan for obtaining relevant historical data is an invaluable aid to the clinician charged with the difficult task of evaluating a patient who has symptoms which are not clear cut.

PART

VI

POLICY ISSUES

The use of drugs and alcohol does not take place in a vacuum. While these substances interact with the physiology of the individuals who use them, those individuals also interact with others. In order to function appropriately in society, there are rules and regulations, norms of behavior, and laws made by government. The following section deals with a few select issues which are germane to someone who wants to understand how drugs are regulated and dealt with in a broader context. The chapters in this section focus on some select topics involving policy issues which are important to anyone who is interested in the larger context of substance abuse. Again, the authors have chosen not to attempt to cover in a comprehensive manner the myriad policy issues associated with substance abuse, but rather to present a few representative and controversial issues.

27

CHAPTER

Drugs in the Workplace

Many of the substances discussed in this book have both legal and illicit use. Alcohol is enjoyed in moderation at appropriate times by many people. The set and the setting associated with substance use constitute important elements in determining whether the substance is enhancing or destructive. Mood-altering substances (with the notable exception of caffeine) do not generally have a place at work. Intoxication is responsible for the majority of accidents and fatalities that occur on the job in the U.S. There are a number of substance abuse prevention and detection programs concerned with the workplace.

☐ Detection

Detection of substances in the workplace can be divided into pre- and post-employment. Many companies now make drug testing routine in the pre-employment physical examination. Each prospective employee undergoes some form of drug testing. Employment is contingent on a negative result. In many circumstances, if the test results are positive, the individual may be employed on a probationary basis. The new employee will then be monitored on a frequent basis to ensure future abstinence.

Such programs have an obligation to refer people whose tests are positive to some form of counseling or treatment center for evaluation.

The second type of detection is ongoing. This is either routinely scheduled or done on a random basis. If testing is done on a scheduled basis, then people are told that they will be tested for drugs at given intervals, usually every six months or a year. Random drug testing is more common, with employees subject to unexpected testing. There are a number of variations of this testing format, the most common being that each day the medical staff selects a two or three digit number at random; each person with a social security number that ends with that number must report that day to the medical office and submit to the test. The armed forces does this each day, and all staff, at all ranks, with a particular number report for a supervised urine test.

It is recommended that if a workplace does engage in random testing that a number of policies are followed. All employees, at every rank, ought to be subjected to this form of testing, with no exemptions. This reduces claims of bias and emphasizes a company's commitment to a drug-free workplace. It also sends a message about the importance of substance abuse and treatment. It is important to include a provision that if an individual does test positive for substance use, there will be an evaluation and treatment program in place to help evaluate the employee's drug use, and if need be, to help him or her with treatment.

In most cases, a person who tests positive for drugs needs to be evaluated and then subjected to more frequent testing. For instance, it may be the case that an employee uses an illegal substance such as marijuana and does not have a "problem" with it; that is, his or her use is infrequent, and has not caused significant impairment in his or her life. If this particular person really does not have a problem with marijuana, then the individual should be able to refrain from drug use for a period of time. The inability to stop using a substance in the face of the threat to end employment is de facto proof of dependence and signifies the need for treatment.

☐ Types of Testing

There are a number of commercially available forms of testing, each with advantages and disadvantages. Most commercial laboratories have testing for routine drugs of abuse. Less commonly available are supervised tests. These are required when a person has a significant incentive to hide his or her ongoing drug use. An anesthesiologist who is threatened with losing a medical license has a strong motive for concealing the misuse of substances. People can be very creative in hiding their drug use. Smuggling in borrowed urine is a common tactic to avoid detection of substance use in urine samples.

A practicing clinician now has the ability to do in-office testing. While it may seem intrusive, testing on the spot as a routine part of the treatment plan can also serve to dispel anxiety and apprehension. Mail order versions of these tests can be found easily by contacting a local medical laboratory (listed in the Yellow Pages), and are available from companies that advertise on the Internet.

Tests routinely examine the most common drugs of abuse such as marijuana, cocaine, amphetamines, opioid analgesics, and PCP. Some drugs, such as MDMA and Ketamine, are not tested for unless specifically requested. Because it is active in such minute doses, LSD is notoriously difficult to detect. These tests are in general reliable and a positive urine almost always assures that the person was using drugs. Much has been made of poppy seeds resulting in positive urines. This *can* happen because poppy seeds contain minute amounts of diacetylmorphine; however, an individual would need to eat a substantial amount of the seed to achieve a detectable level. One bagel or roll with a few seeds, for example, would not be enough to create a positive test result.

Urine Testing

Urine drug screens are the most common form of testing. They test for the metabolites of any drug which is excreted in the urine. The advantages include the relatively low cost and the ready commercial availability of the tests. The disadvantages include the intrusiveness of supervised testing and the fact that many professionals do not like handling urine samples. In addition, there are times when subjects really cannot produce urine. Another important disadvantage with urine testing is that if a person has just ingested the substance, it will not have been metabolized and excreted in the urine immediately and the test may be negative.

Most urine testing investigates drugs only at a threshold but the more expensive tests can look for lower cut-off levels. Different substances take different lengths of time to leave the body; therefore, both the duration of use and the quantity ingested affect this. One puff on a marijuana cigarette will be detected in the urine, but probably for only two or three days after the event. A heavy marijuana user who stops using may have positive urines for a month or even longer. This is because of marijuana's fat solubility; it stays in a person's system and leeches out over a considerable length of time. There is much variability to the length of time a substance produces a positive urine, but as a rule of thumb, most urines will stay positive for a substance used for about a week after the use.

This of course depends on the substance used, as well as the amount, in addition to the variabilty of each individual's metabolism.

Urine tests have been the prefered pre-employment drug screen. Many employers are not concerned that their employees have never used a substance of abuse, or even that they used something six months ago (which might be detected in a hair sample.) They are concerned that a potential employee not have a significant drug problem. Negative urine samples at least ensure that the individual has the ability to stop using drugs for a week, demonstrating at least some measure of control over use.

Blood Testing

Blood-level tests are available for many drugs of abuse. Advantages of testing blood include the reliability of the test and the ability to test for recently ingested drugs. The disadvantages include the cumbersome nature of testing, the need for a medical professional or trained phlebotomist to take the blood, and the expense. This type of testing is best reserved for hospital and emergency situations.

Hair Testing

Drug metabolites permeate the entire body and become entwined in the elements that produce mammalian hair. Hair follicles retain a record of what the person has ingested for three to four months previously (or for as long as the hair is available to be tested.) The advantages of hair testing include the ability to detect remote use, as well as the ease and non-invasive nature of testing for the subject. The disadvantages are that the technology is new and has not yet been subjected to vigorous scientific testing. Though most of the involved technology is patented, some of the commercial establishments have been reluctant to subject the tests to vigorous scientific scrutiny.

The other major problem with hair testing is more subtle. Hair may be positive for an individual that has used drugs, but really does not have a "problem" with them. An individual advised of a pre-employment test ought to be able to stop smoking, taking, or shooting drugs for a week to produce a clean urine. If he or she cannot, this is clear evidence of a drug problem. Someone may have used a small amount of an illicit substance several months previously, the evidence of which would show up in his or her hair. Whether this should prevent a person from being employed is a matter of significant debate.

Saliva Testing

Drug tests will likely soon be commercially available for the testing of saliva. This has about the same profile as urine testing, but has the advantage of being both less intrusive and more difficult to fake. It has the disadvantage of being a new technology and one that has not yet been rigorously scrutinized.

New Technologies

In the years to come, it will be possible to monitor an individual's drug use even more extensively. Devices are currently being tested that would be worn by an individual as a very small skin patch which is sensitive to drugs in sweat. The drug use can be measured after the patch is removed. Other versions are even more sophisticated. As soon as a substance is detected in sweat, a signal is sent to a central authority alerting them about the drug use. Similar signals are sent if the patch is removed. In the future, these devices may be used by law enforcement agencies in order to measure a person's compliance with parole. How these technologies are applied to the work force or the general population remain to be seen. The subtle tension between individual liberties and public policy are complex and sensitive issues which come into play with the newer forms of drug testing.

☐ The Employee Assistance Program (EAP)

Almost all work environments with a medium to large population of employees have an EAP. In some cases, as in very large corporations, the EAP may exist as part of the corporate structure. In this case, the staff of the EAP may be employees of the same corporation as the employees they are evaluating and treating. In other instances, there are independent EAPs whose services are contracted by the company like any independent consulting firm. The staff of the EAP specialize in treating a variety of problems common in the workplace. These include issues of disability, discrimination, and harassment. EAPs differ from human resource departments in that they assist with a *problem* once it is identified. The staff of an EAP can be very helpful in dealing with an employee who is suspected of abusing substances. EAP staff should be very knowledgeable about community resources for substance abusers and can be invaluable in helping with reimbursement issues for a given patient who seeks treatment.

28

CHAPTER

Drugs and the Law

Since the early part of this century, the federal government has attempted to control the manufacturing, distribution, and use of psychoactive drugs. The United States government is a Federalist system where there are state and community regulations over the sale and behavior associated with substance use. These laws vary widely from state to state and region to region. Walking down the street in Manhattan with an open beer may result in arrest or a summons, while in parts of the South an individual is able to purchase open pints of beer while in a car at drive-through windows. This chapter provides a synopsis of the most important regulations concerning psychoactive substances. This is a labyrinthine topic filled with nuances and contradictions, but a discussion of at least the basic issues associated with drugs and the law is warranted for anyone interested in the issues involved with substance abuse, its treatment, and the policies surrounding it.

The Controlled Substances Act, 21 U.S.C. Section 801 ff. was originally passed as Title II of the Comprehensive Drug Abuse Prevention and Control Act of 1970. It is the legal framework that differentiates permissible medical drug use from prohibited drug abuse. This places all known and regulated substances in one of five schedules. These schedules are divided in terms of the likelihood of abuse and the therapeutic benefit. Schedule I drugs are deemed to have no potential therapeutic benefit and a high likelihood of abuse. An example of these are heroin or Quaaludes. Schedule II drugs have a high likelihood of abuse, but some compelling therapeutic benefit. An example of this is cocaine, which is an effective local anesthetic and particularly useful in certain surgical procedures, especially those involving ear, nose, and throat operations (it is a potent vasoconstrictor and is therefore useful in these highly vascularized areas of the anatomy). Schedules III, IV, and V are reserved for drugs which have much less abuse potential.

The Controlled Substances Act does not cover any drug that is not named. For example, MDMA ("Ecstasy ") was not named as a substance of abuse in the original act. Its sale and distribution in the early 1970s and 1980s was therefore legal. In 1985, it was put on Schedule I on an emergency basis. This status was made permanent in 1986. The scheduling of a drug is often motivated by science as well as by politics. The fact that marijuana is a Schedule I drug is highly controversial. A substantial number of people believe that it does indeed have legitimate medical/therapeutic value and, at the same time, are well aware that it has a serious abuse potential. The medical use of marijuana is a subject which has come to the forefront recently and continues to be a source of debate within the substance abuse treatment community.

The Drug Enforcement Agency (DEA) has the ultimate authority for scheduling drugs and enforcing scheduling. The Food and Drug Administration (FDA) has an advisory role in these proceedings, but not ultimate authority. In recent years, the FDA has been increasingly involved in advocating that the Federal government play a more active role in regulating and monitoring substances such as herbal remedies and food supplements.

The sale and distribution of two other substances of abuse—nicotine and alcohol—are legal with the exception of their sale to minors. Neither is under the jurisdiction of the FDA or the DEA. They are not considered part of the federal drug control policy and their regulation has been left to the individual states. This has occurred despite the fact that these two drugs account for more than half a million deaths per year. The distinctions between some of the regulations of these substances have begun to erode in recent years, and the FDA has attempted to assert its role in the regulation of nicotine as an addictive substance.

There is often some variability as to what activities are legal or prohibited in terms of certain substances. There are some substances which are illegal to buy or sell, but not illegal to own or use. An example of this occurred during Prohibition when there was a prohibition of the manufacture and sale of alcohol (except for medicinal and religious purposes) but not of individual possession or use.

In 1997, the federal anti-drug budget exceeded 15 billion dollars, with most money allocated for reducing the supply of drugs entering into or manufactured in this country. Every cabinet department has a substantial anti-drug program. In 1988, Congress created the Office of National Drug Control Policy (ONDCP), headed by a cabinet-level position and intended to coordinate federal drug policy.

Because of both bureaucratic inertia and the American propensity to pander to voters calling for more law and order, the federal efforts at drug control have concentrated on law enforcement and on reducing the drug supply. In bureaucratic parlance, this is "supply reduction."

Almost all rational analysis has indicated that reducing demand and increasing treatment is a far less expensive and far more effective strategy. Still, the great majority of money goes toward law enforcement. Two well-evaluated and effective prevention programs, the Life Skills Training (LST) and Students Taught Awareness and Resistance (STAR), are quite valuable in reducing the incidence of new smoking, drinking, and marijuana use in teenage citizens. These programs cost between $15 and $25 per pupil for supplies and training. By contrast, the cost of one year of outpatient treatment is $5,000; inpatient treatment costs about $18,000. In even sharper contrast, the cost to the taxpayer of incarceration for a year is $25,000. It is hoped that in the future, the issues of treatment and education will become more of a priority.

Criminal penalties for the possession, sale, and manufacturing of controlled substances exist on local, state, and national levels of government. There is an enormous amount of variability in both the laws themselves and the rigor with which they are enforced. Arrests for marijuana possession are much more common in the South than they are in California, where a more permissive attitude prevails.

This variability extends worldwide. Certain countries are quite tolerant of drug use, while others have draconian laws for even modest possession. As an example, in Singapore, an individual found with any amount of marijuana may be hanged.

☐ The Debate over Legalization

The legal status of many substances of abuse is the topic of endless debate. That some substances, such as alcohol and tobacco, are legal is evidence of hypocrisy to some, justice to others, and bafflement to many. Many individuals support tougher drug laws and would advocate the use of the death penalty for drug-related crimes. On the other side of the issue is a large number of people who believe that all substances of abuse ought to be made legal in America. Supporters of this view often state that the emphasis on law enforcement in drug policy in this country leads to needless social problems and an unnecessarily substantial prison population. They point to the unfairness that these laws place on members of minority groups, who are more likely to be arrested and prosecuted for drug-related crimes. As evidence, those that support full legalization note that over one third of all African American men in their twenties are either in prison or on probation, mostly because of crimes either directly or indirectly related to drugs. Proponents advocate the liberalization of laws but also support increased monitoring and treatment of problems resulting from drugs.

☐ Availability

The availability of a drug can be divided into three components: (a) physical, (b) economic, and (c) psychological. Physical availability refers to the actual substantive availability of any drug in the community. An example is the relative ease with which alcohol is accessible in most parts of the United States despite legal drinking-age restrictions. The ready availability of alcohol is in part responsible for the high rates of its abuse. The rate of heroin abuse on Easter Island, a small island in the South Pacific, is quite low, perhaps non-existent. The reason is simple: Heroin is almost impossible to obtain in such a remote and isolated place.

Economic availability involves the cost of any substance. The laws of supply and demand apply to drugs as they do to everything else. Certain substances are quite expensive, making them unaffordable to poorer people. This was the case with cocaine in the late 1970s and early 1980s, but this changed with the introduction of crack cocaine. Per ounce, crack is in fact more expensive than other drugs, but the packaging makes it more affordable. A corollary can be found with alcohol. There is an economic difference between purchasing a bottle of whisky and buying a shot in a bar. Some people cannot afford the $15 to buy a bottle of whisky, but many can afford to purchase one or two shots in a night (even though, ounce-per-ounce, the shot is far more expensive.) The same principle is true for crack; almost anyone can come up with the $2 to $4 required to buy a vial of crack. That is a major reason why it became so popular in the poorer areas of the inner city—it is cheap to get a single dose, and therefore much more economically available.

A final element of availability is psychological. This refers to the many internal and external prohibitions people have concerning different drugs. Availability is related to the prevailing moral and social climate. The more "permission" an individual has to use a substance, the more likely he or she is to partake of it. This "permission" is metaphorical and can come from one's community as well as one's own internal psychological structure. Caffeine is an addicting substance that has enormous availability. There are almost no communities with cultural prohibition of the use of caffeine. In sharp contrast is a drug like injected heroin. Most people have an aversion to needles, and the majority of Americans believe that using heroin is deviant. The level of psychological availability is inversely proportional to the presence of sociopathy in those who use a given drug. This is why many clinicians hold the view that their heroin patients show more signs of sociopathy than their alcoholic patients. Heroin, for most people, is less psychologically available than alcohol.

Most analysis suggests that legalization would effect the economics of substance abuse by driving the price of drugs down. Supply and demand apply here. One of the chief reasons that drugs are so expensive is that the consequences for selling are so severe. The economic incentive must be great to motivate people to take such risk. Legalization would remove that economic incentive and make drugs less expensive. As prices would go down, drug use would increase.

Finally, the legalization of drugs would increase the psychological availability of these substances. The illegal status of many substances provides a deterrent for the majority of individuals. Legalization of drug use would, in a certain sense, sanction the use of drugs such as heroin, crack, and marijuana.

Interestingly, the American experience with Prohibition has often been considered a failure. However, it did have some unintended positive effects: Alcohol consumption did plummet, as did the complications of alcohol abuse; rates of domestic violence decreased, and for years after, the rates of cirrhosis greatly diminished.

In recent years, the residents of the town of Barrow, Alaska, had voted to prohibit the sale and consumption of alcohol. Barrow is the northernmost significant municipality in Alaska and is very remote, and therefore supplies are difficult to obtain—thus, the prohibition of alcohol was quite effective in removing the supply. The result was a dramatic decrease in car accidents, domestic violence, and emergency room visits. In October of 1997, however, the ordinance was repealed by a narrow margin. It will be interesting to follow the consequences of this.

Legalization could take many forms, from total abandonment of any restriction to "de-criminalization," or the lessening of penalties associated with drug-related crimes. In the middle of those that hold these opposing viewpoints are those that advocate strict regulation of drugs and increased treatment, but a removal of the emphasis of law enforcement on substance abuse policy. People involved with both sides of the debate can be quite passionate. This will continue to be an ongoing, complex, legal, scientific, and emotional issue in the foreseeable future.

29

CHAPTER

Prevention and Education

The most effective public health strategies in dealing with substance abuse must rely on prevention. It is almost always easier and more cost-effective to deal with a problem or issue before it develops. This is abundantly true of issues involving substance abuse.

Unfortunately, the bulk of resources in the United States has been devoted to interdiction. More dollars are spent on police efforts and programs to stop drugs from entering the country than on prevention. While based on the good intention of keeping drugs away from people, the demand for drugs and the vastness of and facility with which our borders are crossed preclude the success of these efforts. Still, Congress continues to allocate more and more money for efforts of interdiction.

Prevention programs can be divided between two types. *Primary prevention* programs aim to prevent substance use and abuse. Such programs tend to emphasize the dangers of drugs and alcohol, and the benefits of non use. *Secondary prevention* programs are those that are aimed at deterring further use and avoiding abuse. (Tertiary prevention is aimed at ending abuse and dependence and emphasizes treatment). "Harm reduction" is most closely related to secondary prevention. Harm reduction efforts, in general, are much more permissive of drug use than secondary prevention programs, but seek to limit the negative consequences associated with approved drug use. An example of harm reduction is the British public health effort to educate people about safer uses of MDMA ("Ecstasy"). Most of this literature emphasizes the need to remain hydrated and to use the drug in a safe environment. Such literature does not explicitly condemn or promote the use of the drug, but rather it remains neutral by implying that if use is inevitable, using safely is an important public health goal.

In the United States, the most common and prominent public health efforts concerning addiction have focused on primary prevention. There are numerous educational and prevention programs in existence. While some have demonstrated effectiveness, the vast majority have been untested. The lack of studies that carefully define the target population and the outcome goals for prevention leave the arena to simplistic and untested strategies. The majority of prevention programs rely on two elements: the acquisition of knowledge and the development of adaptive coping skills. The reasoning behind this is that the more informed an individual is, the better equipped he or she will be to make choices. Many of these programs have targeted "gateway" drugs such as cigarettes, alcohol, and marijuana, and have emphasized the acquisition of knowledge about their dangers. *Knowledge about drugs and their use, by themselves, are not enough to prevent abuse.*

The most traditional approaches have been educational. They have aimed to increase knowledge about the consequences of drug use and to promote anti-drug attitudes. Empirical studies have generally demonstrated that such approaches are ineffective at best. At worst, this purely educational and "scare tactic" approach may serve to increase substance abuse by increasing the curiosity of the targeted adolescents.

Another approach has been to ignore the subject of substance abuse itself and to focus on trying to increase self-esteem and enhance responsible decision making. The theory behind this has been that substance abuse, especially in adolescents, is much more likely to occur in individuals who are under stress and who have issues with low self-esteem. These approaches have largely been discredited.

Unfortunately there is little consensus about which efforts and programs are most effective. Very few well-controlled investigations have occurred in this arena. The absence of convincing experimental data has hampered agreement about what principles should be employed, either in individual programs or larger public health efforts.

The above description is not intended to be bleak or nihilistic. Rather it is intended to emphasize how important it will be to elucidate which interventions or policies are most effective. These are complicated disorders and problems, and the reliance on one salient factor, such as lack of knowledge, low self-esteem, or some other factor, to the exclusion of other elements, is simplistic. The fact of the matter is that rates of use of dangerous substances do rise and fall for a variety of complex and intertwined individual, familial, societal, and regulatory reasons.

It seems likely that the most successful programs will employ a multifactorial approach to both policy and education. These will involve rational public health policies to promote treatment, and not merely rely on interdiction. Prevention approaches will not only deal with substance abuse issues but also teach children a second set of skills: coping mechanisms and behaviors that do not rely on drugs and alcohol. In addition, they recognize the need for larger family and community efforts to promote communication and eliminate, or at least reduce, those factors that may lead to drug abuse. Perhaps most important will be recognizing the difficulty that substance abuse issues present as well as the complexity of any effective effort to deal with them. There is a real need to target specific populations and to realize that being sensitive to different populations is extremely important.

For a more complete description of programs that have undergone at least some testing, the reader can visit the National Institute on Drug Abuse home page at http://www.nida.nih.gov. They may also be contacted at the following address:

National Clearinghouse for Alcohol and Drug Information (NCADI)
P.O. Box 2345
Rockville, MD 20847–2345
(800) 729-6686

ART

VII

SPECIAL POPULATIONS AND SPECIAL CONSIDERATIONS

CHAPTER 30

Special Populations and Special Considerations

The clinician needs to stay informed about the groups he or she treats and be sensitive to their special nature. The groups discussed below are intended to be representative of those populations the clinician is most likely to encounter, and whose unique issues in relation to substance abuse merit a specific, brief discussion. There are a few very important populations that naturally stand out in terms of their special needs as pertains to substance abuse treatment issues. Persons interested in substance abuse and its treatment are advised to be aware of the special needs of specific populations encountered. The following are offered as a smattering of some of the most germane "special" populations.

☐ Children of Substance Abusers

Personality is an entity which can be understood as the prevailing and persistent manner in which an individual relates to his or her internal world and to the external world. It is the stable expression of drives and motives. Personality involves elements of temperament, intellectual ability, and emotion. It also includes various emotional, psychological, and spiritual coping mechanisms that make up the way an individual feels about himself or herself and interacts with others.

Professionals who deal with substance abusers have recognized that the children of users have often developed distinctive coping mechanisms and strategies. Although these personalities were first described in the adult children of alcoholics (ACOA), they may exist among the children of any substance abuser. The ensuing discussion will focus on alcohol, because it is the most common problem and the one most studied, but the principles apply to families in the grips of any addiction.

There is a long and rich history of the description of and treatment of patients who come from alcoholic and drug-abusing families. This tradition stretches back long before some of the terms commonly used now were given the names by which they are now known. Some of the pioneers of psychology were very interested in addiction and its many consequences. Jung was involved with the early stages of AA. Later on, in the 1960s and 1970s, researchers such as Miller and Masson began to clarify the effects of child mistreatment and abuse. This time saw a swelling of interest in trauma and its effect on children, in particular the effects that the chaos of an "alcoholic household" would have on children. Many studies were done, and were published in both scholarly journals and the popular press. Some of the names which have been most associated with these studies include Claudia Black, Melanie Beatty, and Charles Whitfield.

Children need stability in order to form their own internal boundaries. This can be understood in both psychological and neurobiological terms. People are born with certain brain characteristics. It is believed that some things are determined as soon as the DNA has formed, such as hair and eye color and potential height. Actual height is influenced by nutrition. Temperament and intelligence (as measured by the standard IQ battery) are also largely fixed. Anyone who has observed infants in a nursery can see that there are placid and lively babies, as well as inconsolable babies and irritable babies. People who have been to a high school reunion will recognize the durability of temperament.

The development of various coping mechanisms for dealing with one's internal and external worlds can change over time. Certain patterns are learned and, in the process, the neurons in the brain become myelinated (the myelin sheath is a permanent covering of neurons much like the sheath on copper wiring). Individuals who are raised in a stable environment develop more stable and resilient "wiring." Those who grow up with chaotic, inconsistent, and unreliable parents develop more unsatisfactory ways of dealing with life's stressors. In order to deal with a world filled with uncertainty and, alcohol, the child of an alcoholic often develops a stereotyped personality. This personality develops as a means of coping with difficult life events and then becomes the personality of the individual. An ACOA may present with any one or a combination of these typical personality types.

Some of these personality characteristics can be adaptive. Many health care professionals come from families where they have been caretakers and rescuers. The impulse to help directed into a career in the helping professions can be a healthy sublimation or re-direction of emotional energy. The problem is that many of these people are unable or unwilling to ask for help for themselves and the rate of "burn out" is high.

The following are descriptions of the types of personalities the clinician may encounter in children of substance abusers. Many of these qualities blend together in the same person. The advantage for the clinician who recognizes these roles is that such knowledge facilitates an understanding of the alcoholic's world and helps in designing more specific treatment strategies. It needs to be stressed that these are personalities and methods of coping that are commonly found in this population. In many cases these individuals have overcome enormously difficult circumstances. Clinicians who deal with this population often marvel at the strength and resilience of adult children of substance abusers.

Common Behavioral Patterns in the Families of Alcoholics

The Addicted One

The children of alcoholics often develop an addiction themselves. This may be to alcohol or other drugs, or be reflected in other compulsive behaviors. This is not only because of the genetic predisposition to substance abuse, but it is a learned behavior as well: A child witnesses behavior in an alcoholic parent which demonstrates that the appropriate way to deal with stress is to drink heavily.

The Bully or Abuser

In order to maintain what seems like control, ACOAs may become physical abusers or bullies. This is often the case with the second born child in an alcoholic family. The second born does not typically receive as much attention as the older sibling, and in order to exhert his/her authority may develop into a bully. In order to feel some measure of relief from the painful situation of living in an alcoholic household, they develop into a hostile, abusive person, erroneously equating that behavior with a sense of personal power, emotional and interpersonal control.

The Compulsive One

This role differs from the addicted type in terms of severity and expression of the compulsion. This individual may be overly neat, orderly, and extremely rigid in personality, insisting on having things done "the correct way." This rigidity is another way of feeling in control and coping with the precarious and unreliable environment in the alcoholic home. If not too severe, these traits may have an adaptive quality. Compulsive traits such as good organizational skills, the sense of being goal-directed, and the ability to persevere are highly valued in both inter-personal and professional spheres.

The Failure

This may also be termed the "inadequate one." This person feels imperfect, rejected, incomplete, deficient, inadequate, and just not good enough. In treatment, they are helped to understand that these feelings of worthlessness are examples of irrational familial beliefs and behavior patterns imposed on children. Adults like these invariably experience problems in realizing their full intellectual and emotional goals and, predictably, have relationship difficulties and ambivalent feelings about being successful in their lives.

The Grandiose One

This behavior pattern is commonly found in the ACOA who develops an exaggerated, but quite fragile, sense of self-esteem. This is the overly "macho" man, or the overly "sexy" woman. An example of this is seen in men who constantly make fun of homosexuals and express aggression towards them. Men who are genuinely confident in their sexuality do not feel threatened by the concept of homosexuality and do not feel the need to spend their time making jokes at the expense of gay people. Ironically, the grandiose ACOA makes these comments to bolster his own tenuous sense of identity and his own deep-seated sense of sexual and/or social inadequacy.

The Martyr

This is the sacrificial individual who organizes his or her life around doing for others. They are often religious and zealously self-righteous. Martyrdom is a form of masochism. The martyr does not feel a secure enough sense of self to give fully to another person. This is altruism. An altruistic individual may make a large donation to a charitable cause and feel very good about this generous act of self-sacrifice. The martyr will give of his or her time, but always feels that he or she is making a cumbersome sacrifice. Such behavior is submissive, self-defeating, maladaptive, and is not borne out of a genuine sense of personal generosity.

The Lost Child

Often the third or later child in an alcoholic family is the "lost child." This is the child that is unable to have his or her needs met, becomes overwhelmed, and withdraws from the world. In both childhood and adulthood, he or she may be unfocused, unmotivated, and appear helpless. ACOAs with this pattern frequently feel that they are the losers in a competition. "Lost" children may tend to try to attach to partners or groups which substitute for their unmet need for a family.

The Overachiever

Usually the first born, this is the individual who attempts to please others and bolster self-esteem with one achievement after another. These accomplishments provide fleeting comfort for the profound feelings of emptiness that linger as a result of developmental deficits. Beliefs such as "I am my resume" or "I am as good as my last accomplishment" abound in overachieving ACOAs who rely excessively on external feedback to fill gaps in their incomplete egos.

The People Pleaser

The people pleaser's submissive and placating posture offers only temporary respite from his or her fears of disapproval or attack from others. People pleasing is a subtle form of manipulation and control. This is the person who has a hard time saying "no" to others and has problems making his or her needs known. Therapy with an adult with this personality configuration involves getting him or her to acknowledge his or her own desires, preferences, and feelings, and learning that it is often perfectly acceptable to say "no." Behavioral strategies such as assertiveness training are often helpful to these individuals in overcoming their passivity and submissiveness.

The Rescuer

This is the person who rescues, "fixes," or helps others. In its extreme form, the individual loses a sense of self in the pursuit of helping others.

Always good in a crisis, ACOAs who are rescuers pride themselves on their ability to come up with logistically sound solutions which can be enormously valuable to others. The compulsion to rescue comes at the expense of ignoring their own genuine emotions and needs. Many rescuers are at risk for depression and/or substance abuse once their attempts to rescue someone fail or if the person dies, leaving them with no organizing focus in their lives.

The Victim

These people live in the past with constant regret over bad decisions and bad outcomes. "If only..." is their constant lament. They toy with getting help, but usually manage to foil even the best plans and almost gleefully admit to running from responsibilities and self-improvement. These are the individuals who lure the fixers, the rescuers, and the helping professionals into attempting to make things right, only to not follow the plan and complain that things have been made worse. By undermining plans which are in their own best interests, they maladaptively maintain some sense of control over their universe. These ACOAs are the "help-rejecting complainers" who populate many substance-abuse therapy groups.

These descriptions are role stereotypes because they are fixed, rigid, and maladaptive in nature. The variations on each theme are as multiple as the people treated. The astute person working with ACOAs will recognize these archetypes. None of them learned the flexibility of role definition necessary to develop a repertoire of coping mechanisms that is a hallmark of mental health.

Therapy with ACOAs is a process toward understanding the underlying motivation behind their coping strategies so that they can learn new, more mature, and more comfortable styles. One intervention commonly takes place in ACOA groups, where these patterns emerge quickly and are readily recognizable to other ACOAs in the group. Once identified, these stereotypical roles can be modified and liberalized. Members can try behaviors and roles employed by others in the group or by the group leader/therapist. Again, it needs to be emphasized that many elements of these coping mechanisms are enormously adaptive, and these patients are very often courageous and valiant individuals who already possess enormous reserves of inner strength.

Ongoing ACOA group sessions offer a venue for expansion of previously constricted roles and for practice of new modes of relating in a safe setting. Group support helps reinforce gains made in sessions and reinforces motivation for continued personal growth.

Adolescents

Adolescence is a time of flux, experimentation, and identity development. It is also the time most individuals first encounter and experiment with alcohol, drugs, and tobacco. Like many social constructs, the concept of adolescence is a sociocultural phenomenon with biophysiological underpinnings. In our society, adolescence usually begins with puberty, continues through the early twenties, and ends in early adulthood with the acceptance of a more adult role in society. There are a few special issues to consider when dealing with adolescent substance abusers.

Experimentation is part of adolescence, so it is not surprising that some degree of experimentation with drugs and alcohol will occur within these formative years. There is some evidence that those individuals who have experimented with drugs are psychologically healthier than either abstainers or frequent users. Most researchers believe that it is important to delay the onset of regular drug use as long as possible to allow time for the development of non-drug-dependent adaptive skills. Consequently, it is probably more important to prevent drug abuse than to try and stop drug use altogether.

Set and setting are very important in determining whether or not an adolescent has a substance abuse problem. In American culture, it is common for adolescents to experiment with alcohol, tobacco, and in some cases, illicit drugs. While most people who voluntarily come to a professional for assessment and treatment of substance abuse have a clear problem with the substance, adolescents may be sent to a professional by anxious parents who become alarmed when, for instance, their adolescent experiments with alcohol and comes home drunk. This is a normal part of adolescence and is not necessarily cause for serious concern. In this example, education and understanding on the part of the clinician are very important, and a follow-up should be scheduled to make sure that a problem does not develop.

Adolescents with substance abuse issues or problems differ from adults with these disorders in a number of ways. The adolescent, for obvious reasons, usually has a shorter history of drug abuse than his or her adult counterpart. Tolerance, craving, and withdrawal symptoms are less common and, in most cases, less severe. The need for physiologic detoxification is usually quite rare. Because of the unique experiences of adolescents, the more traditional therapeutic techniques and approaches do not resonate, and using them is met with failure. As an example, so rare is the adolescent who can relate to the AA concept of hitting "rock bottom," let alone even understand the concept. An explanation for such a lack of understanding is that early and middle adolescents may not have completely achieved the stage of formal operational thinking. The inability to relate to such common themes familiar in addiction treatment as denial, surrender, and a higher power, may not represent resistance per se, but an inability to fully grasp such concepts.

A clinician working with this population must recognize the narcissism and natural self-centeredness which is part of normal adolescence. This includes feelings of invincibility, a lack of empathy, inability to fully comprehend the concept of the distant future, the relation between present actions and distant consequences, and the common belief that adults can not possibly understand or relate to their problems. Rather than being pathological conditions, these feelings are part of normal adolescence. "Talking down" to an adolescent by being patronizing or by pathologizing normal developmental behavior is a serious error, and one that will almost certainly result in alienating the adolescent, thus eliminating the possibility of a therapeutic alliance.

Relations

The clinician who chooses to work with this population must recognize that he or she has a patient who comes attached with others. Adolescence is the time of incomplete separation from family and parents. The adolescent must always be considered in the context of the family, as diversely manifest as that might be. It is often advisable to include parents and older siblings in at least part of the treatment. It is key that the clinician not enter into a collusive relationship with the adolescent regarding self-destructive behavior from substance abuse. Parents and other family members must be considered in any form of treatment because the adolescent is not a "free agent." He or she almost always lives with and is financially dependent upon the adults in his or her life. As a result, treatment of drug- and alcohol-abusing adolescents becomes particularly difficult when it concerns issues of confidentiality and trust. Knowing whether or not to inform parents about certain situations are decisions which call for sound clinical judgment and flexibility and thoughtfulness on the therapist's part.

It is possible to encounter cases where the adolescent has been clearly abusing drugs for a long time. The effects and behavior could be obvious to any outside observer, but the family "just didn't know." In such cases, it is important not to invoke recrimination, but rather to emphasize an appropriate treatment plan and create a system of monitoring for future troubles.

> Lorraine is a 15 year-old young woman who lives in a trailer park with her mother and step father. For many years she was a bright and concerned student, almost always making at least Bs in school. Lately she has been smok-

ing marijuana with her friends, all day, almost every day. She has stopped going to school on many days and spends her time at home locked in her room, usually smoking marijuana and listening to acid rock music. Although her room reeks of marijuana, and she has become slovenly, her mother just shakes her head saying "kids these days..."

In the above example, the adolescent is in serious trouble. Her educational years are being jeopardized by her marijuana dependence. Someone working with her and her mother needs to educate them that this kind of behavior is neither normal nor healthy. That is the first step in dealing with any substance abuse case: recognizing that there is a problem.

There is a pseudo-maturity to many young adolescents that can be misleading to both parents and professionals. Most adolescents, even rebellious ones, actually crave structure, rules, and consistency. The clinician dealing with the adolescent must walk a tightrope, treating them with respect, but not as a fully developed peer.

Adolescents have rituals which change with every generation. A popular current phenomenon is the all night dance marathon, called a rave, which is attended by young people. These raves are sites of widespread drug use. The majority of people who go to raves will use marijuana, LSD, methamphetamine, GHB, Rohypnol, and/or MDMA. Although the use of these substances may be quite dangerous, attendance at these events may be considered normative. Clinicians should be aware that adolescents may be using "club drugs" in addition to the more "traditional" agents such as alcohol and marijuana.

Another perennial problem among adolescents is binge drinking (as well as excessive use of other substances). This type of behavior is sometimes culturally sanctioned. At many college campuses, excessive drinking, especially among younger students at the beginning of the semester, is considered normal behavior. While it may be common, it can be quite dangerous. Condemnation will not be likely to result in a change in behavior; however, the clinician should not be lulled into condoning the behavior, and thereby giving tacit permission. In recent years many educational institutions have begun to recognize this problem, and have instituted policies and programs to deal with binge drinking and its consequences. Banning alcohol altogether has resulted in decreased consumption in some locations. Another strategy has been educational, making students aware of the dangers of bingeing, as well as the simple policy of demanding that only non-alcoholic beverages be served at social events, or at the very least non-alcoholic beverages he makes available.

Treatment Issues

Treatment programs often have specialized or separate adolescent tracks. Prevention/education programs aimed at adolescent substance abuse can be very helpful in developing healthy and mature coping skills that do not rely on alcohol and drugs. There is, however, little consensus and even less scientific evidence about which programs and policies are the most effective.

Given the particular profile and characteristics of adolescents, a few concepts are likely to be useful in designing and implementing prevention and treatment programs. Adolescents rely upon peer pressure, role models, and imitation in achieving an independent identity. Teenagers are much more likely to respond to programs and policies that emphasize the "here and now." Emphasis should not be placed on future consequences of drug abuse, but rather upon the negative impact substance abuse has upon his or her present social, family, and academic life.

Just as the adolescent is a part of his or her family, social issues have a great impact on the adolescent and substance use. Especially in lower income families, the social problems which accompany poverty and economic depravation intersect with issues involving substance abuse. Especially influential are the shattered family structures and absent authority figures in some adolescents lives.

> Jim is a fourteen year-old African American adolescent who lives with his grandmother and aunt. His mother is a crack addict who maintains intermittent contact between failed stints in rehabilitation hospitals. A freshman in high-school, Jim recently began drinking alcohol with his friends and, at their urging, has experimented with cocaine. During a recent Friday night party, Jim drank so much that he ended up passing out. Worried friends called the police who took him to the hospital for observation, where he spent the night, and was then released into the custody of his grandmother. They were referred to the outpatient substance abuse clinic for teenagers for an evaluation.

It is unlikely that Jim needs inpatient treatment at this point. He does, however, need help, and the application of a few resources now may have a substantial impact on subsequent behavior.

His substance abuse is influenced by his peers. It would be important, if treating this patient, to help him find more healthy outlets and develop relations with more positive friends. Although not stated, he likely has many issues about being the son of a crack-addicted mother. Such children often have problems with self-esteem, and someone working with Jim would need to help him develop a positive self-image without drugs. Any sensible therapy program would include a substance abuse component. Big Brothers/Big Sisters, or a similar program that pairs him with a positive role model, might be a useful addition in a case like this. Research indicates that for many adolescents a major positive connection with a healthy role model can make a significant difference in the recovery process.

In summary, this is a difficult population to effectively treat and calls for tolerance, mature judgment, and innovation in response to provocative and self-destructive adolescent behavior surrounding substance use. The distinction between natural adolescent curiosity necessary for normal growth and development, and the signs of an emerging problem with addiction, is a constant clinical challange.

□ The Elderly

The elderly are more likely to abuse substances than almost any other segment of the population. This is particularly true in the case of substances such as alcohol and benzodiazepines. While the rates of abuse for some substances, like crack cocaine, are lower than in younger age groups, the elderly are just as biologically vulnerable to addiction as their younger counterparts. Although many former substance abusers appear to "mature out" of drug use as they get older, the aging process is no insurance policy against continued or newly-formed patterns of substance abuse. Although rare, there *are* 80 year-old crack abusers and 90 year-old heroin abusers.

The substances that are more likely to be abused by elderly patients are alcohol and prescription medications, and these should be asked about in any routine screening of an older person. Alcohol use is frequently abused by elderly people and rates of alcoholism are slightly higher for the elderly than for the general population. This is due to a variety of factors. Alcohol use is socially acceptable for many senior citizens. They grew up in an era in which alcohol consumption was a regular part of the culture. Since the rates of anxiety and depressive disorders climb with age, seniors who have these disorders may be self-medicating an anxiety or depressive condition.

The other reason for an increased rate of alcoholism in the elderly is physiological. As people age, they are less able to process alcohol and their tolerance is diminished. It takes less alcohol to become drunk, and to develop a problem with drinking. The aging, now-retired businessman who used to be able to handle two to three Scotches without feeling the effects, may no longer be able to do so. Force of habit will promote continuation of the drinking pattern with different, often disastrous results.

The second set of substances that are abused regularly by the elderly are prescription medicines, especially the sedative-hypnotics, benzodiazepines, and painkillers. Since older people are more prone to conditions which require painkillers, the elderly receive more prescriptions for this kind of medicine. They also tend to have more than one doctor, some of whom may give them multiple and/or redundant prescriptions. It does not take long to become physiologically dependent upon analgesics. This is a common presentation in the elderly.

> Agnes G. is a retired postal worker, now in her seventies. Last spring, she fell and broke her ankle. This required an orthopedic operation and months of rehabilitation. Her orthopedist prescribed a powerful opioid medicine to help with the pain. At first, this was necessary. Agnes was embarrassed about asking for more from her orthopedist, so she asked her internist, who gave her a large supply. She also asked her cardiologist, and her endocrinologist as well. For the past few months, although she no longer has an orthopedic problem (her ankle has healed well) she finds that she cannot stop the use of the analgesic without feeling terrible. As a result, she has acquired several new doctors, almost all of whom are willing to prescribe her medicine when she describes her ongoing pain symptoms. She is embarrassed to let anyone know about her problem.

The above example illustrates several unique attributes of substance abuse in the elderly. Initially, Agnes had a legitimate reason to use painkillers but soon became physiologically dependent. Her many doctors probably do not talk to one another regularly and thus she is able to maintain her addiction. In addition, she views herself as an upstanding citizen and is even more embarrassed than her younger counterparts about admitting to having an addiction.

Sleep and anxiety problems are common in elderly people. As a person ages, his or her sleep patterns change. The ability to achieve REM sleep, the most relaxing and restorative phase of sleep, is severely diminished. The older one gets, the less sleep one needs and is able to get. Someone who is used to sleeping eight hours a night may no longer need even six. Habit and the popular misconception that the elderly need more sleep prompt many senior citizens to go to bed earlier than necessary. Not getting "my eight hours" of sleep is viewed as a sleep disturbance rather than part of the natural aging process. Busy physicians often prescribe sleep medication, usually benzodiazepines, to address this complaint. While benzodiazepines are very useful drugs, they do generate dependence. Furthermore, high-dose benzodiazepines can themselves cause depression, or they may cause disinhibition or increase confusion, all of which are significant risks in elderly populations.

In treating benzodiazepine withdrawal, abrupt cessation of the drug may lead to seizures. To prevent this, a very slow taper of the benzodiazepine, sometimes over the course of months, is recommended for elderly patients. Some individuals seem to not have enough "natural" benzodiazepine and may need to be on small supplemental doses to deal with anxiety and even chronic sleep disturbances. If benzodiazepine treatment is necessary, the moderately long-acting benzodiazepines such as Klonazepam are the first choice over the very long-acting ones such as diazepam and Dalmane. Dalmane has three metabolites, one of which is extremely long-acting and, hence, particularly problematic.

> John is a 78 year-old retired factory worker. He has been able to weather the travails of life quite well, but these past few months he has been tested too much. His wife of 54 years has died, as has the last of his close friends. He is mildly depressed, but most concerned about his inability to sleep. He sought the advice of his family doctor, who gave him Dalmane to sleep. John liked being able to sleep, in fact preferred it to being awake, and has now seen several internists who have all prescribed Dalmane for his sleep problem. None have inquired about depression, and John now spends most of the day and night asleep, taking Dalmane and not attending to the activities he used to love.

The above example is all too common. An alternative medication plan can include the use of short-acting benzodiazepines such as Lorezapam for selected older patients who do not respond to the aforementioned drugs, or a short course of Zolopidem. Education on the principles of good sleep hygiene and an appreciation that older people metabolize drugs more slowly and consequently require lower doses of prescribed medications to achieve the desired clinical results should accompany any medication plan for the elderly. Because of the importance of sleep in the elderly and in substance abusers in general, the principles of good sleep hygiene are included at the end of this chapter.

The clinician needs to be sensitive to the special needs of the elderly. This may include an awareness of the heightened sense of shame that a loss of control may mean for an older person. A senior may want to think of himself or herself as a dignified mentor; however, this does not mesh well with the concept of substance abuse.

In this country, seniors are often the subjects of discrimination. "Ageism" adds to the stress already experienced by elderly people and is an extremely potent co-factor in the development of substance abuse. The aging process is hard in some other ways, as the powers of the body and mind diminish. Memory loss, medical illness, and a sense of isolation are states which set the stage for abuse of alcohol and drugs. The loss of power and control, both economic and personal, that come with aging, adversely affect one's self- esteem.

Principles of Good Sleep Hygiene

–Regular times for going to bed and getting up are mandatory, with less time allotted than was needed at an earlier phase in life.

–No caffeine after 12 noon, and no caffeine at all if the sleeplessness persists.

–The bed is for sleep and sex; no other activities should take place there (this involves psychological conditioning for the bed).

–Moderate exercise at least five hours before bedtime is helpful.

–A warm bath or shower before bed may be helpful.

–Foods rich in tyrosine, especially warm milk, may be helpful before bed.

–It is not advisable to watch television in bed.

–If sleep does not come, one should get out of bed and engage in some activity which is boring and repetitive (e.g., read, but not anything too stimulating).

☐ The Codependent Relationship

The person with a substance abuse or dependence problem is often enmeshed in an array of maladaptive relationships and interpersonal connections. The people involved with abusers have their own set of maladaptive behaviors. In general, their actions often do not match their stated intention. A wife may complain bitterly about her husband's drinking and yet, without protest, will pick up a case of beer on the way home; a father may be alarmed at his child's drug use, but continues to dole out a liberal allowance. This behavior is called "enabling" and those who engage in it are described as "codependent." Charles Whitfield defines codependence as *a disease of lost selfhood, a condition of any suffering and/or dysfunction that is associated with or results from focusing on the needs and behavior of others.*

Codependency is a comprehensive, multidimensional, and maladaptive pattern of coping with the chaos caused by a substance abuser. It usually develops over time and although it exists in degrees of severity, it is deeply ingrained. Often times, a "codependent" person comes from a family where a similar pattern of drug abuse or alcoholism existed. Such persons gravitate to familiar emotional landscapes and repeatedly choose relationships with people similar to the ones with which they grew up.

Codependency differs from "enabling" behaviors in the comprehensive nature of the syndrome. Enabling refers to a specific behavior or action which helps or allows the substance abuser to continue his or her pattern of addiction. The spouse who buys drugs or alcohol for his or her partner is enabling that person to continue to abuse. The physician who fills prescription after prescription of pain relievers for the same patient without questioning why this is occurring is enabling the dependence on painkillers to continue.

Codependency refers to the feelings, emotions, patterns of behavior, and attitudes of the person in the dysfunctional dyad. It involves issues of self-esteem and worth, as well as feelings of helplessness, either life-long or learned, on the part of the codependent individual. In the above examples the spouse has a variety of complex reasons to buy the drugs or alcohol for his or her partner. The physician also has complex psychological reasons that allow for the continued dispensing of medications that may be doing far more harm than good.

From a psychological standpoint, most therapists believe that people are living and employing defense mechanisms in as adaptive a way as they can. An individual faced with an untenable interpersonal environment such as an alcoholic family, may develop a wide array of defenses for dealing with that chaotic family climate. These mechanisms may include minimizing the extent of the chaos, withdrawing from the emotional life, or denying the existence of the surrounding problems (see the section on common behavior patterns of ACOAs, earlier in the chapter). While these mechanisms are in one sense adaptive, they are also not helpful and certainly not ideal. There is an AA concept that living with a partner or family member who is alcoholic is like having a pink elephant in the living room, one that everyone ignores, tip-toes around or pretends is not there, but is ever-present.

In treating an individual substance abuser, it is vital to identify the codependent relationships in his or her life. These are the people who, unintentionally, will undermine sobriety and treatment. Either counseling that person or suggesting one of several effective treatments (Al-Anon is a classic example of an effective treatment approach for many individuals with issues of codependency) can be very helpful. The therapy for an individual with issues about codependency may be individual, family, educational, or take place in a group setting. Therapy involves helping that person recognize his or her feelings, and develop healthy behaviors so that they do not resort to drug use. Sometimes the simple act of suggesting a useful reading about the subject can be extremely helpful.

When codependency is successfully treated, a spouse may say to her husband, "I recognize that a part of me feels compelled to get you the case of beer. I want to please you but to do so will enable you to continue your addiction and will undermine us both. I love you and therefore will not aid in your self-destruction. I will not get any beer and if you do not help yourself, then I will help myself and leave you." A father will learn to say to his child, "I love you and want to help you get off drugs. Supporting your drug-taking in any way is not a healthy way for me to deal with my guilt. I have locked my wallet up where you cannot get at it. I will help you get help, but I will not help you get drugs."

Promoting autonomy, teaching people how to behave as interdependent adults, and removing substances from the interpersonal equation are all goals when working with people in codependent relationships.

Gay and Lesbian People

Gay and lesbian people are included as a special population in terms of substance abuse for several reasons. This segment of the population has some unique issues about which the informed clinician should be aware. Sexual orientation and behavior exist on a spectrum for most people. Over the last 30 years, as part of a social and political movement, many homosexual individuals began to identify themselves specifically as "gay," "lesbian," or "bisexual." The term "gay" should be understood as not only representing the sexual orientation of an individual but also a cultural identity. The term generally refers to someone who has accepted his or her identity and recognizes that sexual identity and object choice is stable and unchangeable. Furthermore, the term gay implies identification in a political and personal way with other gay people.

The expressions of sexuality are as varied and diverse as humans themselves. The ancient Greeks believed that ideal love existed only between men, often men with a wide discrepancy in age. This concept is complex, and most theorists believe that it was partly attributable to the low social status accorded to women. Love, a higher expression of connection that includes a sexual component, was thought to exist only between two men.

At different times in recent history, the cultural identity of gay persons was more or less accepted. There was a vibrant gay subculture in the early part of this century in Europe and the larger cities in the U.S. In Berlin, before the Nazi takeover in 1933, there were more gay bars than there are in New York City today.

In recent years, gay men and women have been increasingly accepted. As an example, television themes that would have been unthinkable even a few years ago, are now common. It should be noted, though, that this acceptance has been far from universal. Sixty-eight percent of Americans still think that homosexuality is always wrong, and the majority of states still have sodomy laws, even between consenting adults. The stress of living as an openly gay person, though less than was true historically, is still formidable. Prejudice, fear, and ostracism face many youths in their attempt to "come out." It is a primary reason for children being "kicked out" of their homes. Gay and lesbian youth are four times more likely to kill themselves than their heterosexual counterparts.

Chronic stress is a contributing factor to substance abuse and alcoholism. Not surprisingly, gays and lesbians who face considerable stress have higher rates of alcoholism and drug abuse. Actual numbers are hard to pinpoint, but most studies suggest that lesbian women and gay men do have higher rates of addiction than the general population.

The gay bar has long been the cornerstone of gay social life. Traditionally, these were the only places where gays could congregate and "be themselves." Despite the fact that there have been efforts to create social events not at bars, nor revolving around drugs, the bar is still a mainstay of gay social life.

Another issue in understanding and treating gay people is that in some parts of this subculture recreational drug use in a social setting continues into an older age than in straight culture. Older people in larger numbers and greater percentages can be found in places where illicit drugs and alcohol are rampant. One possible explanation for this may be that most gay men and women were not allowed to have an honest and emotionally productive rebellious phase of adolescence. Certain developmental tasks such as dating and "getting over" the novelty of reckless behavior, including drug use, occurs at a later time than in straight culture.

In certain parts of this subculture drugs are rampant. "Circuit parties" are a prime example of events that have become increasingly popular among affluent, usually white, gay men. These are large gatherings that take place over weekends in various cities and usually involve several parties and dancing. Drugs, though not a requirement, are the norm at these events. Many individuals claim that drugs heighten their experience. Stimulants, in particular, facilitate staying up as late as possible on a dance floor and permit partying through the night.

There are a number of drugs that are commonly used by gay and lesbian people. These include MDMA, ketamine, GHB, methamphetamine, and amyl nitrate "poppers." In addition, more "conventional" drugs are widely used as well. It should be emphasized that the vast majority of gay men and women do not attend circuit parties. A particularly affluent and visible subset of the gay and lesbian population, however, do attend these events.

Treatment Issues

The clinician who treats a gay or lesbian person needs to be aware of and sensitive to how much prejudice there is against gays and lesbians. Negative attitudes towards homosexuality can adversely affect an individual's experience in treatment and an ability to form a therapeutic alliance with a clinician who harbors anti-gay sentiments. In groups, psychological casualties can be the result for someone who is sincerely attempting to deal with his or her substance abuse problem in individual or group therapy, and in trying to be honest reveals aspects of his or her sexual orientation or behavior only to be rebuked or shunned. This bias which exists in much of society is real and should not be used in the service of denial. If someone has a drug problem which needs to be addressed, the person should be treated with sympathy, but not permitted to use prejudice as an excuse for continuing substance abuse.

> Ted is a 33 year-old single banker in a Midwestern city. He at first used cocaine in a social setting, especially on Saturday nights when he went dancing at the local gay disco. In addition, he used numerous other drugs such as Ecstasy (MDMA), Special K (Ketamine), and "Crystal" (Methamphetamine). Lately he has been doing more and more cocaine and it has begun to affect his work, but only slightly. His urine toxicology was positive in a rare random drug test at work. His employer mandated that he be sent to a drug counselor. The drug counselor had not heard of many of the drugs Ted used, and said that anyone who used drugs like that was an addict. He insisted that Ted join a Twelve Step-based group run by the counselor. This group included many older men, most of them members of the Teamsters union with whom the drug counselor also had a contract. In the first meeting several of the members made homophobic remarks which were not challenged by the group leader, but seemed to promote solidarity among the other members. Ted attended groups for the next few weeks, but then stopped going. His employer was informed of this, and he was terminated. His subsequent course was poor.

The previous example illustrates several important points about treating gay and lesbian people, as well as substance abuse in general. The counselor made several mistakes in Ted's treatment. No matter what opinion one may have of it, some gay men and women do use drugs recreationally, and although this cannot be seen as healthy, it is within the cultural norm. Secondly, he put Ted in a group where he had little in common with the other members and was likely to be met with scorn and prejudice. The treatment of addiction usually involves the promotion of honesty and self revelation. In the above example, Ted has numerous reasons, other than his possible addiction, not to be self revelatory. The counselor was neither sensitive to, nor even aware of, the special problems Ted might face. In addition, he seems to be the kind of inflexible counselor who believes there is only one way to deal with this problem (this is invariably "his way"). While he might help some individuals, in the above case his approach is met with abject failure.

In recent years there have been an increased recognition of substance abuse problems in the gay and lesbian community. Several treatment programs have special tracks for gays and lesbians. Furthermore, in some areas there are Twelve Step meetings advertised specifically for gays and lesbians. There are also "mixed" meetings that are "more gay friendly than others" as well as a few treatment programs that cater especially to gay and lesbian individuals.

☐ The Health Care Professional

Health professionals are more susceptible to addiction disorders than the general population. Anyone interested in substance abuse needs to recognize the particular vulnerabilities of the health care professional and several unique features of identification and treatment that apply to this population.

Working in health care entails the kind of chronic stress which is a leading factor in pre-disposing someone to addiction. The self-medication hypothesis holds that an individual may turn to certain substances in order to deal with painful affects. A particularly "stressed-out " intern or nurse may have feelings of isolation and anxiety and begin to drink more and more, eventually crossing the line into alcoholism. Another individual may do the same with marijuana, or use a stimulant to "keep up." All these paths can lead to the development of an addictive pattern of substance use.

The second reason for the increased incidence of addictions is the availability of certain substances. Physicians, and in some states, nurse practitioners, can prescribe controlled substances such as opiates and benzodiazepines. Abuse and addiction are especially common in those individuals whose subspecialties necessitate ready access to substances. Anesthesiologists are known to be susceptible to becoming dependent on narcotics and sedatives at a much higher rate than the general population or those professionals in subspecialties where there is not such easy availability. Ketamine, an anesthetic used in pediatric and veterinary procedures, is often diverted to recreational abuse by veterinarians and child anesthesiologists. Ear, nose, and throat doctors, who use cocaine as a topical or local anesthetic are more vulnerable to cocaine abuse and addiction, also based on increased exposure to potential substances of abuse.

Once addicted, these individuals are sometimes enabled by their profession and the public. Many health care professionals are held in high esteem by their peers; this makes it difficult for people to admit that a colleague, mentor, or friend has a problem. Patients do not want to see their surgeon, in whom they have great faith, as an addict or an alcoholic. The traditions of collegiality and professionalism among health care workers tends to exclude outsiders and makes independent monitoring more difficult. In the case of an impaired physician, a conspiracy of silence may develop among the staff which enables the addiction to continue. There is a long history of prominent medical practitioners who have been flagrant in their addictions and erratic behaviors. Historically, this behavior has all too often been tolerated.

In light of the trend toward secrecy among addicted health care professionals, identification of substance abuse for the practitioner needs to be handled as it would be with any other individual. Clues to addiction may include erratic and inconsistent behavior and frequent absences from work. It is helpful and realistic to have a higher degree of suspicion with individuals in health care when it comes to assessing the possibility of a substance use disorder.

Treatment principles are generally the same as with other addicts but ought to include sensitivity to the unique role and knowledge of the health care practitioner. There are specific programs and meetings for physicians. AA meetings for physicians are termed Caduceus meetings and can be powerful tools in recovery. (The caduceus is the symbol of two intertwined snakes on a staff that is a symbol for the medical profession.) The prognosis for an addicted health care professional is actually quite good. Since there is so much to lose if the addiction continues, the treating professional has a lot of leverage in dealing with these patients. The threat of losing a license is a powerful incentive to accept the treatment recommendations. Often medical and professional societies have specific and specialized programs and committees to deal with this type of problem among their membership.

In recent years, many professional schools have instituted programs for identification of impaired health care professionals. These programs operate outside of normal administration, are sensitive to issues of privacy, and are therefore less threatening to students and professionals. Students know that if they develop an addiction or if they suspect a colleague of being impaired, they have a constructive resource available to them. Most states have a board associated with the medical society, but separate from it, to advise on problems with addiction. These organizations may be contacted in the case of a suspicion of a physician's addiction and then the case is investigated. If someone suspects that a health care colleague has a problem with drugs or alcohol, that person has a moral obligation to contact the authorities. Furthermore, the informant, as long as he or she is acting on good faith, is protected from future prosecution, even if the allegation is not substantiated.

The adage "Physician heal thyself" embodies the philosophy governing many efforts aimed at identifying and treating addicted health care professionals.

☐ Women's Issues

Women substance users have some special concerns and issues. The first has to do with physiology, especially in relation to alcohol. Due to the presence of a lower percentage of gastric alcohol dehydrogenase than found in their male counterparts, it takes a smaller amount of alcohol for a woman to reach a state of intoxication. The amount and distribution of fat is also different for women and men. These factors, combined with the relative lower weight of women compared to men means that it takes less alcohol to intoxicate a woman than a comparable man. Another factor involved is hormone levels, which effect alcohol metabolism. Intoxication depends on the rapidity of alcohol intake, as well as the blood-alcohol percentage. Since women do not immediately metabolize alcohol as rapidly as men, an equal amount of alcohol achieves a higher blood level. The clinical relevance of this fact is that a level of drinking which would arouse some suspicion and concern in a clinician if the patient were a man would raise even more if the patient were a woman.

The second special concern about women has to do with social context. In some parts of many cultures it is less acceptable and more stigmatizing for a woman to have a substance abuse problem. The clinician must be aware of this stigma and the shame associated with it. In many instances these feelings may make it more difficult for a woman to acknowledge her substance abuse than her male counterpart.

> Alice is a 55 year old school teacher who was recently widowed. She was transferred to a new school in the district, one with more difficult and violent children. Rationalizing that she needs relief from the stress, Alice has begun to use large amounts of the tranquilizers and painkillers her husband had stored up in the course of his long illness. Increasingly isolated, she knows that she is developing a problem but does not know where to turn.

The past few decades have seen a number of changes in women's social standing. The growth of the women's movement has meant greater social freedom. Along with this increased freedom has come increased rates of substance use and abuse. This is seen dramatically in the increase in nicotine addiction among women. Rates of other forms of substance abuse in women have risen as well.

Women are more likely to have certain psychiatric disorders and conditions than men. This is the case particularly with depressive and anxiety disorders. These disorders are often associated with higher rates of substance abuse, particularly in the case of alcoholism and abuse of prescription medications. Women are more likely than men to be victims of physical and sexual abuse; the resulting post-traumatic stress disorders are also increased risk factors for substance abuse.

In severe substance abuse, women may resort to self-destructive actions. Women addicted to crack are vulnerable to exchanging sex for drugs. A person who is desperate to get another dose of crack will be willing to do almost anything. Female substance abusers are prone to physical abuse from men who supply or pay for their drugs. A woman in this state is essentially emotionally and physically unprotected. As such, she may not be diligent at maintaining the guidelines of safe sex practices, may put herself at risk for HIV or other sexually transmitted diseases, or find herself in the path of threats of physical violence.

> Lisa is a 42 year-old former actress and temp worker who has developed a crack addiction over the past three years. She currently has no fixed address, and lives alternatively with her brother and his lover and at the apartments of her few remaining friends. Since starting to use crack, she finds it hard to believe what she has been willing to subject herself to. Her activities have included sex with violent and abusive men, sometimes in groups. She says that when she is on a binge she will do anything for another hit of the drug, "and I mean anything." She has recently tested positive for the HIV virus and is certain she got it while having sex with one of the many men who promised her money or crack in exchange for her having sex with him.

In terms of treatment, it is important for the clinician to be aware of the special needs of the woman who wants help with a substance abuse problem. There are specific treatment programs which are tailored to the needs of women (one of these, is described in Chapter 25). Many women's groups and female professionals are available to work with substance using women. If these resources are not available in a given area, the clinician needs to be aware of the special issues women face and try to make a sensible and sensitive treatment plan which factors in the elements which are unique to women.

Pregnancy

Pregnancy and substance abuse is a difficult area, where the needs of the individual, society, and the unborn intersect. It is an issue with significant legal and moral repercussions. In American culture, up until the 1960s, women routinely smoked cigarettes and drank alcohol during pregnancy. Most people thought these were not particularly dangerous behaviors.

It has become blatantly clear that substances abused during pregnancy—even moderate amounts of substances that outside the context of pregnancy might be tolerable—can be exceedingly harmful to the unborn. The phenomenon of "crack babies" in the 1980s made this undeniable. The babies of mothers on crack were born underweight, inconsolable, and premature. These children do not appear as damaged when they grow up as most people originally anticipated. They do, however, show some neuropsychiatric abnormalities. Alcohol use during pregnancy can cause "fetal alcohol syndrome" which is characterized by distinct facial characteristics and mental retardation. Babies born to opiate addicted mothers go through a painful withdrawal syndrome themselves after birth. These babies have an increased possibility of being infected with the HIV virus from their mother if she is HIV positive.

Pregnancy is a good time to deal with an addicted person because the pregnant mother may be much more willing to accept help and treatment than when she is not pregnant and, therefore, does not have the added responsibility of an unborn child. The knowledge that she will be bringing a new life into the world may be sufficient motivation to try to achieve abstinence.

When treating addicted women who are pregnant, it is prudent to try non-pharmacological interventions at first. The question of medication use in a pregnant woman is a complex one and needs to be considered carefully. While efforts should be made to avoid using pharmacotherapy with pregnant woman, the clinician must weigh the consequences of treatment without the use of medication. A mother who stops methadone will likely relapse with street heroin. The potential for using dirty needles and the kind of behavior associated with opiate addiction is likely to be far more dangerous to the baby than methadone. Similarly, a mother who is profoundly depressed while off antidepressants may be more dangerous to her baby than she when she is not depressed and on medication. Many of the medications routinely used to treat addiction and comorbid conditions do not seem to cause profound problems in the developing fetus. The use of prescription medications is always a difficult judgment which may not take into account more subtle possible changes in the brain caused by medicines taken during pregnancy.

A compelling nexus of the clash between the rights of the individual and the state exists in the question of what the state's role is in keeping the unborn safe from a drug-using mother. On one end of the ideological spectrum are those that believe the rights of the mother are paramount, and until born, the child is not of consequence. On the other are those who believe that after the sperm and egg are united, the unborn child ought to deserve the same rights as any citizen. These individuals are almost always in favor of abortion being illegal. Dr. Herbert Kleber, an expert on drug policy, believes that a mother has the right to terminate the pregnancy at an early stage of conception; if however, a severely substance abusing mother chooses to carry a child to term, then the state has the obligation to see that the unborn is kept from as much harm as possible and the mother remain drug-free during the pregnancy. That is, if the decision to keep the child and not have an abortion has been made, then the state has at least some obligation to try and create a safe environment for that child, even before birth. This is an emotional topic and many people disagree with Kleber's position, viewing it as a needless violation of civil liberties or an intrusion by the state into the issue of pregnancy rights. It is likely that this topic will continue to be very controversial and hotly debated in the coming years.

PART

VIII

COMMONLY ASKED QUESTIONS ABOUT SUBSTANCE ABUSE

31

CHAPTER

Commonly Asked Questions About Substance Abuse

☐ Is abstinence the only way?

It depends upon where the person is along the continuum of drug use to abuse. An individual who has had one or only a few episodes of abuse may be sufficiently chastened by the experience such that he or she will return to controlled use. An example of this would be the student who, appalled at her irresponsible behavior while intoxicated on marijuana at a school dance, takes a look at her recently excessive drug use, stops using marijuana, and adapts a more healthy life style. Another example is a college-age person who drinks excessively in an attempt to win social approval from his peers, and who comes to clinical attention because his parents are concerned. This individual may be educated by experience and start drinking in moderation. In both examples, the individuals described have not lost the capacity for moderation, and the episodes of abuse have been quite brief.

Substance abuse problems come in a variety of forms. Most people who come to treatment do indeed have severe problems. The rational clinician should not make the mistake of colluding with the addicted individual and rationalizing the possibility of controlled use of the offending substance. By the time a person gets to the clinician, he or she has usually lost the capacity for moderation and control. Abstinence is the necessary goal. This is especially true in the early stages of recovery. The thoughtful clinician will empathize with his patient's desire to return to the early stages of use (the honeymoon phase) when control and euphoria without consequences probably were possible, but will not allow the patient's rationalization and denial to interfere with the principles of good treatment. In cases of people with difficult addictions, abstinence is the goal and the only way.

☐ Does abstinence from one substance mean that abstinence from other substances is necessary?

The literature on this subject is mixed and, as always, good clinical judgment, rather than rigid dogma or excessive permissiveness, is warranted. In general, people become addicted to one substance, and that is not necessarily predictive of loss of control over other substances. That person is, however, more vulnerable to future addictions than a non-substance-using individual. A person who is physiologically dependent on caffeine does not necessarily lose the capacity for controlled drinking. The problem is that many substances of abuse are disinhibiting and are likely to lead to relapse with the primary substance. The classic example of this is the cocaine-dependent individual who does not have an independent problem with alcohol, but who, whenever he or she drinks, gets irresistible urges leading to a severe relapse with cocaine.

The individual with a cocaine problem who wants to drink is putting himself or herself in harm's way. Such individuals should be cautioned that using other substances puts their recovery in substantial jeopardy. The clinician has to be firm about this, especially at the beginning of treatment. In the case of cocaine abuse treatment, even though alcohol may not be the problem, the patient may need to be treated for alcohol abuse as well. Even mild intoxication can make the recovering addict susceptible to a relapse. Many clinicians consider disulfiram an effective tool in the treatment of cocaine abuse. Disulfiram has no pharmacologic relation to cocaine, but patients on it can not drink alcohol, and "slips" or repeated lapses into cocaine use are substantially lessened.

☐ How do I answer if a patient asks about my own substance use?

The clinician must recognize that while the patient is asking a real question, it is being asked for a specific reason which may bear little relation to the stated question. Try to understand the real question (that is, the question behind the question) first, before jumping in. Answering defensively, evasively, or with unnecessary self-disclosure may have a negative impact on therapy or interfere with treatment later on. Therapeutic neutrality, and some degree of anonymity on the part of the therapist, is quite useful in allowing the patient to explore his or her own feelings and attitudes. For a therapist to immediately blurt out that he or she is in recovery and achieved that with the rigorous use of AA will make it much less likely that a patient would feel free to voice his or her objections to that program. The goal is recovery and treatment *for the patient.* This can be achieved in many different ways, and—while a therapist may advocate a given path—there are different paths for different people.

A first response might be, "How will knowing about my experiences be helpful to you?" The most likely reason a patient is asking the clinician is that he or she is there for help and understanding. Saying to the patient something like, "I think you are asking me that question because you want to make sure that I understand how out of control you feel with this problem and how hard it has been for you. Please let me assure you that I understand how hard it is" can be enormously helpful. In our experience, this response is extremely effective in lessening the anxiety of the patient and the therapist in the great majority of cases.

In some cases, patients may be more persistent and insist on knowing if a therapist has ever had any personal experiences with drugs, is in recovery, or still uses substances in a social way. At this point, the therapist's comfort level with self-disclosure becomes important. If a therapist is in recovery, then it can be perfectly acceptable to reveal that. Again, the important point is to find some common ground. To the persistent patient who keeps asking a therapist not in recovery if he or she drinks, a useful response might be, "Yes I still drink on occasion, when it is appropriate. It sounds like in your earlier years you drank like your peers, but then things got out of control. My drinking never took that course, but I appreciate what happened to you with alcohol." Another response which may be useful is, "I think that too much discussion about me will take the focus off you and your treatment, but I think you want to know that I understand you."

Similarly, if a therapist has had experiences with harder drugs and the patient is persistent, a response such as, "I can assure you that I truly understand how compelling cocaine is." The answer does not completely discuss the therapist's experience, but does let the patient know that the clinician understands what the patient feels.

Caution must be used in situations where the therapist feels that the treatment will be threatened if he or she admits use. Explain to the patient that you are there to help him or her, and that your personal life is not an issue in treatment. An example of this might be a group that is mandated to meet. Such a group is likely to be hostile in tone, and information about the clinician's own use will be used by the group in the service of denial. Neither the therapist nor the patients benefit in that case.

Finally, if the patient's questions cause undue anxiety in the therapist, then it is the clinician's responsibility to look at the source of that anxiety. The clinician's discomfort may be due to inappropriate guilt about perfectly acceptable behavior. For example, alcohol, if used moderately, can be beneficial in a number of ways. The clinician need not be guilty about responsible drinking. If the anxiety produced when a patient asks about substance use on the part of the clinician is substantial, then it is a good time for the clinician to take an honest inventory of his or her own relationship to drugs and alcohol.

☐ What do I do if my patient arrives intoxicated to a session?

The patient is trying to tell you something by arriving at session drunk or on drugs. If the clinician suspects present intoxication, then an honest, supportive, but firm confrontation is usually in order. We advocate confronting suspected intoxication, because one of the meanings of showing up in this way may be a test to see if the clinician can tell when the patient is on drugs and alcohol. It is always disconcerting to learn, later in the course of treatment, that the patient was drunk or high during most of his or her first month's sessions. It is embarrassing to the clinician and not helpful to the person in need. When confronted with the question of use, most people will, at least if they are in a position where there is not an immediate negative consequence to drug use, be honest. If the patient continues to deny use, then a breathalyzer or drug-test kit in the office is often useful in confirming drug use. Such kits can be bought commercially, but their actual use is often unnecessary, since at the point before administration, the patient often admits to drug use.

In the rare instance where the clinician suspects intoxication but the test is negative, and the patient is not intoxicated, admit that you misjudged the situation. In a non-defensive manner, explain to the patient that you are there to help him or her, and that your experience and knowledge has caused you to be suspicious. The patient will likely find this comforting and, although he or she may give you a hard time about it, the therapeutic alliance will probably be strengthened by your honesty.

The patient's act of arriving at your office while intoxicated can be interpreted to mean that at least one part of the substance abuser wants to be detected. The patient that does not make it to your office at all is sending quite a different message, the most likely being that the person really is out of control with drugs and alcohol and is testing to see if you can handle this problem.

Despite the fact that the patient who arrives in an intoxicated state may feel provocatively toward the therapist, it is never appropriate to respond with anger. This is a person in need of help and his or her present state is confirmation of this fact. The clinical focus has to be centered on dealing with this present situation and arranging appropriate follow-up.

If the patient is intoxicated, the clinician must decide how impaired the patient is. A "normal" session is not possible under these circumstances. Trying to conduct a "regular" session with the patient even mildly impaired gives the patient the wrong message: that intoxication is okay and that normal activities can occur while drunk or high. If the person is only mildly intoxicated, for example has used a small amount of marijuana, or had a glass of wine, then he or she may be safely sent home, either supervised or by public transportation; such a patient should never be allowed to drive home alone.

If the patient is severely intoxicated, then care must be taken. The severely intoxicated patient should not be simply sent away from the office. This is dangerous for the patient and irresponsible on the part of the clinician. Calling a friend or relative to come pick up the patient is often a good solution. If this is not possible, letting the person stay in the waiting room while time passes may be necessary. If the patient is severely intoxicated and disruptive, then call the police or the Emergency Medical Service (EMS). All of these solutions depend on the severity of the intoxication and the nuances of the situation.

Charles is a 35 year-old accountant, who is married with one child. He had been in the evaluation phase with his clinician, Dr. Norton, discussing problems related to depression and alcohol use. In the first two sessions Charles denied that alcohol was much of a problem at all, but did admit to some issues with it. On the third session, at 10 AM Charles arrived with alcohol on his breath. He appeared mildly intoxicated. Dr. Norton confronted him, and after some initial resistance he admitted to having "a couple of shots" to steady his nerves that morning. The therapist gently explained that he did want to treat him, but that they could not conduct a regular session. Dr. Norton now realized that Charles really did have a drinking problem, as evidenced by his being drunk on a weekday morning. The doctor told him he could not let him leave the office and drive his car, and asked him what he proposed. Charles was annoyed, but after some thought they both called his wife who agreed to leave work and come in and get him. Charles waited in the waiting room and, when his wife arrived, the therapist met with both of them. Dr. Norton determined that Charles did not need hospitalization for detoxification (he was not physiologically dependent on alcohol). He explained to his wife the seriousness of the situation and noted that the situation was hopeful since Charles was now entering into treatment. He arranged to meet with them both again the next morning, before either Charles or his wife had to be at work, and enlisted the help of Charles' wife in keeping him sober before the next meeting.

☐ What is the best treatment for an individual patient?

Substance abuse can be understood as a disease, and a complicated one. It involves numerous substances, many different effects, and the infinite complexity of the human animal. A respected professional simply saying to a patient who has begun to use drugs or alcohol, in a sincere fashion, that he or she is genuinely concerned, is a highly effective intervention. Most patients, if they receive a warning, actually quit, or at least moderate back to acceptable levels. For example, any individual who receives a DUI (a conviction for driving under the influence of alcohol) is by definition abusing alcohol. The educational efforts for these offenders are very effective. Most people who are charged with a DUI stop their excessive drinking and do not get another DUI in the future.

Often it is not that simple. It is important that the clinician realize that not every program or approach is effective for every person. The clinician needs to take a careful history and then be creative in designing an individualized treatment plan. Factors such as the severity of the addiction, the social support available to the patient, the history of what therapies have been effective in the past, as well as the patient's treatment preferences, become vitally important. People very often know what would be useful to them. The therapist may elicit this information by asking, "you know yourself better than anyone else; what do you think will help you get off drugs or alcohol?" The skilled clinician will take the patient's response into account when making a recommendation for a reasonable treatment plan.

The most common mistake made in treating substance abusers is the rigid adherence to one method. Sometimes, as in an intervention, rigidity is necessary to force the patient to confront his or her denial and to stop self-defeating behavior. In that case a definitive, non-negotiable plan is completely appropriate. Even if he or she disagrees with a given treatment plan, the substance abuser will learn something from it. At other times, rigidity is counterproductive and will likely result only in the patient fleeing. The goal is recovery, and in most instances abstinence. There are many paths to that goal. For example, a patient who is addicted to crack cocaine and wants to go to a Yoga colony in the country for a length of time may be presenting a reasonable plan. Although not geared for drug treatment, as long as measures are taken so the patient cannot go into town and buy crack cocaine, the plan may be a good one, and help the patient achieve abstinence. When faced with a non-traditional plan, it is a good idea to establish a written contract with the patient that if this method does not succeed in helping him or her achieve abstinence, a more traditional approach will be employed.

☐ What do I do if my patient has been sober from alcohol for six months and now wants to return to "social drinking"?

First, suggest that this is ill-advised. Get ready to do everything in your power to stop this self-defeating decision; reason, call the family, offer him or her literature. Presumably, if the person was in treatment the alcohol addiction was severe. The best evidence demonstrates that once a person has become addicted to a substance, then he or she can never resume controlled use of *that* substance. In the case of someone who saw you because he or she was concerned, but the addiction did not become full-blown, this may be a different story. Take the patient seriously, and suggest that he or she wait for at least one year, preferably two, before attempting this high-risk experiment.

An example of when attempting to drink socially again might be a reasonable request is the unusual situation where an employee is sent for evaluation after appearing drunk at a Christmas party. Though rare, sometimes a person really does not have much experience with alcohol and might not have known better; he or she simply had "a few too many," and wound up acting foolishly. In this instance, a monitored but controlled experiment might be acceptable. Do make sure that you involve collaterals—the family, a friend, or anyone—that will call you, the clinician, if the situation gets out of hand.

In the case of someone who was truly dependent on alcohol and insists on experimenting, there is not much you can do. Try to delay until the person's better judgment prevails. If that does not work, then it is important to come up with a plan about what to do if the drinking gets out of control. Get a written contract with the person such as "If I cannot limit my drinking to no more than two drinks on any given occasion, I agree to take disulfiram for the next year." Such a contract can have enormous leverage in the future. Some patients do seem to need to experiment to prove to themselves that they really are "addicted." Be philosophical about these situations; these are chronic and relapsing conditions and part of being involved with this work is tolerance of relapse.

If the patient does insist on resuming drinking on a "social" basis, the best approach is to maintain a skeptical attitude. Accept the patient, but not the behavior. It is important to help the patient see if this "experiment" is an earnest one, or a camouflage for a self-destructive act. The student who wants to try an experiment like this during finals week is probably acting out something other than healthy curiosity. A similar situation might be when a patient decides he or she wants to conduct this "experiment" when the therapist is out of the country. If the patient is insistent, plan the experiment at a time when a relapse would do the least harm. Have the patient keep a diary of the experiment and make sure you see him or her more frequently during this time.

You might want to see this patient early in the morning (making sure he or she knows you charge for missed sessions). A missed session will be almost incontrovertible evidence that the patient was out of control the night before. If you know the patient well, you will also be able to tell if your patient is suffering from a hangover.

☐ What advice would you give a patient who used drugs in the past whose children are asking about his or her drug use?

As tempting as it might be, it is not good practice for parents to lie to their children. In the case of a very young child, the parent should find out why the child is asking. This might lead to a discussion on the dangers of drugs, and a direct answer to the question is often unnecessary. In the case of very young children, parents probably ought not to reveal their own drug use and should postpone such a discussion until the child is older and better able to understand and integrate the information.

For older children—honesty ought to be employed. Parents who elect to tell their children should be very careful not to glamorize their drug use. Children do not need to know all of the gory details. Romanticizing past drug use and giving too much information can give tacit permission and make substance use more enticing. Parents may want to talk about their own negative experiences, and the destructive effects that drugs or alcohol has had on their family and friends. Children can be told honestly that the parents grew up in a different era, when not as much was known about the destructive effects of alcohol and drugs.

Although this is a scary topic for many people, it can be a wonderful opportunity for the family to communicate in an authentic and supportive manner. Children, especially teens, if greeted with honesty, openness, and seriousness in such a discussion will be more open to discussing a variety of issues with parents in the future. Reward honesty in the children and congratulate them for being brave enough to bring up this difficult topic.

Parents should also try to become as knowledgeable as possible about the topic. Knee-jerk denunciation of substances, without the authority of knowledge, can lead to mistrust on the part of the child. Prepare for this conversation by becoming informed and discussing the topic with one's partner so that the transmission of accurate information and genuine emotional expression will be the results of this important exchange in family life.

Additional Reading

The following are provided as recommended readings on both general and specific issues with regards to substance abuse for those who would like more information on some of the topics discussed in this book. This list is in no way meant to be exhaustive, but to represent a smattering of reliable readings for those readers who wish to gain a greater understanding of some selected topics.

General Texts

Standard Texts

There are many, many books on the subject of substance abuse. The two texts currently considered "standard texts" in the field are:

Galanter, M., & Kleber, H. D. (1994). *Textbook of substance abuse treatment.* Washington, DC: American Psychiatric Press. (A new edition should be available in 1999.) (In press, 1999.)

Lowinson, J., Ruiz, P., Millman, R., & Langrod, J. (1997). *Substance abuse: A comprehensive textbook* (3rd ed.). Baltimore: Williams & Wilkins.

General Scholarly Publications

American Psychiatric Association. (1994). *Diagnostic and statistical manual of mental disorders* (4th ed.). Washington, DC: Author.

American Psychiatric Association. (1995) Practice guideline for the treatment of patients with substance use disorders: Alcohol, cocaine, opioids. *American Journal of Psychiatry, 152*(11 suppl.), 2–59.

Goodman & Gilman. (1995). *The pharmacological basis of therapeutics* (9th ed.). New York: Pergamon Press.

Kaplan, H. I., & Sadock, B. J. (Eds.). (1995). *Comprehensive textbook of psychiatry* (6th ed.). Baltimore: Williams & Wilkins.

Robson, P. (1994). *Forbidden drugs: understanding drugs and why people take* them. Oxford: Oxford University Press. (This contains an excellent, although slightly dated, bibliography and reference section.)

Ruden, R. (1997). *The craving brain.* New York: Harper Collins.

Stockley, D. (1992). *Drug warning: an illustrated guide for parents, teachers and employers.* (2nd ed.). London: Optima Books.

Weil, A., & Rosen, W. (1983). *Chocolate to morphine: understanding mind-active drugs.* Boston: Houghton Mifflin.

General Information Texts

Coombs, R. H., & Ziedonis, D. (Eds.). (1995). *Handbook on drug abuse prevention: a comprehensive: strategy to prevent the abuse of alcohol and other drugs.* Allyn and Bacon Inc.

Doweiko, H. E. (1998). *Concepts of Chemical Dependency.* Brooks/Cole Publishing Company.

Frances, R. J., & Miller, S. I. (Eds.). (1998). *Clinical textbook of addictive disorders.* New York: Guilford Press.

Galanter, M., & Kleber, H. D. (Eds.). (1994 and *in Press*). *The American Psychiatric Press textbook of substance abuse treatment.* Washington DC: American Psychiatric Association Press.

Jonnes, J. (1997). *Hep-cats, narcs and pipe dreams: a history of America's romance with illegal drugs.* Johns Hopkins Press.

Kuhn, C., Swartzwelder, S., & Wilson, W. (1998). *Buzzed: The straight facts about the most used and abused drugs from alcohol to ecstasy.* W. W. Norton and Company.

Lowinson, J., Ruiz, P., Millman, R., & Langrod, J. (1997). *Substance abuse: A comprehensive textbook.* Baltimor: Williams and Wilkins.

Marlatt, G. A. (1998). *Harm reduction: pragmatic strategies for managing high risk behaviors.* New York: Guilford Press.

Marlatt, G. A., & Vandenbos, G. R. (Eds.). (1998). *Addictive behaviors: readings on etiology, prevention, and treatment.* American Psychological Association Press.

Ruden, R. A., & Byalick, M. (1997). *The craving brain: the biobalance approach to controlling addiction.* New York: Harper Collins.

Schuckit, M. A. (1995). *Educating yourself about alcohol and drugs: a people's primer.* New York: Plenum Publishing.

Sparks, B. M. (Ed.). (1998). *Go ask alice.* Aladdin Publishing Company.

Tarter, R. E., Tammerman, R., & Ott, P. J. (Eds.). (1998). *Handbook of substance abuse: neurobehavioral pharmacology*. New York: Plenum Publishing.

Yalisove, D. L. (Ed). (1977). *Essential papers on addiction (essential papers in psychoanalysis series)*. New York: New York University Press.

Assessment and Treatment

Beattie, M. (1996). *Codependent no more: How to stop controlling others and start caring for yourself*. Hazeldon Foundation.

Blaine, J. D., & Julius, D. A. (Eds.). (1996). *Psychodynamics of drug dependence*. Jason Aronson Publishers.

Brizer, D. A., & Castaneda, R. (Illustrator). (1996). *Addiction & recovery for beginners (Writers and Readers Documentary Comic Book, 77)*. Writers and Readers Publishing, Inc.

Carnes, P. (1994). *A gentle path through the twelve steps: The classic guide for all people in the process of recovery*. Hazeldon Foundation.

Christopher, J. (1988). *How to stay sober: Recovery without religion*. Prometheus Books.

Galanter, M. (1993). *Network therapy for alcohol and drug abuse: A new approach in practice*. Basic Books.

Jarvis, T. J. (1995). *Treatment approaches for alcohol and drug dependence: An introductory guide*. New York: John Wiley and Sons.

Kaufman, E. (1994). *Psychotherapy of addicted persons*. New York: Guilford Press.

Levin, J. D., & Weiss, R. H. (Eds). (1995). *The dynamics and treatment of alcoholism: Essential papers*. Jason Aronson Publishers.

Margolis, R. D., & Zweben, J. E. (1998). *Treating patients with alcohol and other drug problems: An integrated approach*. American Psychological Association.

Meyers, R. J., & Smith, J. E. (1995). *Clinical guide to alcohol treatment: The community reinforcement approach*. New York: Guilford Press.

Miller, W. R., & Rollnick, S. (1992). *Motivational interviewing: Preparing people to change addictive behavior*. New York: Guilford Press.

Powell, D. J., & Brodsky, A. (1998). *Clinical supervision in alcohol and drug abuse counseling: Principles, models, methods*. Jossey-Bass, Inc.

Trimpey, J. (1996). *Rational recovery: The new cure for substance addiction*. Pocket Books.

West, J. W. (1997). *The betty ford center book of answers: help for those struggling with substance abuse and for the people who love them*. Pocket Books.

White, R. K. (Ed.). (1998). *Addiction intervention: strategies to motivate treatment-seeking behavior (Haworth Addictions Treatment)*. Haworth Press.

Specific Substances

Beck, J., & Rosenbaum, M. (1994). *Pursuit of ecstasy: The MDMA experience (SUNY Series in New Social Studies on Alcohol and Drugs)*. State University of New York Press.

Clayton, L. (1998). *Amphetamines and other stimulants*. Hazeldon Foundation.

Cohen, R. S. (1998). *The love drug: Marching to the beat of ecstasy (Haworth Therapy for the Addictive Disorders)*. Haworth Press.

Goodwin, D. W. (1994). *Alcoholism: The facts*. Oxford: Oxford University Press.

Henderson, L. A., & Glass, W. J. (1997). *LSD: Still with us after all these years*. Jossey-Bass, Inc.

Higgins, S. T., & Katz, J. (1998). *Cocaine abuse: Behavior, pharmacology, and clinical applications*. Academic Press.

Karch, S. B. (1997). *A brief history of cocaine*. Boca Raton, FL: CRC Press.

Lee, R. S., & Lee, M. P. (1997). *Caffeine & nicotine*. Hazeldon Foundation.

Sherry, C. (1994). *Inhalants (Drug Abuse Prevention Library)*. Hazeldon Foundation.

Sloman, L. R. (1998). *Reefer madness: The history of marijuana in America*. St. Martin's Press.

Smith, S. L. (1997). *Marijuana*. Rosen Group.

Stratton, K., Howe, C., & Battaglia, F. (Eds.). (1996). *Fetal alcohol syndrome: Diagnosis, epidemiology, prevention, and treatment*. National Academy of Social Insurance.

Yesalis, C. E. (Ed.). (1992). *Anabolic steroids in sport and exercise*. Human Kinetics Publishers, Inc.

Specific Populations

Burkstein, O. G. (1995). *Adolescent substance abuse: Assessment, prevention, and treatment (Wiley Series on Personality Processes)*. New York: John Wiley and Sons, Inc.

Coombs, R. H. (1997). *Drug-impaired professionals*. Cambridge, MA: Harvard University Press.

Covington, S. (1999). *Helping women recover: A program for treating substance abuse*. Jossey-Bass, Inc.

Glick, R. (Ed.). (1990). *Drugs in Hispanic communities*. Rutgers University Press.

James, W. H., & Johnson, S. L. (1997). *Doin' drugs: Patterns of African American addiction*. Austin: University of Texas Press.

Kaminer, Y. (1994). *Adolescent substance abuse: A comprehensive guide to theory and practice* (Critical Issues in Psychiatry). New York: Plenum Publishing.

Leite, E. (1989). *Different like me: A book for teens who worry about their parent's use of alcohol/drugs*. Johnson Ins.

Miller, D. K., & Blum, K. (1996). *Overload: Attention deficit disorder and the addictive brain*. Andrews Publishing, Inc.

Ross, G. R. (1993). *Treating adolescent substance abuse: Understanding the fundamental elements*. Allyn and Bacon, Inc.

Siney, C. (1995). *The pregnant drug addict*. Butterworth Heinemann Publishers.

Underhill, B. L., & Finnegan, D. G. (Eds). (1996). *Chemical dependency: Women at risk*. Harrington Park Press.

Weinstein, D. L., & Geller, A. (Designer). (1993). *Lesbians and gay men: Chemical dependency treatment issues*. Harrington's Park Press.

☐ Additional Readings For Selected Chapters

The following is a list of additional readings for selected chapters:

Historical Perspectives (Chapter 2)

Jones, J. (1996). *Hep-Cats, narcs, and pipe dreams: A history of America's romance with illegal drugs*. New York: Scribner.

Musto, D. (1987). *The American disease: Origins of narcotic control*. New York: Oxford University Press.

Neurobiology of Addition (Chapter 3)

One of the best reviews of this material is Eliot Gardener's chapter in Lowenson et al., mentioned above.

Alcohol (Chapter 7)

Goodwin, D. W. (1992). Alcohol: Clinical aspects. In *Substance abuse: A comprehensive textbook* (3rd ed.). J. H. Lowinson, P. Ruiz, R. B. Millman, & J. G. Langrod, (Eds.) Baltimore: Williams & Wilkins.

Valliant, G. (1982). *The natural history of alcoholism*. Cambridge, MA: The Harvard University Press.

Hallucinogens (Chapter 8)

Iverson, L. L., Iverson, S. D., & Snyder, S. H. (Eds.). (1995). *Handbook of psychopharmacology*. New York: Plenum Press.

Weil, A. (1972). *The natural mind.* New York: Houghton Mifflin.

"Club Drugs": MDMA (Chapter 9)

Eisner, B. (1992). *MDMA: Ecstasy*. Ronin Publishers.

Cohen R. (1998). *Marching to the beat of ecstasy.* New York: Hapworth Press.

Goodwin, D. W., (1992). Alcohol: Clinical aspects. In: J. H. Lowinson, P. Ruiz, R. B. Millman, & J. G. Langrod (Eds.). *Substance abuse: A comprehensive textbook* (3rd ed.). Baltimore: Williams & Wilkins.

Marijuana (Chapter 10)

Grinspoon, L. (19__) *Marijuana, the Forbidden Medicine.* New Haven, CT: Yale University Press.

For completely favorable, biased, but up-to-date information about marijuana, *High Times* is a monthly magazine whose theme is marijuana. It can be found at any large newsstand.

Nicotine (Chapter 11)

Gold, M. S. (1995). *Tobacco.* (*Drugs of Abuse, Volume 4*). New York: Plenum Publishing Corp.

Opioids (Chapter 12)

Jaffe J. (1995). Opioid-related disorders. In H. I. Kaplan & B. J. Sadock (Eds.). *Comprehensive textbook of psychiatry* (6th ed.). Baltimore: Williams & Wilkins.

(This is a scholarly, readable, and comprehensive chapter.)

Stimulants (Chapter 13)

Kosten, T. R., & McCance-Katz, E. (1995). New pharmacotherapies. *Review of Psychiatry, Vol. 14*, pp. 105–126. Washington, DC: American Psychiatric Press, Inc.

Kleber, H. D. (1988). Cocaine abuse: Historical, epidemiological and psychological perspectives. Journal of Clinical Psychiatry, ______

Spitz, H. I., & Rosecan, J. S. (1987). *Cocaine abuse: New directions in treatmetn & research*. New York: Brunner/Mazel.

Twelve Step Programs (Chapter 20)

Alcoholics Anonymous (2nd ed.). New York: AA World Services.

Kurtz, E. (1979). *Not God: A history of alcoholics anonymous*. Center City, MN: Hazelden Press.

Robertson, N. (1990). *Getting better—inside A.A.* New York: Outlet Publishers.

Family Therapy (Chapter 22)

Kaufman, ___. (1985). *Title*. City: Publisher.

McGoldrick, M., & Gerson, R. (1985). *Genograms*. New York: Norton.

Network Therapy (Chapter 23)

Galanter, M. (1993). *Network therapy for alcohol and drug abuse: A new method in practice*. New York: Basic Books.

Therapeutic Communities (Chapter 24)

Mitchel, D., Mitchel, C., & Ofshe, R. (1982). *The Light on Synanon: How a country newspaper exposed a corporate cult*. Seaview Press.

Comorbidity/Dual Diagnosis Issues (Chapter 26)

Wetzler, S., & Sanderson, W. (Eds.). (1997). *Treatment strategies of patients with psychiatric comorbidity*. New York: John Wiley & Sons.

Drugs in the Workplace (Chapter 27)

Scanlon, W. (1991). *Alcoholism and drug abuse in the workplace: Managing costs and care through employee assistance programs*. Westport, CT: Praeger-Greenwood Press.

Prevention and Education (Chapter 29)

Falco, M. (1996). *What works? The making of a drug-free America.* New York: Pergamon Press.

(1996). *Making the grade: AA guide to school drug prevention programs.* Washington, DC: Drug Strategies.

In addition, the National Center on Substance Abuse at Columbia University is a five year-old foundation which studies policy on substance dependence, and publishes numerous tracts and studies. They are located at:
152 West 57th Street, 12th Floor
New York, NY 10019
212 841–5200
www.CASACOLUMBIA.org

Special Populations and Special Considerations (Chapter 30)

Seligman, M., & Marshak, L. A. (1990). (Eds.). *Group psychotherapy with special populations.* New York: Grune & Stratton.

The Codependent Relationship

Whitfield, C. (1991). *Co-dependence: Healing the human condition—the new paradigm for helping professionals and people in recovery.* Deerfield Beach, FL: Deerfield Communications.

Beattie, M. (1989). *Codependent no more.* Center City, MN: Hazelden Publishers.

Black, C. (1990). *Double duty.* New York: Ballantine Books.

Adult Children of Alcoholics

Tony, A., & Dan, F. (1990). *The laundry list: the ACOA experience.* Deerfied Beach, FL: Deerfield Communications.

Group Psychotherapy (Chapter 21)

Brook, D.W., & Spitz, H. I. (Eds.) (In press). *Group psychotherapy of substance abuse.* Washington, DC: American Psychiatric Press, Inc.

Spitz, H. I. & Spitz, S. T. (1998). *A pragmatic approach to group psychotherapy.* New York: Brunner/Mazel.

☐ Readings for Topics Discussed in Various Chapters

Psychodynamics and Substance Abuse

Khantzian, E. J. (1980). An ego-self theory of substance dependence: A contemporary psychoanalytic perspective. In D. J. Lettieri, M. Sayers, & H. W. Perason (Eds.). *Theories on drug abuse.* NIDA Research Monograph #30. Rockville, MD: National Institute on Drug Abuse.

Relapse Prevention

Wilson, P. (1992). *Principles and practice of relapse prevention.* New York: Guilford Press.

Marlatt, G., & Gordon, J. (Eds.). (1985). *Relapse prevention: A self-control strategy for the maintenance of behavior change.* New York: Guilford Press.

Withdrawal

Miller, N. S., & Gold, M. S. (1991). *Alcohol and other drugs: Dependence and withdrawal characteristics.* New York: Plenum Books.

Kosten, T. R., Gawin, F. H., Morgan, C., Nelson, J. C., & Jatlow, P. (1990). Evidence for altered desipramine disposition in methadone-maintained patients treated for cocaine abuse. *American Journal of Drug and Alcohol Abuse, 16,* 329–336.

Meyer, R. E. (1986). How to understand the relationship between psychopathology and addictive disorders: Another example of the chicken and the egg. In R. E. Meyer, (Ed.). *Psychopathology and addictive disorders.* New York: The Guilford Press.

AUTHOR INDEX

SUBJECT INDEX

For Product Safety Concerns and Information please contact our EU
representative GPSR@taylorandfrancis.com
Taylor & Francis Verlag GmbH, Kaufingerstraße 24, 80331 München, Germany

www.ingramcontent.com/pod-product-compliance
Ingram Content Group UK Ltd.
Pitfield, Milton Keynes, MK11 3LW, UK
UKHW022217190926
475702UK00003B/405
* 9 7 8 1 1 3 8 4 5 1 9 1 9 *